THE ROMAN CULT OF MITHRAS

THE ROMAN CULT OF MITHRAS

The God and his Mysteries

MANFRED CLAUSS

TRANSLATED BY RICHARD GORDON

Routledge
New York

Published in North America in 2001 by
ROUTLEDGE
29 West 35th Street
New York, NY 10001
www.routledge-ny.com

By Arrangement with Edinburgh University Press

English translation and Further Reading © Richard Gordon, 2000

First published in German as Mithras: Kult und Mysterien
© C. H. Beck'sche Verlagsbuchhandlung, Munich, 1990

The publishers gratefully acknowledge the assistance of Inter Nationes
in the publishing of this English language edition.

Typeset in Goudy Old Style
by Hewer Text Ltd, Edinburgh, and
printed and bound in Great Britain by
The University Press, Cambridge

Cataloguing-in-Publication data is Available from the Library of Congress

ISBN 0 415-92977-6 (HB)
ISBN 0 415-92978-4 (PB)

Contents

List of illustrations

This list gives material, size, and present location of the monuments, where known, and the source of the illustration used here. Dimensions are in metric units. V. denotes: Vermaseren, *Corpus*.

I would like here to thank the museums listed above, but particularly Dr Ingeborg Huld-Zetsche and Profs Reinhold Merkelbach and Elmar Schwertheim for assistance in procuring the illustrations.

Preface to the English edition

The cult of Mithras has fascinated ancient historians for a century now, thanks chiefly to Franz Cumont's indefatigable energy in collecting and interpreting the texts and monuments. One cannot of course today accept all his views and constructions – some of them indeed seem to me quite wrong. But in general, all criticism of details aside, his work calls to mind Friedrich Nietzsche's remark, 'We should honour the errors of the great: they are more fertile than the truths of lesser men.' Students of Mithraism, myself included, owe an enormous debt to critical engagement with Cumont's views.

My interest in the study of Mithras as the focus of a Roman mystery cult now goes back a decade and a half. Alongside an analysis of the social composition of almost 500 small, sometimes tiny, Mithraic congregations in the Roman empire, I published some while ago a general interpretation of the cult, drawing upon all the wide range of literary, epigraphic and archaeological evidence. It is an honour to have it now translated into English. For this edition, the basic structure has not been altered, but in some places I have taken note, at least briefly, of important new finds and discussions, and included references to them in the notes. The notes themselves are intended primarily to provide references for statements in the text, but the further literature cited in them should also enable the interested reader to follow up questions that could not fully be dealt with given the scope of the book. It may indeed be that, despite all one's efforts, much still remains opaque. But, in studying what is after all a mystery-cult, should we really expect anything else?

The book has found an ideal translator in Richard Gordon. I would like to thank him warmly for the patience and the intelligence he has brought to the task. I am also grateful to him for supplying many references and corrections of slips and errors. My further thanks are due to John Davey for arranging for the English translation.

Translator's preface

Although the cult of Mithras was in many ways the most unusual of the new religions of the Roman Empire, as well as the last to become popular, it has long had a special place in the educated folk memory of the English-speaking world. In England, that place was demonstrated by the extraordinary public interest aroused by the discovery of a head of Mithras on the Bucklersbury House site in the City of London in September 1954, the site of the Walbrook Mithraeum. The cult-niche of the Mithraeum at Dura-Europos in Syria, excavated in 1933–4, is prominently displayed in the University of Yale Art Gallery, and many US public and private collections boast a Mithraic relief. This educated interest rests partly on the fame and haunting quality of Rudyard Kiplings' poem 'Song to Mithras' – itself one of the leitmotivs of the later volumes of Anthony Powell's *Dance to the Music of Time* (1951–75) – but also on the fascination of an iconography which is as suggestive as its precise meaning is obscure.

The English-language edition of Franz Cumont's *The Mysteries of Mithras*, which has hardly been out of print since its publication in 1903, is now seriously, one might say hopelessly, out of date, not least on account of the archaeological discoveries of the past century. Its only recent competitor, M. J. Vermaseren's competent but rather uninspired *Mithras* (tr. 1963), has long been unavailable. Manfred Clauss's *Mithras* offers just the reliable and balanced introduction for undergraduate teaching and for the general reader, taking account of all important recent archaeological discoveries, that was needed to replace Cumont. At the same time, a word about its background may be useful.

The book was written during the late 1980s, at a time when Reinhold Merkelbach's *Mithras* (1984) had made a considerable impact in Germany, though not elsewhere. Merkelbach's book was characterised by bold, imaginative writing, and bold, imaginative theories. Clauss's aim was partly to present a corrective to Merkelbach's propensity to speculate. Hence his emphasis on the archaeological material, and his resistance to going beyond what it allows one to say. Moreover, the book was of course written for a German-speaking public, which has naturally influenced its choice of material, its focus on the Rhine-Danube frontier rather than, say, Italy or Dura-Europos.

Since the late 1980s, thanks to the work of David Ulansey and Roger Beck, interest in a possible astronomic-astrological reading of the Mithraic cult-relief has grown very substantially. This development could hardly have been foreseen a decade ago. Given Clauss's distaste for speculation, I do not think that, had he been writing the first edition now, he would have come to a conclusion much different from the one he expresses in the Foreword; but he would no doubt have discussed the problems involved more fully than he does. I have pointed to some astronomic-astrological features in the captions to the illustrations, and listed some relevant bibliographical material in English at the end of the translation.

Foreword

A hundred years ago, the Belgian Franz Cumont was the first scholar to publish all the evidence for the cult of Mithras then available, the literary sources, inscriptions, and archaeological monuments, in his great two-volume work *Textes et monuments figurés relatifs aux mystères de Mithra* (1896–9). The ample introduction to this collection of documentary evidence made him the dominant authority on the cult for more than half a century after its publication. Quite apart from his familiarity with the material, this dominance was mainly due to the sheer coherence of his account of the cult: he seemed to have an answer for everything. But there was a contingent reason too: in the years after 1900 Cumont brought out the 'Conclusions' of *Textes et monuments* more or less unchanged to provide a brief introduction in French, English, and German; and for decades this was actually the only work of its kind available.[1] It is obvious now that Cumont's authority tended throughout this period to muffle dissident views.[2] He vigorously defended the position that the cult of Mithras developed from Iranian antecedents, and so postulated a dualism between good and evil. Indeed, he ended up by discovering a Mithraic eschatology. His fundamental assumption was that the religion consisted essentially in its theology, and he tended therefore to play down the rôle of ritual and worship. The aim of this book is to make good that neglect.

Between 1956 and 1960 Maarten J. Vermaseren published his *Corpus Inscriptionum et Monumentorum Religionis Mithriacae*, a new collection of the epigraphic and monumental evidence, which had become necessary owing to the steady increase in material over the intervening years. In Mithraic studies Vermaseren rapidly acquired a status similar to Cumont's, though he never became so rigidly dogmatic. Today his two volumes provide access to the great bulk of the archaeological evidence, and in fact constitute the standard work in the subject.[3] He also wrote a general account of Mithraism, which was translated into several languages but is now out of print.[4]

Vermaseren's heroic achievement soon stimulated a remarkable renaissance in Mithraic studies. A recent research report covering new finds as well as synthetic work since Cumont lists just under five hundred titles.[5] Two facts may serve to illustrate this development. There have been three international conferences, at Manchester (1971), in Teheran (1975), and at Rome (1978), their proceedings all published in bulky volumes.[6] Furthermore, a journal devoted exclusively to the study of Mithra, the *Journal of Mithraic Studies*, was founded in 1976, of which three volumes appeared up to 1980. Both in the conference proceedings and in the journal two topics tended to dominate the discussion, and they are, in my view, the reason why both the conferences and the journal ran out of steam. On the one hand, many of the individual articles focused on the issue of Mithraism's supposed Persian or Iranian links, which in the final analysis can never be demonstrated; and on the other, a great deal of space was devoted to rather unconvincing speculation about astrological issues. Roger Beck, Michael Speidel and David Ulansey have all read into the representation of Mithras killing the bull a star-map of great complexity and subtlety.[7] The participants in the Mithraic panel that met under the aegis of the IAHR Congress held at Rome in 1990 mostly tended to pursue the same themes.[8] In my view, however, although the Mithraic cult-reliefs depict a sacred narrative in which the heavenly bodies and beliefs about them certainly play a part, they are not a map of a journey through the realm of the fixed stars.

Of recent scholarship, I may mention three writers who have taken a more original turn. First of all, we owe to Richard Gordon the most penetrating critique of Cumont's general thesis.[9] His most important work, 'Mithraism in the Roman Empire', unfortunately, however, remains unpublished.[10] Robert Turcan has stressed, especially in *Mithras Platonicus* and in his introductory text *Mithra et le mithriacisme*, the degree to which the cult was influenced by current philosophical thinking.[11] This point, as well as many others, has been followed up in the general account by Reinhold Merkelbach.[12]

One can hardly do better, with regard to the problem of the sources for the cult of Mithras, than to cite A.D. Nock's vivid comparison.[13] Imagine a historian attempting at some distant date in the future to write about contemporary twentieth-century Christianity. He has at his disposal the following:

- a few chance allusions in Jewish religious texts,
- the ground-plans and structure of a few churches, stripped for the most part of their ornaments,
- some altars and carvings, together with some fragments of stained glass,
- a few pages from baptismal registers.

We should add that our imaginary historian also has available around 700 diverse representations of the crucifixion from many different sites, some of them including other scenes from the Passion. It would be hard indeed to describe Christianity on such a basis; and it is likewise extremely hard for us to give an account of the cult of Mithras. The material is quite simply ruinously incomplete. This fact makes it all the more worthwhile trying to fit the Mysteries into the wider context of Roman cult-practice.

The evidence used in this book is essentially the archaeological remains – the Mithraic temples and their contents, the inscriptions and the reliefs, whose iconographic conventions are those of Hellenistic and Roman tradition. Evidence for the cult has been found at some 420 sites. There are about 1,000 inscriptions, and 700 depictions of the bull-killing (only about half of them complete); and in addition 400 monuments with other subjects.[14] These facts more or less demand that cult practice be given much more weight than putative theological claims: for the truth is that we possess virtually no theological statements either by the Mithraists themselves or by other writers.

At the end of this study, we shall nevertheless have to accept that many questions remain unanswered. We may well be left with a sense of bafflement; perhaps too with a recognition that the past is indeed another country.

Abbreviations

Abbreviations of classical authors and texts as in *Oxford Classical Dictionary*;[3] of Christian texts, as in *Lexikon der antiken christlichen Literatur*, S. Döpp and W. Geerlings (eds) (Freiburg iB: Herder, 1998). Other abbreviations, and the names of journals cited more than once, are:

ArchAel	Archaeologia Aeliana
AE	L'Année épigraphique
ANRW	Aufstieg und Niedergang der römischen Welt
Beard, North, Price	M. Beard, J.A. North, and S.R.F. Price, *Religions of Rome* (Cambridge: Cambridge University Press, 1998), 2 vols
BMC	*Catalogue of Greek Coins in the British Museum*
CCL	Corpus Christianorum. Series Latina (Turnhout)
CIL	Corpus Inscriptionum Latinarum
CRAI	Comptes rendus de l'Académie des Inscriptions et Belles-Lettres
CRBM	H. Mattingly and R.G. Carson (eds), *Coins of the Roman Empire in the British Museum* (London: British Museum, 1923–62)
CSIR	Corpus Signorum Imperii Romani
EPRO	Études préliminaires aux religions orientales dans l'Empire romain
FIRA	S. Riccobono *et al.* (eds), *Fontes Iuris Romani anteiustiniani*[2] (Florence: S.A.G. Barbera, 1968)
HABES	Heidelberger Althistorische Beiträge und Epigraphische Studien
Henig, RRB	M. Henig, *Religion in Roman Britain* (London: Batsford, 1984).
IDR	I.I. Russu *et al.* (eds), *Inscriptiile Daciei Romane* (Bucharest: Editura Academici Republicii Socialiste Romania, 1975–88)

IGLS	L. Jalabert and R. Mouterde *et al.* (eds), *Inscriptions grecques et latines de la Syrie* (Paris: Librairie orientaliste Paul Geuthner, 1929–)
IGUR	L. Moretti, *Inscriptiones Graecae Urbis Romae* (Rome: Istituto Italiano per la Storia Antica, 1968–79)
JMS	Journal of Mithraic Studies
JRA	Journal of Roman Archaeology
JRS	Journal of Roman Studies
LIMC	L. Kahil (ed.), *Lexicon Iconographicum Mythologiae Classicae* (Zurich and Munich: Artemis Verlag, 1981–97)
Migne, PG	J-P. Migne (ed.), *Patrologiae Cursus, series Graeca* (Paris: J-P. Migne, 1857–66)
Migne, PL	J-P. Migne (ed.), *Patrologiae Cursus, series Latina* (Paris: J.P. Migne, 1844–65)
Paroemiogr.	E.L. von Leutsch and P.G. Schneidewin (eds), *Corpus Paroemiographorum Graecorum* (Göttingen: Vandenhoek and Ruprecht, 1839–51)
PGM	K. Preisendanz and A. Henrichs (eds) *Papyri Graecae Magicae*^{2} (Stuttgart: Teubner 1973–74)
P.Oxy	Oxyrhynchus Papyri
RE	G. Wissowa, W. Kroll *et al.* (eds.), *Paulys Realencyclopädie der classischen Altertumswissenschaft* (Munich: Alfred Druckenmüller; later Stuttgart and Weimar: J.B. Metzler, 1893–1980)
RIB	R.G. Collingwood, R.P. Wright *et al.* (eds), *The Roman Inscriptions of Britain*^{2} (Far Thrupp, Stroud: Alan Sutton, 1995)
RICG	A.S. Robertson, *Roman Imperial Coins in the Hunter Coin Cabinet, University of Glasgow* (Oxford and Glasgow: Oxford University Press, 1962–82)
ZPE	Zeitschrift für Papyrologie und Epigraphik

Epigraphic conventions:

( ) round brackets, enclose the resolution of a word abbreviated in the original
[ ] square brackets, enclose restored text
(!) denotes a mistaken form or spelling in the original
/ represents a line-break in the original
// denotes that a text is distributed over different parts of the stone, or is interrupted by a figural representation

Contexts

CHAPTER 1

Mitra and Mithras

It is convenient to term the Persian and Hellenistic deity Mitra, to distinguish him from the god of the Roman mystery-cult. Mitra was an ancient Indo-European divinity, a member of a pantheon which can be reconstructed by means of evidence from North India and Iran. The earliest document to name the god dates from the second millennium BC: on a fourteenth-century clay tablet from Boghaz-Köy in modern Turkey, the former capital of the Hittite empire, Mitra is invoked as a guarantor of an agreement between the Hittites and a neighbouring people, the Mitanni (V 16). But Mitra is not only the god of treaties, of agreements, he is treaty or contract personified. In Avestan (the eastern dialect of Old Iranian), *miθra-* means 'treaty' or 'contract'.[15]

We have slightly more information about Mitra in Persia. The earliest known equation of the god with the Sun is to be dated to the fifth or fourth century BC.[16] This is the likely date of the great *yašt* (hymn) to Mithra in the collection of the older Avesta. The hymn vigorously extols the god 'who has ten thousand spies, is strong, all-knowing, undeceivable' (10 §27, tr. Gershevitch). White steeds pull his golden chariot with its single wheel (32 §136), an evident allusion to the Sun's chariot. Mitra was thus the Sun-god, who sees all. Moreover, the god 'in the morning brings into evidence the many shapes . . . as he lights up his body, being endowed with own light like the moon' (33 §142). In the *Vendidad* (*Videvdad*), an East Iranian text written by a Median magus in the Hellenistic period, we find the following passage:

> Then Ahura Mazda spoke: 'When a person dies, when a person's life has come to an end, when the demons, the upholders of the lie, the evil ones, have utterly divided him up, then on the third day after death the shining goddess appears with the dawn, and gives light, and Mithra, whose weapons are good, arises blazing like the Sun, and ascends the mountains.'
>
> (*Vendidad* 19.28–29)

In the dualistic Zoroastrian system, Mitra is the light that brings good, forever battling with darkness; it is Mitra who strives against evil spirits and puts them to flight. We must surely be reminded here of the epithet of the later Roman Mithras, *invictus*, Invincible, Unbeaten.

In texts such as these, we find Mitra identified with the Sun, which recalls Strabo's report that Mitra is the Persians' name for the Sun (in Greek, Ἥλιος, *Helios*) (15.3.13, 732C).

Mitra was god of the oath, protector of oaths. He was a god of good faith, of agreements, of loyalty. Plutarch has an anecdote of how the Great King reminded one of his servants that he had bound himself to loyalty by shaking hands and by swearing by Mitra: 'Tell me (the truth), keeping faith with the light of Mitra and the King's right hand' (*Vit. Alex.* 30.8). At the end of the fourth century AD, Mitra as the sun-god was still being invoked by the Persians to witness their oaths. In 383 the Roman Emperor Theodosius I sent Stilicho, then still a young man, to the Persian court to complete a treaty. The poet Claudian describes the ceremony. First incense was burned on the altars, and the sacred fire borne out from within the temple. Then the magoi sacrificed young bulls. The king of the Persians himself poured a libation from a gleaming offering-dish, invoking as witnesses to the oaths Ba'al, with his secrets, and Mitra, who as the Sun governs the course of the planets (*Laud. Stil.* 1.58–63).

With the destruction of the Achaemenid empire by Alexander and the Diadochi, the cult of Mitra retained its importance in some of the Hellenistic successor states in the area of modern Turkey.[17] Six kings named Mitradates, 'Gift of Mitra', ruled the kingdom of Pontus on the northern coast of Asia Minor. The last of them was also the most famous, namely Mitradates Eupator (120–63 BC), the great enemy of Rome. During the Principate, the city of Trapezus (Trabzon) issued coins showing Roman Mithras, traditional god of the city (V 14).

In Cilicia, too, the metropolis Tarsus issued coins in the mid-third century AD with the canonical scene of Mithras killing the bull (V 27, fig. 1). In connection with this region, Plutarch reports that the famous Cilician pirates, who came from here, were the first to introduce secret rituals in honour of Mitra (*Vit. Pomp.* 24.5). This may have been the case, but it proves nothing about the origins of the Roman mystery-cult. From Cappadocia, we know of just two inscriptions in honour of Mitra, one of which, at Faraşa, probably states that the dedicator performed a ceremony to or for the god according to the ritual of the Persian magoi (V 19: ἐμάγευσε Μίθρῃ).

The significance of Mitra in Armenia may be judged from the fact that the literal meaning of the Armenian word for temple is 'temple of Mitra'. Shrines for the god still existed in the fourth century AD. His importance is also clear from an incident described by the historian Dio Cassius, in which Nero conferred the throne of Armenia upon Tiridates I. In the course of the ceremony, Tiridates knelt before Nero and declared, 'Lord, I am . . . your slave. And I have come to you as my god, to pay homage to you just as I do to Mitra.'[18]

1. *Tarsus, metropolis of Cilicia Pedias and the 'three provinces': rev. of bronze* aes, *Mithras killing the bull (AD 238–44): BMC Cilicia, Tarsus no. 258, pl. 37.4. The radiate crown, Mithras' stance and partial heroic nudity all diverge from the norm in the western mysteries.*

In Commagene, as in Pontus, there were kings named Mitradates. We may also recall the identification of Mitra with the Greek sun-god, for which the monument of Antiochus I of Commagene on Nemrud Dagh, at 2,000 m the kingdom's highest mountain, provides the classic example. This is the cult-centre (*hierothesion*) and mortuary tumulus which the Christian rhetor and poet Gregory of Nazianzen towards the end of the fourth century describes, with the pride of the local patriot, as the eighth wonder of the world (*Anth. Pal.* 8.177). Antiochus ruled from *c.*75 to *c.*35 BC; both his father and his son were named Mitradates.

As his inscriptions declare, and the sculptures and reliefs demonstrate, Antiochus accorded the figure of Mitra special honour in the divine pantheon of Commagene. Mitra is the only one of the deities represented in the complex to have his own priest.[19] The king bore the title 'Just God' (θεὸς δίκαιος), an epithet also used for Mitra (V 18). Antiochus celebrated his birthday as an appointed feast-day on the sixteenth of each month, that is, the middle day, which was dedicated to Mitra. If Antiochus were in fact born on the sixteenth, this would be mere coincidence. But it is more probable that the date of the royal birthday was fixed with reference to Mitra. Among the so-called *dexiosis*-scenes, reliefs showing the king shaking hands with different deities, there also survives one with Mitra (fig. 2). The god (r., with the rayed nimbus) wears garments otherwise worn exclusively by members of the Commagene royal house; no other god wears them. The significance of this had been adumbrated much earlier, in the Achaemenid period. Mitra was the god of the Iranian kings, a god of the rulers as well as of the followers subject to them.[20] In all the various representations of the god

2. *Nemrud Dagh, Commagene: stele from the West Terrace of the* hierothesion *of Antiochus I, Mitra (r.) shaking hands with Antiochus. One of four similar stelai representing the king with the gods of his foundation (IGLS 1, 1 ll. 54–7). The object in Mitra's l. hand seems to be a* baresman, *the ceremonial bunch of tamarisk-twigs already associated with the god's worship in the Avestan Hymn (fifth cent. BC).*

in Commagene, however, it is not Mitra alone who is depicted but a bevy of syncretic divinities, whose names are listed in the inscriptions in various combinations: the one here at Nemrud Dagh is Apollo-Mitra-Helios.[21] There is an obvious link between Mitra, Apollo and Helios: all are solar deities.

It should be emphasised that the purpose of this summary account is not to suggest that such ideas were taken over directly into the Roman mystery-cult. On the contrary, no direct continuity, either of a general kind or in specific details, can be demonstrated between the Perso-Hellenistic worship of Mitra and the Roman mysteries of Mithras. The oft-repeated attempts to trace a seamless history of Mithras from the second millennium BC to the fourth century AD simply tell us something quite general about the relative stability, or, as it may be, flexibility, of religious ideas. We cannot account for Roman Mithras in terms borrowed from Persian Mitra.[22]

In view of the difficulty of demonstrating continuity, it also makes little sense to explain the poor showing of the mysteries of Mithras in the Greek-speaking world, both old Greece and Asia Minor, by invoking a supposed hostility towards a cult that proclaimed itself 'Persian'. Two examples will serve to indicate that prejudices of this kind did not exist. From the 190s Roman troops garrisoned the town of Dura-Europos, on the River Euphrates, against the threat of the neo-Persian Sassanian empire; the soldiers, however, had no objection to being initiated into the mysteries of Mithras. That anti-Persian feelings existed is made clear, for instance, by Diocletian's law against the Manichees. After the emperor had personally crushed a revolt in Egypt in AD 297, he published an edict there against Manichaeism, which he denounced as a sect stemming from 'the Persians who are our enemies'.[23] But not long afterwards the same emperor dedicated an altar to Mithras, calling him protector of the empire (*fautor imperii*) (p. 28). His altar was to a Roman god.

There is another reason too for thinking that it makes little sense to treat the mysteries of Mithras as but one stage in a longer evolution. The mysteries cannot be shown to have developed from Persian religious ideas,[24] nor does it make sense to interpret them as a fore-runner of Christianity.[25] Both views neglect the sheer creativity that gave rise to the mystery-cult. Mithraism was an independent creation with its own unique value within a given historical, specifically Roman, context.

The mysteries of Mithras came into being in Rome or in Ostia. We are not compelled to assume the existence of an 'unknown religious genius', as the Swedish historian of religion Martin Nilsson put it.[26] But there is a certain justification for doing so. Alexander of Abonouteichos in Paphlagonia (Asia Minor) showed in the second century AD how easy it was, with the aid of a new oracle and a completely new god – albeit one calqued upon an earlier cult – to begin from scratch. Of course the mysteries of Mithras combine new with old: the cult was enriched by elements taken from Hellenistic and oriental mysteries; it absorbed astrological knowledge, and even a few Persian words and technical terms, such as *nama*, 'Hail!' or 'Long live . . .!' As Iranian words, they have no significance outside the cult – which does not mean that the initiates were familiar with their original meaning. For the Mithraic community, the value of such utterances lay within the world of their mysteries; at the same time, they constructed a welcome distance from the world outside. We must nevertheless grant that, despite numerous conferences and round tables, and an almost overwhelming number of publications, the central issue of the emergence of the mysteries remains controversial.

CHAPTER 2

Religious perspectives in the Roman empire

Some preliminary remarks on the wider context are called for if we are to understand the mysteries in their proper time and place. First, the habits of mind of the people who worshipped Mithras. It may sound a truism, but living as we do in the twentieth, and now twenty-first, century we must unthink a great deal if we are to understand conditions in the ancient world. Just take a passage from the philosopher Plotinus, who wrote the following account of himself around the middle of the third century AD:

> Often have I woken up out of the body to myself and have entered into myself, going out from all other things; I have seen a beauty wonderfully great and felt assurance that then most of all I belonged to the better part; I have actually lived the best life and come to identity with the divine.
>
> (*Enn.* 4.8.1, tr. A.H. Armstrong)

This is the language and style of a philosopher, but we may be sure that an average worshipper, without any philosophical training, would have found it even easier than Plotinus to attain such unity with the divine. For in a polytheistic society the word God has none of the submissive overtones of awe and distance that it has, for example, in Christianity. By contrast, all pre-Christian religiosity is characterised by what I would term a limitless access to all godhead. Public and private life, down to the tiniest everyday details, was inflected with countless religious rituals and observances. This had its effect on people in the ancient world, just as did the religious symbols of diverse origin that were to be found in houses, in streets and other public places, in the fields.

In Greek popular tradition, a god differed from a human in being immortal, and endowed with superhuman powers, which bestowed that immortality: human beings were in fact mortal gods, a god an immortal human. The cleft between god and human was not unbridgeable, and could indeed be bridged by every mortal. Any person could, through meditation, attain mystic unity with god. Though we nowadays can still talk to God, we cannot become a god.

We cannot separate this view of divinity from the cosmology that subtended it.[27] This cosmology, widespread among intellectuals but also amongst other social groups, was a precipitate of the views of Aristotle and the Hellenistic astronomers. The entire vast construct of the kosmos was understood as a manifestation of divine order in which the earth had its place. Aristotle had, as it were, drawn a line within the universe. Above this line, beyond the moon, lay the unchanging heavens, where the innumerable stars had their being, the host of an immutable dispensation. Below it, this side of the moon, lay the earthly world of chance, mutability, death. Within this gigantic construction with its numerous habitats, the earth appeared minute by comparison with the vastness of the universe beyond, a poor dwelling-place constructed from all the refuse and jetsam of the cosmos. This earthly world thus took on a hostile aspect, became alien.

This cosmology had its counterpart in a view of human life; human experience, in great things and in little, was shaped by it. The following passage from the Christian bishop Cyprian of Carthage in the mid-third century, with its blend of cliché and pathos, has been repeatedly cited:

> The world has grown old, does not enjoy that strength which it formerly enjoyed, and does not flourish with the same vigour and strength with which it formerly prevailed . . . The farmer is vanishing and disappearing in the fields, the sailor on the sea, the soldier in the camp, innocence in the market-place, justice in the courts, harmony among friendships, skill among the arts, discipline in morals.
> (*Ad Demetrianum* 3, tr. R.J. Deferrari (adapt.))

There can be no doubt that Cyprian's tone here is apocalyptic, and is intended as a warning. Many people surely shared his view, irrespective of the real conditions prevailing in the mid-third century. At any rate, the growing demand for oracles reflects the same feeling of insecurity as that evoked here.

Experience at the level of the individual, at home in the family, for example, or in relation to death, was in keeping with the same general view. We live now in ever smaller families: many people hardly know what it is to have a brother or a sister, let alone to lose one. In the ancient world things were very different. What we today call socialisation took place in the context of big families, with many siblings. Death too was a daily occurrence at all social levels, and in all age-groups. This did not mean that people were indifferent to death, but they were familiar with it, and they surely had therefore a different relation to life and to religion.[28] The predominant pattern of mortality was one of widely variable individual age at death, with a very uncertain and unpredictable individual life-expectancy. Life in fact consisted of a more or less long, more or less important earthly component, and a more significant post-mortem component in the other world. Dying was just a transition. A perspective such as this understandably influenced religious practice, which sought, far more urgently than now, refuge and, especially, help and protection, not simply within one religious community but in a whole variety of them.

In this account of the kosmos, there was one source of hope for humankind. For in every person there was a link to the better world of the heavenly bodies, namely the soul. In the soul is to be found a fraction of changeless Being, of what is forever itself, a particle of light deriving from that Light which, before it fell into our bodies, dwelt in the sphere of the fixed stars. The soul's passage through the planetary spheres is described by the Platonist Macrobius, around the turn of the fifth century AD, in his commentary on Cicero's 'Scipio's dream':

> The soul, having started on its downward course from the intersection of the zodiac and the Milky Way to the successive spheres lying beneath, as it passes through these spheres, not only takes on the afore-mentioned envelopment in each sphere by approaching a luminous body, but also acquires each of the attributes which it will exercise later. In the sphere of Saturn it obtains reason and understanding, in Jupiter's sphere the power to act, in Mars' sphere a bold spirit, in the Sun's sphere sense-perception and imagination. In Venus' sphere the impulse of passion, in Mercury's sphere the ability to speak and interpret and in the lunar sphere the function of molding and increasing bodies.
>
> (*In Somn.* 1.12.3–4, tr. W.H. Stahl)

The idea of such a passage was widespread, though individual fantasy had plenty of room to manoeuvre when it came to details. The scientific aspect of such doctrines appealed to the reason, for they were based upon current astronomical views. But equally one could take pleasure in the images and symbols, such as those of the Mithraic reliefs, and draw from popular narratives the comforting promise that the soul is immortal.

In this connection, we must turn to dreams and visions. In our culture, seeing visions and hearing voices are generally considered signs of mental illness. But they belong to a group of experiences whose religious character was never doubted in the ancient world, for all that their shadowy nature made definition elusive. Gods drew near to humankind in the images that appear during sleep, to communicate for example that they wished for a votive. One Mithraist set up an altar *somno monitus*, 'admonished in a dream' (V 304). We are nowadays inclined to translate images into abstract ideas. We tend to understand mythological and religious images primarily as allegorical guises for conceptual claims. But in ancient religion images, or rather the ways in which people perceived images, were based upon a quite different psychology. They were apprehended directly, rather as a dream operates with images. In all likelihood, such images did not need to be explained conceptually: their meaning was grasped instinctively, their imaginative burden interiorised, and then in turn further expressed in myths, legends and folk-tales. The fourth-century AD grammarian Servius found a neat phrase for this ancient view of images and narrative reliefs: 'we should understand that in religious contexts simulation is allowed to be veridical'.[29] Suggestion becomes reality. Our modern explanations, if they manage to hit the mark at all, are always impoverished by comparison with the unmediated experience available to the ancient worshipper.

After death the soul can find its way back again, can re-ascend. Its home is beyond the sphere of the fixed stars, it yearns to return there all the while it is compelled to dwell in the prison-house of the physical body. Seneca captures this human longing for the other world:

> Some day the secrets of nature shall be disclosed to you, the haze will be shaken from your eyes, and the bright light will stream in upon you from all sides. Picture to yourself how great is the glow when all the stars mingle their fires; no shadow will disturb the clear sky . . . Then you will say that you have lived in darkness, after you have seen, in your perfect state, the perfect light – that light which you now behold darkly with vision that is cramped to the last degree. And yet, far off as it is, you already look upon it in wonder; what do you think the heavenly light will be when you have seen it in its proper sphere?
>
> (*Ep.* 102.28–9, tr. R.M. Gummere)

This vision of light was influenced by one of the changes that came about in the Hellenistic period: star-worship entered the Greek, and later the Roman, world from the Near East. Philosophy conducted in the Greek tradition was influenced in many ways by the tenets of this astral piety.

Among these stellar cults, Ba'alim from Syria, originally divinities of life and natural growth, but which had by now become astral or celestial gods under the influence of Babylonian religion, enjoyed particular favour. Divinities such as the Jupiter of Doliche in Commagene (Dülük in South East Turkey), or the Jupiter of Heliopolis (Baalbek in the Lebanon), had reached Italy already in the late Republic. Their importance grew during the Principate, especially in the Severan period. Julia Domna, wife of Septimius Severus (reigned AD 193–211), was the daughter of the high priest of the Ba'al of Emesa. With the accession to the imperial throne of Elagabalus in 218, a high priest of this cult actually ruled over the Roman empire. Finally, Aurelian (AD 270–5) elevated the Syrian sun-god under the name of Sol

Invictus to the rank of high god of the empire, and transported the cult-image, probably from Palmyra, to Rome.

More important than actual worship of these gods, however, was the theology which accompanied them. The celestial and solar divinities of the East were crucial in the shift towards belief in a supreme deity. This belief, by which the Sun, a male god both in Greek (*Helios*) and in Latin (*Sol*), was promoted to an all-powerful godhead whose life-giving power extended throughout the universe, became fused with the monotheistic tendencies of rationalist philosophy. And so it was that in the course of the Principate a solar pantheism – the idea that the Sun is all-powerful, and that Sol comprehends most gods – spread all over the Roman world. The Sun did not merely denote the heavenly body, a constituent of the material world, but was conceived also as the apprehensible manifestation of the Highest Being, the one all-powerful God. Reverence for the visible heavens became veneration for a God who had created the universe and set it to work.

At the same time there rapidly gained ground at all levels of society a belief in the power of fate, a belief whose visible symptom was astrology. It became fashionable to have one's horoscope cast and to enquire what the stars might declare to be the most propitious moment for undertakings great and small. The Emperor Augustus had his horoscope published, and issued coins that bore his zodiacal sign, Capricorn. Constantine commissioned astrologers to work out the most favourable juncture for the foundation of his new capital, Constantinople.

At the same time there were raised numerous voices that promised to free humankind from bondage to Fate. Graeco-Roman tolerance in matters religious had led to a confused Babel of cults and creeds. The most notable of these were the so-called mystery religions, one of which was Mithraism.

CHAPTER 3

Mystery religions[30]

In the ancient world, the term 'mysteries' was used to refer to secret cults throughout the period from the seventh century BC to the fourth century AD. All shared two basic features: the injunction to silence, intended to prohibit ritual details from reaching the outside world; and the promise of salvation to initiates.

The mystery-cults were voluntary associations of believers. Anyone who wished to join and fulfilled the requirements necessary to membership might be admitted, wherever he or she came from and whatever his or her social status (though social status did not simply cease to count). Such cults – and here they differed from Christianity – were generally not exclusive. Becoming a member of such an association did not preclude taking part in official public cult, whether state or civic, or initiation into other mysteries. There was no difficulty about being able to accept new religious ideas while continuing to believe in old ones.

Mystery-cults are characterised by a range of features typical of all such religions. Their special mark was an initiation-ritual which was secret – precisely, a mystery. The burden of the secret was the knowledge of the initiand's transformation. It was believed that participation in the cult transformed a person, and that this transformation was necessary before he or she could partake of the salvation offered. Salvation might comprehend anything that human beings yearn for, preservation from the changes and chances of this earthly life, or protection from illness and misfortune; but above all the soul's salvation after death. This present and future salvation was normally understood as immortality, or as union with the transcendent Deity. The mystery-cults shared the conviction that deliverance and salvation are the aim of all human existence on earth, and that they are to be attained by ceremonial replication of the god's experience. Imitation of a god's deeds was a well-proven means of acceding to the god's status. Identification with divinity, which we have mentioned already (p. 9), symbolised indeed that one had achieved salvation.

It was knowledge of this secret which bound the initiates one to another and distinguished them from non-initiates: it was a fundamental assumption of such cults that one could only attain the desired salvation once one had been initiated. The name of the divinity who bestowed salvation, on the other hand, was generally known, and likewise who was a member of which congregation, and where they met. In the case of Mithras, for example, outsiders must surely have known about the cult-relief showing the god as bull-slayer, and also the narrative describing the sacred deed, the cult-legend. What was restricted was solely the ritual, the ceremonial, and thus access to deliverance: because only the community of the initiated knew the means by which salvation might be acquired.

Initiation was preceded by a variety of purification rituals, such as fasting and sexual continence. After these preliminaries, there took place the actual ritual of initiation, with the transmission of the religious message: the initiates learned secret phrases, signs of recognition, symbols, emblems. There followed finally the main ceremony, the vision of the deity, in which light-effects commonly played a part, and then at last union with the godhead. The individual human being shared in the divine, experienced his or her own divinisation, that would give salvation and deliverance on the day that his or her soul left the earthly body. Such divinisation required a particular state of mind, a special religious mood for reception of the holy, a heightened state of feeling and imagination that was content to leave a great deal unexamined in the half-light of adumbration, but open to impressions and emotions aroused by the striking ritual representation of the god's true being and myth. In each mystery-cult, it was the power of the secret formulae employed, the richly symbolic rituals and dramatic performances, not to mention the dressing up in special garments and the shared meals, that ensured acceptance of the salvation offered.

It is this in context that the cult of Mithras belongs, as we meet it in the Principate by way of an abundance of archaeological evidence, and a pitiful remnant of literary testimony.

CHAPTER 4

The nature of the evidence

Mithras is just one god in the pantheon of ancient deities, related to many, identified with many. We should resist the inclination to view this multifariousness, this impulse to syncretistic identification, as signs of infirmity and decadence. That is how the Christians saw it, and they reacted accordingly. It was in reply to Christian charges that Symmachus formulated his famous phrase, 'There is no single way to the Truth'[31] – nor, we could add, 'to salvation'. The cult of Mithras offered one among several ways. Its attractiveness is indisputable; which is of course not to deny that only a tiny fraction of the population of the Roman empire was initiated into it.[32]

The cult is found from Britain to the Black Sea, from the Rhine to the Nile, over a period of almost 300 years, during which conditions in the Empire altered considerably. This means that, even if the main tenets, the most important features, remained the same, the mysteries must have undergone many changes. Change was all the easier in that there was no higher-level organisation, so that the cult was free to alter in accordance with the wishes of its members in their small congregations. For that very reason, it is unsatisfactory to speak of the mysteries of Mithras as a unified religion. To do so makes things simpler, but it also gives a false impression. No doubt we cannot avoid doing so; we should nevertheless remain alert to the problem.

There was a whole variety of local and regional variations and influences. Those on the Rhine were different from those on the Nile. For example, we find Mithras represented as a hunter at Vicus Med(-) (Dieburg) behind the Main-*limes* in Germania Superior (V 1247), just as he is at Dura-Europos in Coele Syria, on the eastern frontier of the empire (V 52).The Palmyrene archers at Dura, who formed a considerable proportion of the Mithraists there, saw Mithras as a mounted hunter with bow and arrow, in the uniform of an officer of their unit, decorated with embroidered facings. At Dura the god is hunting gazelles, at Dieburg hares. Local everyday differences show up, though we cannot always recognise them as easily as in this example. Many differences between the reliefs must be due to local tastes or artistic traditions. Local difference may even extend to the way in which the name of the god is written: at one of the mithraea at Apulum in Dacia (Alba Iulia, Romania), for example, it is noticeably often spelled Mythras (V 1939, 1943, 1945). I can here give only an occasional impression of the great variety of these repeated differences, and sometimes – unavoidably – that will involve merely listing a series of archaeological finds.

Because Mithraic congregations regularly remained small (p. 105), the religious views of their members were largely contingent upon social rank, occupation and educational level. When a religion is in transit, and spreads widely in both space and social location, often only the language and the imagery remain constant, not the content and substance: for the value of a sign depends upon its context. A mainly military congregation would have different religious interests and different emphases, would interpret symbols differently, from, say, one consisting primarily of slaves. Only very few Mithraists, surely, were in a position to read the dialogues of Plato.[33] It makes a considerable difference whether such a cult is practised in an urban context, such as Rome or Ostia, or by farmers in the mountains of Bosnia.[34] Lastly, the influence of other cults or religious movements brought about local changes, depending upon how strongly they were absorbed. The philosopher Celsus provides evidence in the late second century AD of the influence of gnostic groups on the cult of Mithras,[35] and that was certainly more strongly perceptible by the banks of the Nile than on the Rhine.

If the cult of Mithras certainly owed something of its popularity to the discreet backing of the authorities, it owed much more to its convincing presentation, its impressive rituals and myth, of which sadly we can follow little and comprehend less. The cult is an example of the primacy of images in the ancient world, in ancient thought, and of the power of the symbolic, of life lived beneath the suzerainty of symbols.

The God and his Mysteries

CHAPTER 5

The growth of the cult

THE EARLIEST EVIDENCE

The earliest securely dated evidence for the cult of Mithras does not stem from Italy but from the provinces; in each case, however, in connection with people originally from Italy. An important example is the dedication of a centurion of the *cohors XXXII voluntariorum civium Romanorum* from Nida, behind the Wetterau-limes in Germania Superior (Heddernheim/Frankfurt am Main), that is, a unit recruited, unlike most auxiliary units, from among Roman citizens – primarily Italians at this period (V 1098). The cohort was stationed in Nida only until the end of the first century AD, when it was transferred to Ober-Florstadt, a little further to the North-East. The inscription is thus probably to be dated before about 90. A cavalryman named Tacitus dedicated his votive altar in the same mithraeum sometime before 110 (V 1092). This example shows that the new cult quickly found support among soldiers: his altar is admittedly dedicated to Fortuna, but carries on the reverse a relief of Mithras dragging the bull. A second mithraeum was built in Nida c.AD 100, which suggests that the cult had already become successful. The date is fixed by the coarse-ware pottery found in the temple.[36]

We also have a terminus *ante quem* for an inscription from Carnuntum in Pannonia Superior (Bad Deutsch-Altenburg, Austria) dedicated by a centurion from Italy serving in the *legio XV Apollinaris* (V 1718). This legion was stationed at Carnuntum until about the end of the reign of Trajan (98–117). The first evidence for the cult in Moesia Inferior is a dedication of c.AD 100 by a slave in the service of an Italian customs-farmer, found at Novae (Steklen, Bulgaria) (V 2269).

The mysteries thus reached both the Rhine and the Danube from Italy. It was soldiers recruited in Italy, and persons in the service of Italian customs-farmers or other Roman citizens from Italy, who carried the new cult to the provinces. We may compare, for example, the process whereby Italians pushed into Dalmatia (the western Balkans) in the first two centuries of the Empire, or the colonisation of Dacia (Romania) that began with Trajan's conquest.

A passage by the poet Statius, written about AD 90, evidently alludes to some Mithraic relief in a mithraeum at Rome. Apollo as a Sun-god is equated with Mithras 'who beneath the rocks of a Persic cave twists the renitent horns' (*Theb.* 1. 719–20). Some aspects of the myth of Mithras were already so well known in Rome by this time that Statius' audience could make some sense of the god's name and what he was doing.

One of the earliest datable inscriptions from the capital, Rome, is to be found on a free-standing sculpture of Mithras slaying the bull (fig. 105), dedicated by a slave who cannot have lacked financial means: *Alcimus Ti(beri) Cl(audi) Liviani ser(vus) vil(i)c(us) Sol(i) M(ithrae) v(otum) s(olvit) d(onum) d(edit)* (V 594). Alcimus was the slave-administrator of one Ti. Claudius Livianus, who is probably to be identified with the praetorian prefect under Trajan, so that the votive is to be dated to the first quarter of the second century AD. This dedication is important for another reason too. It shows that Sol and Mithras were already identified with one another in one of the earliest known inscriptions. It is also worth noting the mention by name of the praetorian prefect. Such a mention does not of course imply that he had been initiated into the mysteries, but it certainly would not have been possible for the slave to dedicate such a monument without his master's knowledge. We can take it that he had approved of members of his slave-household being admitted to the cult of Mithras. We know nothing about the early legal status of such congregations, but we can hardly assume that a religion which very soon won adherents in the army, and in the clerical grades of the imperial administration, was long left unregulated. It must very quickly have been recognised as an approved cult (*religio licita*).

The cult spread from Italy, then. In view of the sheer amount of evidence found there, we can probably point specifically to the area of Rome and Ostia. The cult in Rome retained some peculiarities well after the first century AD, though we have no firmly datable monuments from the early period. Among these idiosyncrasies we can list the term *spelaeum*, ritual cave, for the mithraeum, which was not replaced by the word *templum* as quickly as in the provinces (p. 42). The iconographic evidence also suggests that in Rome greater emphasis was laid, and over a longer period, on the bull-slaying itself than elsewhere. Whereas in Italy only one monument in ten alludes to additional themes from the myth, in the provinces one in four does so.

EXPANSION

By the middle of the second century AD the cult had penetrated virtually the whole extent of its later territory. The number of mithraea increased constantly, and as a result the epigraphic evidence begins to multiply. Mithraism had by this time long transcended its early social catchment and had begun to find adherents from a wider spectrum. Slaves became freedmen, soldiers after their retirement became prosperous civilians; and no doubt both groups ascribed their social advancement, among other things, to their god (p. 142).

From the reign of Marcus Aurelius (161–80), and particularly from that of his son Commodus (180–92), we find in mithraea inscriptions dedicated *pro salute imperatoris Caesaris*, for the health and safety of the emperor. Such expressions, often associated with the fulfilment of vows, were one of the most characteristic forms of the imperial cult.[37] They stress the emperor's rôle as guarantor of peace and security, and in this connection invoke Mithras as the source of these blessings. There could thus develop a close link between personal religious obligations and the imperial cult. Over the long term, Mithraic votive-inscriptions that name the emperor, and thus assume the dignity of a quasi-official act, could not have been dedicated without the authorities' knowledge. That is especially true in the case of dedicators who were soldiers, administrative slaves belonging to the customs-farmers, or imperial slaves and freedmen.

We may cite here the example of an inscription from Histria in Moesia Inferior (in the Dobrogea, Romania) that lists the founders of the mithraeum there: the fact that it is dated by the (imperial) priesthood of the legate, who was also the city's patron, gives the text a quasi-official character (V 2296). The openness of Mithraic votives in this connection can further be illustrated by an example from Immurium in Noricum (Moosham, Austria). Here a benefactor's name has been erased, probably at the time when local opponents were eliminated during the widespread political conflicts of AD 196.[38] Such gestures were of course also a mark of the congregation's loyalty towards the emperor.

Under Commodus, *invictus*, Invincible, became part of the semi-official imperial titulature, an epithet that Mithras had borne from the very beginning. The parallel induced a centurion of a *vexillatio Brittonum* stationed at Volubilis in Mauretania Tingitana (Morocco) to put up an inscription at his own expense for Mithras, *invictus (deus)*, *pro salute et incolumitate Imperatoris Caesaris Lucii Aelii Aurelii Commodi pii invicti felicis Herculis Romani*, 'for the safety and deliverance of the Emperor (Commodus), dutiful, invincible, favoured of god, the Roman Hercules'.[39] Similar considerations may have influenced the dedicator of an inscription from Rome, a priest of Sol Invictus who offered an altar to Silvanus *salvis Aug[g(ustis)] invictis*, 'in view of the safe preservation of the invincible emperors' (V 502). Both inscriptions imply a parallelism between Imperator *invictus* and Invictus Sol, which may well have smoothed the way for their complete identification in the formula Sol Invictus Imperator. Dedications *D(eo) S(oli) I(nvicto) Imp(eratori)* have actually been found in mithraea, for example on the cult-relief set up by C. Amandinius Victor, a military *bucinator* (bugler) at Durnomagus (Dormagen) on the Rhine in Lower Germany (fig. 46).[40]

There is no doubt that it was a self-identification with Hercules the Invincible that prompted Commodus to take the epithet *invictus*. The notion, however, was by no means exclusively associated with one god alone, and many Mithraists, like the centurion at Volubilis, must certainly have taken advantage of the indeterminacy of the vague *invictus* in the imperial titulature to associate it with their god. And so, from the second half of the second century up to the fourth, we find the emperor ever more frequently included in the group of those for whose sake a statue or a votive-inscription was dedicated to Mithras (p. 39).

Such texts were sometimes cut for special occasions. Two imperial freedmen, for example, set up an inscription at Rome in honour of the return of Septimius Severus from his Parthian expedition in AD 202, *pro salute et reditum et victorias* (!), 'for his safe return and victories' (V 407). A priest of the cult, together with other members, had a temple built for Deus Sol Invictus, adorned with the god's statue, also on the occasion of the emperor's safe return from war (V 626).

It is, I think, significant that we come across inscriptions of this kind from all over the Roman empire where Mithraism is represented, offered by dedicants from all the social groups that favoured the cult. Two *seviri* of the *colonia* of Carnuntum in Pannonia Superior, L. Septimius Valerius and L. Septimius Valerianus, jointly dedicated both a relief and an altar, and had the mithraeum restored (V 1659, 1661). The altar they erected to honour Septimius Severus, the relief for him together with his son Caracalla. The occasion for these gestures was no doubt their having been freed by the emperor. To have become *seviri*, presidents of a college of priests composed of freedmen, they must quickly have made good in the provincial city. In recommending their imperial benefactor to Mithras, they saw a fitting means of demonstrating their loyalty to the imperial house to which they owed their citizenship.

The cult of Mithras never became one of those supported by the state with public funds, and was never admitted to the official list of festivals celebrated by the state and the army – at any rate, in so far as the latter is known to us from the *Feriale Duranum*, the religious calendar of the units at Dura-Europos in Coele Syria; the same is true of all other mystery cults too. This of course does not exclude the possibility that the emperors and their circle may have felt a more than casual personal sympathy for the cult, but they certainly tolerated, perhaps even encouraged, their subjects' adherence. We can point to a connection, at least at the individual level, between state cult and the mysteries of Mithras in those cases in which initiates were also provincial high priests or city *flamines*. The same point can be made about the equestrian *sacerdos* of the *domus Augusta* under Commodus, who in addition was a Mithraic *pater*, Father.[41]

Sol Invictus Mithras was a god of the contract and of loyalty, and thus pre-eminently congenial to the political order. The fit became still closer when Sol Invictus was heralded, at first sporadically under different emperors, then loudly and persistently from Commodus and the Severans. The emperor himself became the vice-gerent of the sun-god, he was *invictus*, *comes* and *conservator*. He thus assumed the same epithets, 'invincible', 'companion', 'protector', that Mithras, the invincible sun-god, had long made his own. In parallel to this process occurred the astonishing spread of the cult in the later second and early third centuries AD, the very period, that is, when Sol appears as a type on coin reverses. Official support for Sol Invictus thus encouraged entry into the mysteries of Mithras. This extraordinary expansion, documented by the archaeological monuments, finds its literary correlate in two books which seem to have appeared around the middle of the second century. A certain Pallas devoted a monograph to Mithras; and then Euboulus, a little later, wrote a History of Mithras, Ἱστορία περὶ τοῦ Μίθρα, in several rolls.[42] Both wrote primarily for a readership in Rome and undoubtedly helped to advertise the cult further.

An initiate into the mysteries of Mithras would view public recognition of Sol, especially on countless coins, as honour paid to the god whom the initiate served, disregarding the fact that others, who were not members of the Mithraic community, did not do so. But the adherents of Mithras surely spoke of the fact that Mithras was Sol, and that it was possible to encounter the official Sol Invictus in their mysteries. As we shall see (p. 107), there was in the cult a whole range of secret utterances (*symbola*), as well as special connotations given to ordinary expressions. But many of the words and terms employed retained their ordinary meaning and served to link the cult to the wider everyday world, with normality and with ordinary religious practice. The epithet *invictus* for Mithras was no doubt one of them.

Friedberg
Ober-Florstadt
Heddernheim/
Frankfurt
Rückingen
Groß-
Krotzenburg
Groß-Gerau
Stockstadt
Dieburg
Ladenburg
Neuenheim
Wiesloch
inset

High
Rochester
Rudchester
Carrawburgh
Housesteads
Whitley
Castle

St Albans
London

Krefeld-Gellep
Dormagen
Cologne

see
inset

Bingen
Mainz
Trier
Osterburken
Gimmeldingen
Heilbronn
Mackwiller
Mundelsheim
Sarrebourg
Fellbach
Ittenwiller
Strasbourg
Künzing
Bad Deutsch-
Altenburg
Biesheim
Riegel
Pfaffenhofen-
am-Inn
Linz
Skt.
Andrä
Stix-Neusiedl
Illmitz
Moosham
Fertőrákos
Mauls
Klagenfurt
Bordeaux
Chiusa
St Urban
Ptuj
Zgornja
Pohanca
Lezoux
Trojana
Rayanov
Sisak
Martigny
Milan
S. Giovanni
Grich
Pritoka
di Duino
Jezerine
Angera
Lodi
Vécchio
Vratnica
Golubić
Sinac
Bihać
Modena
Bologna
Ivóševci
Split
Crikvine
Sentino
Bolsena
S. Gemini
Montoro
Mérida
Fiano Romano
Rome
Ostia
Marino
Lanúvio
Capua
Posillipo

Skikda
Cirta

Diana
Lambaesis

Volubilis

km0   500

The Roman Empire

Mithraic sites mentioned in the text and captions

Bad Deutsch-
Altenburg
Szentendre
Szőny ● Budapest
Ilmitz ● ● Alcsut
Nagytétény

Alba Iulia
Veţel ● ● Doştat
Sarmizegetusa
Reşca
Hinag ●
Slăveni
Belgrade ● ● Kostolac
Jajce ● ● Rogatica
Konjic ●
Bijelo Polje ● Paraćin
Golema Kutlovica ● Kreta ● ● Steklen
Kumanovo ● ● Lopata ● Sofia ● Stari-Nikup
Biljanovac ● Radomir
Gaganica ● Vetren

Histria
Tirguşor
Vasile Roaita
Gant La Mangalia

Kerch'

Trabzun

Boghaz-Köy

Kayseri
Nemrud
Dagh

Faraşa ●

Tarsus ● ● Dülük

Andror

Hawarti

Dura-Europos ●

Sidon
Sia'

Alexandria

Anyone who worshipped Mithras as Sol Invictus Mithras could certainly believe that he was participating in the official cult of Sol, even though the cult of Mithras itself was neither official nor public. The followers of Mithras saw their god as protector of the imperial house, because the emperor recognised Sol Invictus; and Sol Invictus had always been identical to their god.

THE FOURTH CENTURY

The bulk of the surviving epigraphic evidence, which is no less difficult to date than the iconographic, dates from the period between AD 150 and 250. Relatively few inscriptions of any kind survive from the second half of the third century, and the cult of Mithras is no exception. It is only at the turn of the fourth century that we have a series of documents which reveal senior public officials supporting the cult. On the basis of these dedications, we can establish a revival in the cult's fortunes after the turmoil of the third century, a revival that included much rebuilding. This was a period of general instauration, not merely of the cult of Mithras, but also of many others – a moment in fact of widespread religious renewal. The inscriptions witness to the erection of new temples, but more frequently still of restoration of old ones.[43]

We may mention first of all the dedication by the Tetrarchs dating to the year AD 308 (V 1698). On the occasion of their meeting at Carnuntum in Pannonia Superior, Diocletian, now in retirement, together with the ruling emperors, the *Iovii et Herculii religiosissimi Augusti et Caesares*, dedicated an altar to Mithras as *fautor imperii sui*, as protector of their empire, and thereby gave expression to an understanding of the god already shared by Mithraists for centuries. Concomitantly, the Tetrarchs had part of Mithraeum III at Carnuntum repaired. At the same time, appropriately enough, a soldier at Ulcisia Castra (Szentendre), also in Upper Pannonia, dedicated his altar *I(nvicto) M(ithrae) Patrio*, to his native Mithras (AE 1926: 72).

In AD 311, the *dux* of the new province of Noricum Mediterraneum restored a decayed mithraeum in the capital Virunum (Klagenfurt), which had lain neglected for more than a half-century: *templum vetusta(te) conlabsum* (!) *quot* (!) *fuit per annos amplius L desertum* (V 1431). The equestrian *dux limitis provinciae Scythiae* dedicated a relief at Axiopolis in Moesia Inferior (Hinag, Romania) (V 2280). A colleague repaired a mithraeum whose roof had fallen in at Poetovio in Pannonia Superior (Ptuj, Slovenia) (V 1614). And at Lentia (Linz) in Noricum a new mithraeum was actually made within an existing building (V 1414).

The last known dated foundation of a mithraeum is at Gimmeldingen/

Neustadt in Upper Germany (south-west of Ludwigshafen). To judge from the inscriptions, all the furniture, including a small relief of Mithras and some altars, was presented by a certain Materninius Faustinus (an indigenous name), who held the grade *Corax*, Raven. He gave not merely the furniture but also the temple itself, which he terms *fanum*, and which was dedicated by the *pater*, the leader of the community, in the year AD 325. Materninius Faustinus also provided the land on which the mithraeum was built, and dedicated it to the god (V 1313–22). The inscriptions suggest some difficulty with Mithraic terms: *Midre* for *Mithras*, for example, and *Carax* for *Corax*. The relief (fig. 3), to be sure, offers the prescriptive actors (p. 78–90): Mithras killing the bull, the torch-bearers (albeit in the less common position, with Cautes on the left, Cautopates on the right [p. 96]), Sun and Moon, dog, snake and scorpion. But the execution suggests that the sculptor no longer had much practice in carving such monuments.

3. *Gimmeldingen/Neustadt an der Weinstraße: the latest datable cult-relief N. of the Alps, dedicated AD 325. Like the owner of the unpublished mithraeum at Bornheim/ Sechtem nr. Bonn, Materninius Faustinus built his temple on his own property. Errors in spelling Mithras' name show that it was usually pronounced 'Mítras'.*

THE PAGAN REVIVAL

Mithras also found a place in the 'pagan revival' that occurred, particularly in the western empire, in the latter half of the fourth century AD. For a brief period, especially in Rome, the cult enjoyed, along with others, a last efflorescence, for which we have evidence from among the highest circles of the senatorial order. One of these senators was Rufius Caeionius Sabinus, who in 377 dedicated an altar M(atri) D(eum) M(agnae) Idaeae et Attidi Menoturano. Sabinus was p(ontifex) m(aior), hierof(anta) D(eae) Hecat(ae), au(gur) pub(licus) p(opuli) R(omani) Q(uiritium), pater sacror(um) Invict(i) Methrae (!), tauroboliatus M(atris) D(eum) M(agnae) Id(aeae) et Attidis Minoturani, a lengthy list of priestly offices, the details of which are of no importance here. As a senior priest of the state religion, he lived in the Regia in the Forum Romanum, near the temple of Vesta. This is the background to the verse text inscribed on the altar, which may be translated:

> High-born descendant of an ancient house, pontifex for whom the blessed Regia, with the sacred fire of Vesta, does service, augur too, worshipper of reverend Threefold Diana, Chaldaean priest of the temple of Persian Mithras, and at the same time leader of the mysteries of the mighty, holy taurobolium.[44]

The demonstrative honour paid in public to so many traditional Roman cults was also a protest on the part of the pagan élite of the former capital against the emperors' increasingly rigid stance in religious matters. In 382, Gratian (367–83), who was the first emperor to have renounced the title of pontifex maximus in 379, had the famous altar of Victoria removed once again from the Senate house, and abolished the state subsidies for the erection and maintenance of temples for pagan worship in Rome. The senator Tamesius Olympius Augentius, the grandson of Nonius Victor Olympius, a senator who was also Senior Father, pater patrum, of a Mithraic congregation, and several of whose inscriptions dating from the years 357–62 have survived (V 400–5), reacted to this move by building a mithraeum at his own expense, and recorded both building and protest in a poem:

> In former days, my grandfather Victor, devotee of the heavens and stars, erected with royal magnificence a temple to Phoebus; his grandson of the same name now outdoes his piety, has built a cave – and for you Rome need not find the resources. For the pious it is better to lay out than to save; who is wealthier than the heir who without ostentation shares his goods with the gods in heaven?[45]

If we are to understand the motives of those involved in the 'pagan revival' we must look a little more closely at their own religious views, which are documented in a whole series of inscriptions. One of their religious centres was the temple of the Mater Magna on the Vatican Hill (the Phrygianum), where they put up numerous altars.[46] The best-known representative of this group, indeed its leader, was Vettius Agorius Prae-textatus, praefectus Urbi in 367 and praefectus praetorio in 384. Among his other offices, he was *pater patrum* in the cult of Mithras (V 420; CIL VI 1779). On his death in 384 he left his supporters without a leader. But they had brought new life to the old priestly offices of the state religion, such as the *pontifices maiores*, the *sacerdotes Vestae*, the *augures*, the *quindecim viri sacris faciundis*, and the *septemviri epulonum*. Most of these senators had undergone the taurobolium, that is, had undergone a ritual in which a bull was sacrificed over a pit containing the initiand; through the blood, he was reborn for eternity (*in aeternum renatus*: CIL VI 510). Mithras was also recruited among the deities, such as Liber, Isis, Hecate or Sol Invictus, the assumption of whose priesthoods, and initiation into whose mysteries, were now once again something to be proud of. One factor in the case of Mithras was that he had for so long been represented among the gods in Rome; another that he was regarded as one of numerous manifestations of the sun-god. The traditional reliefs of the bull-slaying continued to be set up, the familiar formulae continued to be employed, but it is difficult to decide how much of the actual cult or myth survived. We should at any rate beware of reading back into earlier periods the analogies with the taurobolium that become apparent in the late fourth century.

The imperial measures against paganism intensified in the reign of Theodosius (379–95). Pagan sacrifice and even visits to temples were forbidden in an edict dated 391 (*Cod. Theod.* 16.10.10). The latest known Mithraic monument, a drawing incised on glass, is dated to the same year (CIL VI 736). On 8 November of the next year, 392, all celebration of any pagan cult, even privately, was absolutely prohibited (*Cod. Theod.*16.10.12). Yet it was precisely in the private sphere that these cults persisted, in some cases for a very long time.

The new surge of interest in Mithras within the wider context of a general revival of traditional pagan religion was not limited to Rome, even if its epicentre was there. Members of the aristocracy took it with them when they left the former imperial capital. One senator at this period dedicated at Pausilypum (Posillipo, now in Naples) a cult-relief to Almighty Mithras (*omnipotens deus Mithras*) (V 174). The senatorial governor of Numidia built a *speleum* (!) *cum [sig]nis et ornamen[tis]* at Cirta (Constantine, Algeria) (V 129). Another example, finally, is the mithraeum of Sidon (Lebanon), where Flavius Gerontius dedicated in AD 389 a free-standing bull-slaying group and other statues now in the Louvre.[47]

THE END OF MITHRAISM

It is difficult to trace in detail when the cult of Mithras came to an end, except in those cases in which mithraea were actually destroyed or fell into ruins (p. 170–2). There is virtually no evidence for its continuance into the fifth century AD. Even in the fourth century inscriptions are uncommon, apart from the special case of Rome and the 'pagan revival' that we have just surveyed. The coarse-ware pottery used for the cult meals might be of some help in deciding how long a temple continued in use, but the material has been examined from this point of view only in very few cases. The coins unearthed in the destruction-levels of some mithraea might also be useful, though it would need to be established that the coins were offerings kept in the temple and not part of buried hoards.[48] Typical here are the finds at Pons Saravi, Gallia Belgica (Sarrebourg, dép. Moselle). The destroyers of the mithraeum found the votive coins that had been gathered and preserved over many years by the little congregation. A total of 274 was found by the excavators: the series begins with Gallienus (AD 253–68) and continues up to Theodosius (379–95), a period of 140 years. This example is characteristic both of the amount of money found in these temples and of the time it took to accumulate. The Christians who wrecked the temple did not steal the money dedicated to the god they detested, but scattered it mockingly all over the floor, just as they did with the rubble of the statues and altars they smashed, and the broken sherds of ritual crockery.[49] These and other coin-assemblages date the end of the cult to the late fourth century AD (p. 171).

CHAPTER 6

Recruitment [50]

We may begin by singling out two groups in which the cult of Mithras had no adherents. First, the mysteries admitted no women. This was a cult in which the female principle played no rôle, either on the divine or on the human level (disregarding standard Roman goddesses such as Juno, Venus, Diana and one or two others, who were in no sense deities central to the worship). As far as the cult's social composition goes, this meant that half of humankind could not be accepted on *a priori* grounds, which was a disadvantage in respect of numbers but did not amount to any great general weakness. For within the wide range of cults in the Roman empire there were also some exclusively for women; and, anyway, in a society dominated by men a male cult was at no particular disadvantage.

It is equally clear, secondly, that the cult of Mithras was not accepted by the ruling élite of the Roman empire. Making every allowance for gaps in the epigraphic record, it is striking that there are virtually no senators among the dedicators of inscriptions and reliefs, apart from the special situation during the fourth century (p. 29). Senators were fundamentally conservative with regard to religious matters, and are very poorly represented in other mystery cults too. [51] Equestrians, except when holding military posts, and decurions, apart from some cases in the Danube area, are almost equally under-represented. Thus those very orders are absent which, on the one hand, disposed of the financial means required to commission inscriptions and cult-reliefs in stone, and for whom, on the other, it was simply a matter of course to document their social superiority *inter alia* by means of inscriptions of all kinds.

As members of Mithraic congregations we find rather soldiers, members of the imperial administration in the clerical and sub-clerical grades, slaves and freedmen belonging to the *domus Caesaris* and private households, and ordinary citizens. In the following section, I have selected *exempli gratia* a few locations which have been generous in the production of evidence, in order to illustrate the social composition of the cult, evidence which could be filled out with examples from other provinces. But we must remember that, in trying to analyse the social composition of the mysteries, we are wholly dependent upon the inscriptions in which the dedicants of votive objects name themselves. We often only know something about the group of those who paid for the initial decoration of a temple. Particularly in the case of a small shrine, a single individual might well be in a position to provide a modest building, together with a few reliefs and altars. In one of the mithraea at Aquincum in Pannonia Inferior (Budapest) were five statue bases, all dedicated by M. Antonius Victorinus, an *aedilis*, one of the four most senior magistrates of the colonia.[52] Such furnishings, at any rate the reliefs and altars, could easily serve for several generations, so that there was no particular reason for later members of the congregation to record their names in stone.

SOLDIERS

The earliest evidence for the cult of Mithras at Carnuntum in Pannonia Superior is to be dated to the first half of the second century AD. As we might expect from the local importance of the legionary camp, the earliest Mithraists recorded there are soldiers (p. 21). It was Italians who brought the cult to the Danube. At Poetovio (Ptuj, Slovenia) in the same province, soldiers only became an important element in the cult's membership when it was decided under Gallienus (AD 253–68) to enlarge and repair one of the town's mithraea. Here we may note another point of significance in military contexts: entire groups of privileged soldiers, in this case of the *legio* V *Macedonica* and *legio* XIII *Gemina*, became members of the cult (as they also did elsewhere), being involved in the dedication of at least four monuments (V 1589, 1591, 1593, 1595). One of them, an image of the rock-birth (fig. 30), is dedicated to Mithras the invincible Sun for the well-being of the administrative staff of Flavius Aper, the equestrian commander in Poetovio, in charge of all, or at least a large proportion of, the troops there: *D(eo) S(oli) I(nvicto) M(ithrae)/ pro sal(ute) officialium Apri prae/positi legg(ionum) V M(acedonicae) et XIII Gem(inae)/ Galli(enarum)* (V 1594). It may well be that these privileged soldiers made their dedications under the influence of their commander, who himself dedicated the largest altar in the mithraeum, for the well-being of the emperor, decorated with reliefs that are of considerable importance for interpreting aspects of Mithraic ritual (V 1584, figs 4, 5; pp. 58, 72).

One of the cult's (to us) best-known adherents, the senator M. Valerius Maximianus, who was among the most successful of Marcus Aurelius'

4. *Colonia Ulpia Traiana Poetovionen-*
sis/Ptuj, Slovenia: r. lateral face of altar
in Mithraeum III, 'Water-miracle'. A
recently-published cult-vessel from Mainz
shows a Father seated on a chair and
shooting a bow. The event in the cult
myth was thus reproduced in a ritual in at
least one mithraeum.

5. *L. lateral face of same altar: the*
weapons of Mithras. The sword refers
to the bull-killing, and so Mithras' gen-
eration, and regeneration, of the natural
world. The bow with quiver, the arche-
typal 'Persian' weapons, alludes to the
'Water-miracle' reproduced on the other
face.

generals, was surely also influential in spreading the cult.[53] As legionary legate at Apulum in Dacia, he dedicated an altar to Mithras. Some years later we find him dedicating two Mithraic altars at Lambaesis, Numidia (Tazoult, Algeria), where he was again legionary legate. It seems almost to have become traditional in this North African provincial capital for the governor to have himself initiated into the mysteries of Mithras, since a number of them after Valerius Maximianus dedicated votive altars. We thus find votive altars dedicated in the second and third decades of the third century for the well-being of the imperial house, and the governor of the day, by senior officers of the legion that garrisoned Lambaesis, the *III Augusta*. And later, around the end of that century and into the fourth, votives were offered by two governors (now a post of equestrian rank).[54] The more interesting of them is Valerius Florus, who was governor in AD 303, and is known to have persecuted Christians. The paradigmatic rôle of those in authority in spreading the cult can also be illustared from elsewhere, such as Aquincum in Pannonia Inferior (Budapest). There were so many members of the provincial governor's staff here who had been initiated into the cult that the *pater* Arpocras could dedicate his altar *pro salute famili(ae)*, for the well-being of the governor's slave-household (V 1777).

Among dedications by soldiers, those by officers and under-officers are more frequent than those by ordinary soldiers. Thanks to their higher pay, they had greater means with which to pay for them; but such an example must also have had its effect upon their men. At Slăveni (com. Gostavătu) on the River Olt in Romania, the junior officers and senior under-officers (*principales*) of a cavalry *ala* dedicated an altar for the well-being of the entire unit (AE 1966: 314 = IDR 2: 510); at Romula (Reşca), a little further north, the ration-clerks (*librarii*) of one unit dedicated an altar together with their chief: *libr(arii) cum Anton(io) Z[oi]lo act(ario)* (V 2177).

In these areas, as well as in the Rhineland, the cult of Mithras was at first rooted in the army, but quickly found followers among the civilian population, at first of course among those who had settled around the various military camps. The cult's special attractiveness for soldiers is often emphasised, particularly in view of the grade *Miles*, Soldier.[55] The divine epithet *invictus* must certainly have appealed to soldiers, but the motif may have had a specific value for quite different social groups. In general we can say that the proportion of soldiers, even in the provinces where the legions were stationed, varies between 10 and 20 per cent, but never rises higher than that. After completing their service, that is, after between sixteen and twenty-five years, depending on the arm, soldiers were discharged, and returned to private life. But they remained attached to the cult of Mithras. One C. Iulius Val(ens) served in the governor's office in Viminacium, the capital of Moesia Superior (Kostolac, Yugoslavia) and headquarters of the *legio VII Claudia*. At the end of his service, he was sufficiently well-off to become decurion of the city, and have the mithraeum extensively repaired at his sole expense (V 2222). We can well imagine that, like others in the town, he had been initiated while serving as a soldier. If the god had helped one survive a no doubt dangerous life in such a profession, it would be natural to entrust the rest of one's life to him, quite irrespective of hopes for an after-life. In this way, while soldiers often provided the stimulus to found Mithraic congregations, once retired they could equally well act as multipliers in their new civilian surroundings.

We may look in this connection at Dacia, whose conquest and annexation began under Trajan in AD 107. The province was then romanised and consequently invaded by a whole variety of religious cults. It is quite uncertain whether the cult of Mithras entered the province with the soldiers in garrison or with the colonists who settled there from all over the empire, *ex toto orbe Romano* (Eutr. 8.6). The only circumstance which might point to soldiers as the colporteurs is that the evidence clusters in the military centres. On the other hand, we should note that one half of all Dacian Mithraic reliefs, and one third of all the Mithraic inscriptions, were found in the administrative capital, Sarmizegetusa (the site once again bears the name).

Soldiers, for example the praetorian cohorts in the capital, might be ordered anywhere in the empire. Four praetorians accordingly spent some time on the island of Andros in the Cyclades at the turn of the second and third centuries AD, perhaps to guard a harbour installation or an exile or two. The mithraeum built by these soldiers from Rome, in which they dedicated an inscription for the well-being of Septimius Severus, Caracalla and Geta, is one of the few so far known from the Greek-speaking part of the empire.[56]

In most areas, the cult had spread from the larger urban centres into the surrounding region. In the case of Carnuntum in Pannonia Superior, it was soldiers and office-holders of the city who carried it with them to their homes in Illmitz, Scarabantia (Fertörákos) or Stix-Neusiedl.[57] Around the beginning of the third century, the cult managed to penetrate the native population, and was widespread particularly in the Rhineland. The distribution of some mithraea in Dalmatia, such as the areas around Prozor and Sinać (Croatia), Bihać (Golubić, Jezerine, Pritoka in North Bosnia), and Konjic (Bosnia-Hercegovina), suggests that the cult was also accepted by the indigenous rural population of Dalmatia.

MINOR OFFICIALS

We find another social group among which the cult flourished at Poetovio (Ptuj, Slovenia). Here it was the slave officials of the customs-post who equipped the earliest of the temples we know of; a similar pattern holds good for many sites in Noricum (Austria) and Moesia Inferior (Bulgaria).[58] The various owners of the slaves came from Italy. Analogously to the case among the military, it is slaves in the senior position of supervisor (*vilicus*) or deputy-supervisor (*vicarius*) whose names we encounter in the documents. This earliest temple, of the mid-second century AD, presents a homogeneous grouping: nine out of eleven bases and altars, with or without a statue on top, were put up by personnel of the *publicum portorium Illyrici*, which at that time was controlled by lessees, the customs-farmers. The votive-altars and bases with statues are mostly similar in size and all are carefully worked. It is also striking that the texts are identically patterned, as may be seen from the following example:

D(eo) I(nvicto) M(ithrae)
OPTIMVS
VITALIS
SABINI(!) VERANI
P(ublici) P(ortorii) VIL(ici) VIC(arius)
V(otum) S(olvit)

'To the invincible god Mithras, Optimus, deputy of Vitalis, slave of Sabinius Veranus and supervisor of the customs-post, has fulfilled his vow' (V 1491). Both in this mithraeum and in the second temple found at Poetovio, which was built around the end of the second century, the worshippers rapidly became more socially mixed. Slaves belonging to the lessees of the customs continued to dedicate their votive offerings, though from the administrative reform under Commodus (AD 180–92) they had the status of imperial slaves. Such slaves, who were generally freed after a period of service, also carried the cult with them into their new social milieu. It is also worth noting that personnel from other customs-posts than Poetovio offered their votives there. This is explained by the fact that for a time Poetovio was the administrative headquarters of the entire Illyrian customs organisation (the *publicum portorium Illyrici*), which meant that some of the personnel spent time there in a professional capacity, and thus had the opportunity to join the Mithraic congregations there. It may not be just by chance that it was precisely such newcomers who were encouraged to dedicate votives in Poetovio.

As an initiate, it was evidently possible to enter another congregation if one moved one's place of residence. This is the obvious explanation for votives by the same person in two different mithraea. Unusual formulae in an inscription, or an unusual relief-type, amid otherwise homogeneous temple furniture, are also indications of such movements. For example, it is only in Italy that the common formula d(onum) d(edit), 'gave as a gift', appears in Mithraic inscriptions to any great extent (p. 22; fig. 105). If it turns up once in Dalmatia, as it does at Burnum (Ivoševci, Croatia), then the likeliest inference is that the dedicator brought it with him.[59] A similar point must apply to the thin plaque, measuring 20×19 cm ($8 \times 7\frac{1}{2}$ in), with a relief of the bull-slaying, that was hung up in Mithraeum I in Nida (Heddernheim) (V 1084). It is virtually unique in the Rhine area and must have been brought by its dedicator from the Danubian provinces.

I have stressed that we must assume that it was Italians who brought the cult of Mithras to the Danube and the Rhine. Throughout the period, Italian immigrants gave fresh supply to already existing congregations in these areas; it is surely no accident that all known priests in Pannonia Superior are of Italian origin. There are similar cases in other Danubian provinces.

THE MITHRAIC COMMUNITY AND THE SOCIAL ORDER

Once Mithraic temples had been established in a given area, the cult spread, as we might expect, within the families of the believers. Up to four members of the same family can be found pooling resources to dedicate a votive. The inscriptions mention brothers, grandfathers and grandsons, but mainly fathers and sons: the cult was clearly passed on from generation to generation. Equally, family connections, as well as professional ones, served to propagate the cult further.

Dedications for the well-being or deliverance of someone, *pro salute*, can tell us a good deal about social relations within Mithraic congregations. Such dedications were, in all cults and not merely mysteries, mainly for one's own well-being and that of one's own family: *pro salute sua* or, much more usually, *pro salute sua et suorum (omnium)*. These are the formulae which, with slight variations, we find on the votive-reliefs and altars. One might also simply say something like *pro se et suis*, 'for himself and his family and dependants'. These phrases include the members of the immediate family, who may also be listed individually: brothers, a wife, children.

However, inscriptions in which Mithraists link the fulfilment of their vow with a formula of good-will towards a third person are distinctly more common (one or two were erected for a friend, e.g. V 1873). In about one half of all cases this third person is the emperor (p. 24). In the others, the dedicators are mainly slaves and freedmen who combine their religious obligations to Mithras with those to their masters or patrons. Most of the slaves are in the privileged position of *actor* (household or estate administrator) or his *vicarius* (deputy). The freedmen sometimes include the family of their former owner in their dedications.

The inscriptions thus mention masters as well as their slaves, patrons as well as their freedmen. But it is always the *servi* and *liberti* who dedicated a votive for the well-being of their masters. In the light of that, it may not be by chance that in some cases the ordinary believers are slaves but the priests free persons. At Atrans, a customs-post in Noricum (Hrastnik-Trojana in Slovenia), for example, we find exclusively votives made by slaves, whereas the head of the community was a Roman citizen.[60]

Social distinctions were not laid aside in Mithraic congregations. There can be no doubt that any individual who had the means, and the Father's permission, to dedicate reliefs, altars or other cult furniture, as well as candles, even food, might do so. Though the social rank of every member of the community was known to all the others, the relevant inscription always carefully notes whether the dedicator was a slave, and what position he held, whether he was a freedman and who had freed him, whether he was a soldier and of what rank, whether he was a senatorial governor even – and so on.

A group of individuals from Micia in Dacia (Vețel, Romania) will serve to illustrate the close interrelationships between Mithraists. P. Aelius Euphorus founded a mithraeum in Micia, a dependent community of Sarmizegetusa. In the same town, he also made a dedication to Silvanus for the well-being of P. Aelius Marus, who is stated as being the lessee of the local grazing-land and salt-pans, *conductor pascui et salinarum*. Euphorus may thus well be the freedman of Marus. Atticus, a slave *actor* of Marus, also dedicated an altar in Micia for the well-being of his master. In Tibiscum (Jupa) nearby, the slave Hermadio, *actor* of Turranius Dius, dedicated an altar for the well-being of the same Marus. The connection here is that the master was married to Aelia Nice, who was probably related to Aelius Marus.[61]

It should be stressed that soldiers, administrative members of the *familia Caesaris*, slaves, freedmen and ordinary Roman citizens all found in the mysteries of Mithras a confirmation, or replication, of their normal everyday social experience outside the mithraeum.[62] Submission to authority, acceptance of a specific rôle within an organisation, identification with the prescribed values, conformity, fitting into the system, all of these were important in the army, the administration and the imperial and slave households. A similar point can be made about the ordinary citizen too: as farmer, merchant or craftsman he was dependent upon the members of the city élites, and equestrians and senators too. The return for being ready to accommodate and defer was the hope of improving one's own position and rising socially. We have here a phenomenon which helped underwrite the stability of the entire Roman social order.

That the ordinary individual should have sought to replicate normal social experience shows how thoroughly he accepted his place and so the entire social order of the imperial system. We may describe this as the typical attitude of the socially ambitious. The cult of Mithras appealed especially to those groups which valued authority and their own social advancement.

Relations within the religious community and within society at large, both interpersonal and between god and man, were structured in the same way, and express analogous values. The mysteries are not to be understood as a compensation for a decline in personal circumstances. On the contrary, it was in most cases, and especially in the Rhine and Danube areas, social risers who turned to this Roman cult; in these provinces, it was one element in a complex process of romanisation.

As just one example of this, I take a Greek inscription from Histria in Moesia Inferior (in the Dobrogea, Romania), which lists ten contributors to the foundation of the mithraeum there in the mid-second century (p. 23). The list contains the names of Roman citizens as well as Greek non-citizens, members of the local city council, and a soldier in the administrative branch, a *beneficiarius consularis*. It is headed by the Pontarch, the priest of Rome and Augustus of the Pontic League. [63]

From a modern standpoint, the cult of Mithras represents one factor in the maintenance of social control in the empire. It is a central function of any religion to formulate and amplify important integrative values. In the case of Mithras, we can see religion acting to underwrite the ideal social norm. The relations between social structure as a whole and that of the religious organisation were extremely close. Against this background, we can understand the efforts of the individual to ascribe his success, both within the cult and in the wider society, to his readiness to obey and his ability to accommodate. He stood for loyalty, including loyalty to the emperor, who himself represented the system as a whole (pp. 23–8).

CHAPTER 7

The mithraeum

This spot is blessed, holy, observant and bounteous:
Mithras marked it, and made known to
Proficentius, Father of the mysteries,
That he should build and dedicate a Cave to him;
And he has accomplished swiftly, tirelessly, this dear task
That under such protection he began, desirous
That the Hand-shaken might make their vows joyfully forever.
These poor lines Proficentius composed,
most worthy Father of Mithras.[64]

According to ancient custom, wrote Euboulus (ap. Porphyry, *De Antr. nymph.* 6), Mithras was worshipped in an appropriate rock-cave, the construction of which Proficentius describes in this poem from Rome by his own pen. Because Mithras killed the bull in a cave, his followers likewise performed the ritual reproduction of this saving act in a cave, or rather in a shrine which reproduced that cave, in a *spelaeum* ('cave'). It is worth noting that this term for the temple is used almost exclusively in Italy or by Italians: in the provinces, by contrast, the word *templum* occurs almost everywhere.[65] We may conclude that the characteristic feature of the mithraeum survived more strongly in the terminology used in Rome and Italy, where the cult originated and first won converts. Statius, our earliest literary evidence, describes it already at the end of the first century as a cult in a cave, *sub rupibus antri* (p. 22). The mysteries reached the provinces through Italian intermediaries, that is, as a Roman cult, so that Mithraists in those areas took over the ordinary Roman term for a shrine, *templum*. The mithraeum is also occasionally called a *fanum* or *crypta*.

THE BUILDING

Mithraea are for the most part small meeting-places for small congregations consisting of a handful of people. The main cellae of the largest temples to have been fully excavated, those beneath the Baths of Caracalla in Rome, and Carnuntum III, are 23m long and rather less than 10m wide (25 × 11 yd) (V 457; 1682). Most are less than ten metres in either dimension. It was evidently important to maintain the intimacy of the ritual meal, so Mithraists preferred to keep founding new, small communities. At Ostia we know of seventeen temples, and in Rome there were undoubtedly many more. Even in a small fort-settlement like Nida (Heddernheim) in Germania Superior, four temples have now been discovered. Since they were so small, a removal was easy enough to effect. One of the mithraea at Nida was in the way of the city-wall that was built c.AD 210, so the congregation simply took its votives with them to the new one. Because the buildings were so small, it was often possible for a single individual to pay the entire costs out of his own pocket. There is a statue base at Volsinii (Bolsena, Etruria) with a brief account of the mithraeum and its contents, all given by a single Mithraist: *Soli Invicto Mitrhae* (!) / *Tiberius Claudius Tiberi filius* / *Thermodon* / *spelaeum cum signis et ara ceterisque voti compos dedit*, 'To the invincible god Mithras, Tiberius Claudius Thermodon, son of Tiberius, mindful of his vow, has given the mithraeum with its statuary, and altar, and the other requisites' (V 660).

Dedicators occasionally mention that they have also vowed to the god the land on which the temple stood. In Mediolanum (Milan), the city council had made available the building plot for the spelaeum, and P. Acilius Pisonianus, *pater* of the community, later repaired the building at his own expense after it had been damaged by fire: *qui hoc speleum* (!) *vi ignis absumtum comparata area a republ(ica) Mediol(anensi) pecunia sua restituit* (V 706). Another member of the congregation also alludes to the city's generous gift, stating on his altar that the land had been provided by decree of the city council, expressed here by means of the usual abbreviation, *l(ocus) d(atus) d(ecreto) d(ecurionum)* (V 707). Elsewhere in Italy, at Montoro and San Gemini (Umbria), the *ordo decurionum* gave permission to rebuild mithraea destroyed in an earthquake.[66]

The architecture of mithraea is quite special, and its characteristic configuration makes it easy to identify such temples in excavations. At Rome and Ostia they often formed part of private buildings, the rooms being made available for the purpose by well-off members. At Ostia itself we find mithraea in all manner of buildings typical of a harbour-town like this: warehouses, shops, baths, apartment-houses. There are quite plain temples, such as the 'Sabazeum', and richly decorated ones, such as the 'Imperial Palace'.[67] Here as elsewhere, mithraea were part of city life. At Lentia (Linz) in Noricum, the temple of Mithras was directly beside that of the Capitoline triad. At Carnuntum and Poetovio, in Pannonia Superior, both a temple of Jupiter Dolichenus and one of the Mater Magna were located close by the mithraea.

As a rule, *spelaea* are subterranean rock-caves (one inscription uses the word *antrum*: V 407), which had to be artificially illuminated. For a Christian writer such as Tertullian, at the turn of the second and third centuries, the temples were *vere castra tenebrarum*, 'in truth strongholds of darkness' (*De cor.* 15). And in the fourth century, Firmicus Maternus declaims mockingly:

> They say (this god) is Mithras, but they perform his initiations in caves that are hidden away, so that, plunged perpetually into the pitchy murk of night, they may shun the grace of the bright and glorious light.
>
> (*Err. prof. rel.* 5.2)

The Mithraist, however, believed that his God came forth all the more gloriously out of this darkness, to give ever-renewed light to the world and his followers.

In rural areas it was occasionally possible for Mithraists to construct the mithraeum directly in an actual cave. In these cases, the natural properties of the landscape (in the Dalmatian hinterland, for example), the cult's prescriptions, and not least financial advantage neatly coincided, since the construction-work was less involved, and repairs less frequent, than was the case with free-standing buildings. Thus the mithraeum at Zgornja Pohanca in Pannonia Superior (Slovenia) was built into a cave beneath a slightly overhanging cliff (V 1457). The cave itself was artificially en-larged, and where the side-walls, which remained rough-hewn, were unsupported, they were underpinned with brickwork. The cult-relief in such natural caves was generally cut directly into the living rock, thus happily combining the message of the Rock-born God with the medium of the rock-carved relief. This is the case, for example, at Rayanov Grich (Croatia) (V 1852). But even here, where the relief is inside a natural recession, the area behind Mithras' head is worked much more deeply so as to make his act take place expressly in a cave, thus creating a double play of significations.[68] In towns, where for the most part caves and grottoes were not to be found, the temple, or at any rate the cult-room itself, was constructed below ground-level, so that one entered it by means of steps, sometimes seven in number. A section taken through Mithraeum II at Nida shows the different levels of the ante-room and the centre aisle of the cult-room (fig. 6). In the late phase of the mithraeum at Dura-Europos on the Euphrates the risers up to the cult-niche were set extremely shallow, so as to be able to fit in seven steps (V 37).

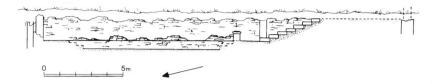

6. *Nida/Heddernheim: section through Mithraeum II (V 1108). To the S, the temple gave onto the street. This is the only certain case in which seven steps led down from the ante-room into the mithraeum proper.*

Occasionally the temple had a portico attached to it.[69] In some cases, between the entrance to the shrine and the main chamber there was an ante-chamber (sometimes more than one), used as a service-room, *apparatorium*. In the plan of Mithraeum II at Aquincum (Budapest), which was excavated in 1888, the largest of these service-rooms is marked A (fig. 7); B is a smaller chamber, while C should be seen as the actual ante-room. (The small squares mark the location of the excavated altars and statues.) Tableware, cult-vessels and other equipment were kept on shelves, or in chests, in these side-rooms, and the ritual meals were prepared there. Depending on the wealth of the congregation, additional side-rooms might be attached to the main mithraeum, where there was a particular spring, for example, or where special groups of priests might gather on certain occasions. This may have been the function of the *leonteum*, the 'Lions' Room', that we find in the inscription from San Gemini mentioned earlier.[70]

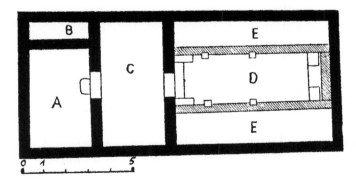

7. *Aquincum/Budapest: plan of Mithraeum II (V 1750). The entrance was by means of several steps down into room A, with two further steps from C into the main aisle D. The small squares near these steps mark votive altars to the torch-bearers Cautopates (l.) and Cautes (r.). When they occur on the podia, the torch-bearers always have this relation to each other.*

The cult-room itself (*crypta*) was constructed according to a traditional scheme, whose design remained virtually constant from Britain to the Black Sea. Its characteristic feature was a central aisle (fig. 7: D) flanked on each side by raised podia (E) for the initiates. They reclined on these during the ritual meal. Fig. 8 shows a cut-away axonometric reconstruction of another temple in the same town.

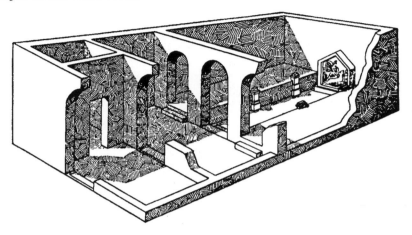

8. *Aquincum/Budapest: axonometric reconstruction of Mithraeum IV (V 1767), phase 1. The similarity of the ground-plan to that of Mithraeum II illustrates how Mithraists tended to refer to a familiar model when they decided to found another mithraeum in the same town.*

If the basic design of the mithraeum was everywhere identical, decoration and execution were variable. At Brocolitia (Carrawburgh) on Hadrian's Wall, the podia were of tamped earth revetted with wickerwork. Those at Koenigshoffen/Strasbourg (Germania Superior) were evidently battened, and perhaps made more comfortable by cushions. An initiate at Ostia, on the other hand, records in an inscription that he had the podia revetted at his own expense in marble (*praesepia marmoravit*: V 233), and that over a total length of 68 Roman feet (> 22 m/24 yd). Another man uses the word *parietes*, 'internal walls', of the podia facings that he had built; and commemorated the gift by means of an inscription on each retaining wall, as is shown by the mortar still attached to the stones (V 1692, 1693).

At Jajce and Konjic in Dalmatia (Bosnia-Hercegovina) the aisle-floor was made of beaten earth (mixed with pebbles at Konjic). A layer of mortar painted bright red covered the floor at Lentia (Linz). Many of the mithraea at Ostia have mosaic floors (fig. 9), which have provided important general

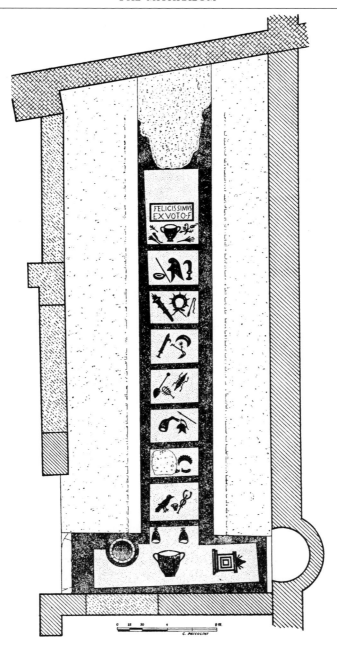

FELICIS SIMVS
EX VOTO F

9. *Mithraeum of Felicissimus, Ostia: mosaic floor (mid-third cent., V 299). Along with the earlier frescoes in the S. Prisca Mithraeum on the Aventine in Rome, this mosaic provides the most important evidence for the grade structure of the mysteries.*

information about the cult. The walls of mithraea were plastered and sometimes brightly painted with red and yellow stripes. Some Italian temples were decorated with scenes of Mithraic rituals.

Although the basic pattern was everywhere identical, we find a great variety of idiosyncratic details, in the wall-paintings, for example, or the individual statues, but above all in the ritual paraphernalia, which varied according to local and regional custom or the individual wishes and preconceptions of donors or congregation. In this regard, the cult of Mithras affords an instructive example of sheer variety of religious expression, notwithstanding the overall uniformity that we must assume in its main rituals and doctrines.

FURNISHINGS

Mithraea housed a variety of statues, reliefs and altars, depending upon the financial resources and religious requirements of the congregation. I take as an example the contents of one of the temples in Stockstadt, on the Main-*limes* (nr Aschaffenburg), that was especially richly furnished. It contained three reliefs of Mithras slaying the bull; three altars with votive inscrip- tions, three decorated in relief, and the fragments of five more; two bases for statues, and 26 statues or statuettes (some deities are represented more than once): Cautopates (2), Cautes, Mithras dragging the bull, Mithras with Sol, the Rock-birth, Sol in his chariot, the ritual meal, Mercury (3), Mars (2), Hercules (2), Victoria, Diana, Vulcan, Hecate, Epona, a male and a female divinity whose identities are uncertain, and two statues each of a lion and a raven. A basin for water and several other fragmentary statues were also found in the temple, which measures *c.*13 × 8 m (14 × 8 yd) (V 1158–1208). In all mithraea there was a great number of lamps and brasiers, which lit up the whole room, or perhaps just individual monuments or paintings.

So far as can be established, there was probably no rule governing the location of all these altars and statues. Some were placed in the area of the cult-niche and in the aisle between the podia; others were built into the podia themselves. Little plaques could be set into the walls. Votives were even sometimes kept in the ante-room. Fig. 10 shows the plan of Mithraeum I at Poetovio. A wooden ante-room, 1.80 m (2 yd) wide, led into the mithraeum proper, whose internal measurements are 5.60 × 5.57 m (6¼ yd). The aisle is 8ft wide, bounded by the podia, which are 20ins high and 4ft 1in (r.) or 3ft 8ins (l.) wide. The figures denote the find-spots of the following statues (the main cult-relief was never found):

1. Altar to I(nvictus) M(ithras)
2. Rock-birth
3. Altar to D(eus) I(nvictus) M(ithras)
4. Altar to *Natura Dei*, with a representation of the rock-birth
5. Altar to *Transitus*, with a representation of Mithras dragging the bull
6. Altar to *Transitus*
7. Cautes
8. Cautes
9. Cautopates
10. Cautopates

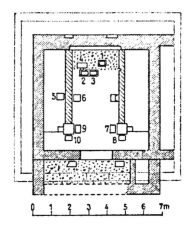

10. *Poetovio/Ptuj: plan of Mithraeum I (mid-second cent., V 1487). The stippled areas denote pebble floors; the floor of the main aisle was of tamped clay. The cult-room was made to resemble a cave by fixing wickerwork to the ceiling and plastering it.*

From this example, we can see that the statues of the torch-bearers (pp. 95–8) stood regularly at the entrance to the main mithraeum, generally on their own bases, just where the podia begin. They were part of what we might call the basic equipment of a mithraeum (one Mithraist mentions that he built the *speleum* (!) *cum omni apparatu*, 'the cave with all its appurtenances': V 747). The smith who made a little silver plaque of the bull-slaying found at Stockstadt set the torch-bearers on little pedestals (fig. 15). In the floor-mosaic that runs up the central aisle of the Mithraeum of Felicissimus at Ostia (fig. 9), the place that belongs to the torch-bearers is occupied by their symbols, two phrygian caps with stars.

At the opposite end of a mithraeum from the entrance, the rear wall was often by means of vaulting converted into an apse-like niche (*exedra*), raised somewhat from the ground. At S. Prisca on the Aventine in Rome this niche was lined with pumice to make it look like a natural cave. This niche was the location of the main cult-relief representing the bull-killing; the top of the frame of these reliefs too was often arched. The niche might on occasion be covered by a hanging (*velum*). One inscription mentions an *aram cum suis ornamentis et bela* (!) *domini insignia habentes* (!) *n(umero) IIII* (V 563), an 'altar with appropriate decoration and four hangings bearing paintings of our Lord': the hangings in front of this relief were evidently painted with different scenes (if the numeral is indeed to be taken with the *vela*). There is some evidence that there was a barrier in front of the cult-niche in the mithraea at Nida, to separate it from the 'nave', as shown here in a reconstruction (fig. 11). The altar – sometimes there were several – was placed in front of the cult-relief.

11. *Nida/Heddernheim: reconstruction by I. Huld-Zetsche of the original appearance of Mithraeum II (cf. fig. 6 above). The gates were suggested by the peculiar indentations in one of the bases found at the top of the steps up to the cult-niche.*

Both nave and niche were alike made to resemble a cave, and thus doubly recalled the image of the kosmos, the World-Cave: as Porphyry puts it, they represented a micro-kosmos.[71] This allusion might be reinforced by vaulting the ceiling: *camaram picturis exornavit*, 'he had the vaulting decorated with frescoes', as a new inscription from Virunum in Noricum has it (AE 1994: 1334).[72] A reconstruction of the mithraeum at Serdica in Thracia (Sofia, Bulgaria) shows what this might have looked like (fig. 12). It could have been done by means of plastered wickerwork, impressions of which have been found in several mithraea. To complete the likeness to a natural cave, the Mithraists covered the ceiling at Groß-Krotzenburg in Germania Superior with rough basalt (a common local stone). In some places the ceiling was painted blue for the sky, with stars in yellow or gold. In other places, little openings, which could be fitted with lamps, gave an imitation of the star-studded vault of heaven. In the natural cave at Kreta in Moesia Inferior (Bulgaria) small rings for hanging lamps from were worked directly out of the rock of the roof (V 2256). The mithraeum thus became an image of the world through which men pass in order to reach God, visible in the background.

12. Serdica/Sofia: drawing of the possible appearance of the interior of the Mithraeum (18.50 × 6.50 m = 20 × 7 yd). Note the five steps up to the cult-niche, and those giving access to the podia. As often in mithraea, there was a supply of water, in this case a sink in the r. podium.

THE CULT-IMAGE

The cult-relief (*typum* or *simulacrum*), with the representation of Mithras' most important deed, the killing of the bull, was set against the rear wall of mithraea, lighted by flickering oil-lamps. In the great majority of cases, this scene occupies the centre of the relief, and takes up most of its surface. The cult-images are generally in bas-relief, more rarely free-standing sculptures (figs 44, 105), in stucco, or fresco (dust-jacket); in the case of natural caves, they may even be carved out of the living rock (fig. 45). The blocks used are often large and correspondingly heavy, and required a special foundation, which may have been given the name *thronum* (V 266). At Immurium in Noricum (Moosham, Austria) the cult-relief rested on a base weighing almost three tons, on which was inscribed the name of the founder (V 1403).

The dedicator of a relief at Nicopolis ad Istrum in Moesia Inferior (Stari-Nikup, Bulgaria) mentions in his inscription that he has dedicated 'the stele [on which the relief was carved], together with the painting' to the god; the relief survives, but the colouring is lost.[73] This reminds us of a point also made by the occasional traces of paint that survive on reliefs: they were brightly painted, and it takes a considerable effort of imagination to appreciate the impression they must originally have made. Working from the traces of pigment on a fragmentary marble plaque from Nida, which provide a good idea of the original tones (fig. 13; pp. 81, 85, 103, 111), Ingeborg Huld-Zetsche has drawn a reconstruction (fig. 14, also rear dust-jacket) using the appropriate colours.

A few of the surviving cult-images were worked on both faces. In the one from Nida the centre panel can be swung on its axis on two pivots top and bottom: the frame remained fixed, but one and then the other central scene could be shown during the course of a ceremony. One face represents the bull-killing, the other the solemn feast of Mithras and Sol (fig. 72).

The different by-scenes that appear on these large reliefs may have served the believers both as objects of silent contemplation and as illustrations of the accounts of the god's different exploits given by the priests. Parts of the relief could have been covered over, or hidden behind a hanging, so as to permit only the relevant portion to be seen. To the left and right of the main cult-image at Koenigshoffen/Strasbourg stood a slender stone column to carry a curtain, by means of which the entire relief could be concealed (V 1335). In one case at Ostia, a curtain of this sort seems itself to have been painted (V 233).[74] It was also possible just to light up a particular part of the whole cult-image, by moving an oil-lamp from scene to scene during the course of the narration. Some reliefs have preserved nails or their traces.

13. Nida/Heddernheim: relief from Mithraeum III (V 1128). The leaf-crown frame of the main scene alludes to the theme of invincible Mithras. There is only one example of a bull-killing scene in which the bull and Mithras face l. instead of r., from S. Giovanni di Duino nr Trieste.

We can also imagine that in the course of such narrations, perhaps when the central bull-slaying scene was unveiled, the attentiveness of the congregation was heightened by ringing a small bell to increase the tension: some mithraea have indeed produced small wrought-metal bells. A little votive plaque made of beaten silver foil from Stockstadt, which still has traces of gilding, shows a bell hanging from the vaulted ceiling of the mithraeum over the cult-image (V 1206; fig. 15, p. 55).

14. The same, drawing by I. Huld-Zetsche (in colour on back cover). The registers and scenes are demarcated by red lines. Note the lion at 7 o'clock, which seems to represent the constellation Leo, connoting the hottest part of the year; and the goat at 4 o'clock, which may denote the star Capra, whose morning rising was associated with fine weather and the end of the sowing season.

We are no longer in a position to read the representations of Mithras' various exploits, as we find them on reliefs with numerous by-scenes or those with panelled frames, in a fixed order. Where there are no panelled frames, one often has the impression that the arrangement of the scenes has been adapted to the configuration of the cult-image as a whole. We thus often find the Rock-birth, but cannot show that it has a constant position in the *c.*100 reliefs in which it occurs (e.g. figs 14, 15, 16, 17, 51, 59). This seems easier in the case of the panelled frames, which are mostly to be 'read' from top to bottom, though even this has been questioned.[75] The scenes occasionally follow the rules of symmetry, for example on the upper register of the relief at Neuenheim (Heidelberg) in Germania Superior, where the 'water-miracle' (pp. 71–4) appears twice (fig. 16; pp. 70, 74, 98). But in most cases we have to assume that the intentions of dedicants and congregations were individual, and are therefore no longer fully intelligible.

15. *Stockstadt: votive plaque in silver foil. The frame in the form of a temple-façade (Mithras' rock-birth in the pediment) connotes the constructed mithraeum (templum), while the arch below connotes its 'real' referent, the cave in which Mithras slew the bull (cf. fig. 69). At the same time, the* aedicola *was a routine frame for a votive (fig. 24).*

This is true particularly in the case of the massive and correspondingly expensive reliefs, which can hardly have been mass-produced. In the mithraea of the Rhine provinces there was generally only one cult-image, often measuring as much as 2 m square, and whose main scene is framed by a whole series of by-scenes from the legend of Mithras, or containing other mythical, sometimes cosmic, symbols. Their specific meaning in relation to the cult of Mithras often remains obscure, but many scenes can be explained at least hypothetically on the basis of analogy, since the mysteries drew to a large extent on Graeco-Roman mythology and religious feeling.

16. *Neuenheim/Heidelberg: complex panelled relief (late Antonine, V 1283). Unusually enough, there is no reference to any event after the death of the bull. The main scene of such reliefs has been seen as a 'theophany', a non-narrative image of the divine presented for veneration, while the panels offer a discursive commentary (S. Zwirn). At Hawarti (Syria) the narrative was painted on the walls.*

By contrast with the mithraea on the Rhine, a local style developed in several Danubian provinces, particularly Dacia (now Romania), in that it became customary to set up or attach to a wall numerous small reliefs, mostly measuring less than 50 × 50 cm (20 in). Here we encounter a sort of mass-production, since the decisive consideration for the person who commissioned such a relief was not the content but the financial outlay. Dacia has provided us with 150 reliefs, almost one quarter of all surviving Mithraic cult-images: there are 78 just from the mithraeum of the provincial capital of Dacia, Colonia Ulpia Traiana (Sarmizegetusa). But, because they are mostly thin plaques only 2–4 cm thick, almost all survive only as fragments. Being produced in such quantities, they tend to be heavily standardised: I illustrate an example from Alcšut in Pannonia Inferior (Hungary) (V 1740, fig. 17). Danubian reliefs regularly, as in this example, have a lower register. Most of these, at least on 'triptychs' like this, carry a settled sequence of scenes: the 'obeisance' of Sol, the feast, the ascent to heaven, all of them subjects that concern relations between Mithras and Sol (pp. 146–55).

17. Alcšut, Hungary: votive relief. Complex reliefs convey a sense of narrative sequence, though not a constant order of scenes. In Danubian reliefs, as here, the Bull-killing tends to separate the narrative of the bull, in the upper register, from the narrative of Mithras and Sol, in the lower register.

ALTARS

A very considerable number of altars has been found in mithraea.[76] Their inscriptions show that they were very often dedicated, apart from Mithras, to the torch-bearers Cautes and Cautopates. It is striking that all Mithraic altars are rather small, are in fact votive-altars. The reason for this is the small size of mithraea. As well as the mass of rectangular examples, we occasionally come across round ones, as well as altars that are triangular or hexagonal in section.

The decorative relief-work of the altars (one Mithraist mentions an *aram cum suis ornamentis*, p. 50) reveals numerous details characteristic of the cult of Mithras: bull's heads, lions, kraters (mixing-bowls for wine) and the torch-bearers. From time to time there appear very finely worked examples such as that of the *pater* (Father) Cn. Arrius Claudianus, still kept in the mithraeum beneath the church of S. Clemente in Rome (V 339). On the front face is Mithras killing the bull (fig. 18), and on either side a torch-bearer; a great serpent swarms up the back. The main persons and actions of large cult-images are here distributed over the four faces: the god sacrifices the bull on the very altar upon which the priest offers the sacrificial victim to him.

18. Mithraeum of S. Clemente, Rome: altar of Cn. Arrius Claudianus (late Antonine). The acroteria heads may represent seasons or wind-gods, since Sol and Luna (lost) are depicted above the cave. Note the lion's mask below the dog (cf. fig. 14).

In Mithraeum III at Poetovio in Pannonia Superior, a large decorated altar stood to one side in front of the cult-relief. The scenes of the handshake between Mithras and Sol, on the front (fig. 19), and of the 'water-miracle', on a lateral face (figs 4, 5), are likewise taken from the general inventory of themes found on large narrative reliefs. Such scenes could only be very summarily represented in the small panels of these reliefs: the larger area of altar-faces made it possible for the sculptor to introduce details for which there was no place in the smaller-scale representations.

19. *Poetovio/Ptuj: altar of Flavius Aper, front (V 1584) (cf. figs 4, 5). The 'handshake' of Mithras and Sol is here connected with the sacrifice of the bull, whose hind-quarter lies on the ground. The two gods are roasting meat on a spit over the altar flame (cf. V 1510). The rôle of the raven is unknown, but may be the narrative prototype of the 'serving' Raven (fig. 69); there is a scene at Dura-Europos where the Corax offers a kebab-stick to Mithras and Sol (V 42. 13).*

An altar from one of the mithraea in Carnuntum is unique in its design and composition (V 1685). Likenesses of the four Seasons and the gods of the four Winds, recognisable in each case by their wings and other attributes, stand erect or kneel round the main body of the altar. Caelus, the god of Heaven, whose subjects include both the Winds and the annual Seasons, occupies the centre of the front face. The figures are all symmetrically arranged. Caelus is flanked by two Seasons, Spring (l.) and Summer (r.). In fig. 20, these three figures stand beneath the inscription on the cornice [pr]o sal(ute) Aug(usti) Deo Invicto, 'For the well-being of the Emperor, to the Invincible God'. On the lateral faces there follow two Winds, resting one knee on a lump of rock and directing a blast of air upwards. The remaining two Seasons are at the rear corners. The face pictured here is the left side, with Favonius, the West-Wind, kneeling, and Autumn standing. On the back of the altar are again two Winds, turned away from one another and resting one foot on a squarish rock. The depiction of the god of Heaven with the Seasons and the Winds fits with the syncretism of the cult, in which the elements and Time played a significant rôle.

20. Carnuntum/Bad Deutsch-Altenburg: altar of the Seasons and Winds from Mithraeum III (early third cent.). The symbolism conveys the Mysteries' stress upon the order of the kosmos, guaranteed by Mithras' sacrifice.

THE MITHRAEUM AND ITS CONGREGATION

The architecture of mithraea reveals important aspects of the cult. By contrast with the case of temples of other divinities, the altar stands inside the sanctuary: all religious ceremonies took place within the building, that is inside the cave. Mithraists thus created for themselves an image of the kosmos, the dwelling-place of humankind, which then became, as the locus of the encounter with Mithras, a new and better home. This cave may even have had a particular attraction as a place where one could withdraw from the outer world for a limited period among a familiar and exclusive group. Worship in such small temples implies an experience of community, whose fellowship was fostered above all by the ritual meals.

In this context it is moreover relevant that the cult of Mithras had no public ceremonial of its own. The festival of the *natalis Invicti*, 25 December, was a public festival of the Sun and thus by no means limited to the mysteries of Mithras. There was nothing in the cult comparable to the great festivals and celebrations of other cults, such as the 'Discovery' of Osiris or the 'Voyage' of Isis, spectacular occasions which attracted great crowds of people. Nor did it possess buildings famous all over the Empire, such as the Serapeum at Alexandria or the Iseum in the Campus Martius at Rome. Unlike the well-known mysteries of Eleusis, for example, which according to Herodotus had 30,000 initiates (8. 65), and attracted 3,000 of them to its festivals, Mithraic congregations were esoteric groups.

CHAPTER 8

The sacred narrative

The story of Mithras' saving action barely finds mention in any literary source. To reconstruct it, therefore, we must rely mainly upon the numerous details of the cult-images. In the Rhine- and Danubian provinces especially, they constitute regular 'picture-books', though we perforce thumb through them with more curiosity than comprehension. We also cannot now reconstruct a satisfactory chronological succession of the god's exploits. I therefore propose to present them in a seqence that I have chosen myself, within the framework offered on the one hand by the birth of Mithras, and on the other by the high point of his achievement, the slaying of the bull.

ROCK-BIRTH

The sequence of images from the mythical account of Mithras' life and exploits begins, so far as we can make out, with the god's birth. The literary sources here are few but unmistakable: Mithras was known as the rock-born god.[77] The inscriptions confirm this nomenclature: one even reads: D(eo) O(mnipotenti) S(oli) Invi(cto), Deo Genitori, r(upe) n(ato), 'To the almighty God Sun invincible, generative god, born from the rock'.[78] Mithras is here invoked as the all-powerful, invincible sun-god, as creator-god, and as rock-born.

An unidentified writer of the second century AD, for convenience termed Pseudo-Plutarch, relates the following story (De fluviis 23.4). Mithras spilled his seed onto a rock, and the stone gave birth to a son, named Diorphos, who, worsted and killed in a duel by Ares, was turned into the mountain of the same name not far from the Armenian river Araxes. Here we have a version of the rock-birth combined in folk-loric manner with Greek myth and given a bit of local colour.

Mithras also appears in the archaeological record as the rock-born god. Many images represent the god growing out of a rock with both arms raised aloft. This symbolism is particularly striking at Rayanov Grich (Croatia), because the representation of the rock-birth there is carved from the living rock (V 1852). After the bull-slaying, the rock-birth is the most frequently represented event of the myth, either as a detail on reliefs or, quite commonly, as a free-standing image. This fact confirms the significance of the rock-birth for the individual worshipper: it is the fundamental pre-condition for all the subsequent exploits, and thus the warrant of salvation. For the *petra genetrix*, the fecund rock, whose image was accorded particular reverence in mithraea, had given life to Mithras.

Just this reverence for the god's birth is shown by the Mithraist who carefully turned an early imperial coin into a medallion celebrating the rock-birth. Perhaps in connection with Augustus' legislation on morals, the Roman *triumvir monetalis* Turpilianus in c.18 BC had the unchaste Vestal Tarpeia (Propert. 4.4) represented on a silver denarius (fig. 21). The illustration shows her, arms aloft, being pressed to death by the Sabine shields (cf. Livy 1.11.5–9). In the second or third century AD, a coin of this type caught the imagination of a Mithraist from Verulamium in Britain (St Albans). It then took only a few changes to turn the denarius into a memento of Mithras' rock-birth (fig. 22).

21. *Silver denarius of P. Petronius Tur-pilianus, IIIvir monetalis (c.18 BC); rev. showing Tarpeia crushed by the Sabine shields: cf. CRBM 1: 6, nos. 29–31; RICG 1: 2, no. 8 (mint of Rome). In the early history of Rome, Tarpeia betrayed the Capitol to the Sabines, and for her pains was pressed to death by their shields.*

22. *Verulamium/St Albans: rev. of re-worked denarius of the same type found beneath the wall of Building IV.1 (second half of second cent. AD, V 827). The moneyer's name and the female features have been erased. In place of the obv. type, a new inscription in Greek was expertly cut: Μίθρας Ὠρομάσδης Φρήν: RIB II.1,1 no. 2408.2 (see Henig, RRB, 189 fig. 91). The names of the Persian high god, represented as a winged solar disk, and the Demotic Egyptian name of the sun-god, Prē, are here linked with Mithras.*

The most common representation of the birth shows Mithras naked, his sole clothing the phrygian cap; and wielding a torch and a dagger (figs 25, 30, 32). His most important exploits are thus adumbrated already at his birth. With his torch he brings light: he is *genitor luminis*, creator of light (V 1676), and, as sun-god, himself also that light. With the aid of the dagger he creates life, by killing the bull. Very occasionally, as on a relief from Colonia Agrippina (Cologne) in Germania Inferior, only the latter is emphasised (fig. 23). We cannot tell for certain whether an unusual monument from Vetren (Bulgaria) also represents this adumbration of the bull-slaying, or is simply clinging to familiar models: both the shape and the manner of the relief are closely similar to those of other Mithraic reliefs of the eastern Danubian area. At the top, right and left, are the busts of Sol and Luna, with Cautes and Cautopates below them; but in the centre, where the bull-slaying normally is, we find the Rock-birth.[79]

23. *Colonia Agrippina/Cologne: Rock-birth from Mithraeum II, found in 1969. In this instance, most un-usually, Mithras holds a bunch of wheat-ears in his l. hand, rather than a torch.*

The rock from which Mithras is born symbolises the kosmos just as does the cave, both the mythical cave, where Mithras will slay the bull, and the mithraeum-cave, where the rituals take place and the cult-myth is reproduced through the reliefs. For that reason, Mithras is represented inside a temple on the Rock-birth, *p(etram) genetricem*, which Senilius Carantinus, who came from the area around modern Metz, *c(ivis) Mediom(atricus)*, dedicated *Deo In(victo) Mi(thrae)* at Nida (V 1127, fig. 24; see also p. 96).

24. *Nida/Heddernheim: votive from Mithraeum III. The 'roof' is cut to represent tiles; the acroteria probably represented wind-gods (fig. 20). This key monument labels the eagle-thunderbolt-orb group on the lateral face shown* as Caelum, Heaven (cf. fig. 29), *and the reclining deity with vase, on the opposite face, as* Oceanus.

Light comes from the firmament, Mithras is the god of light, the new light which bursts forth each morning from the vault of heaven behind the mountains, and whose birthday is celebrated on 25 December. A late antique Syriac commentator describes this festival, and correctly observes that it later developed into the birthday of Christ:

> It was in fact customary among the pagans to celebrate the festival of the Sun's birthday on 25th December and to light bonfires in honour of the day. They even used to invite the Christian population to these rites. But when the teachers of the Church realised that Christians were allowing themselves to take part, they decided to observe the Feast of the true Birth on the same day.[80]

It may be that the Mithraists also celebrated the birthday of their god in public in a similar manner.

Normally, just Mithras' naked torso appears in representations of his birth, but occasionally he is shown more or less entire, as, for example, on a relief from Rome (fig. 25), where, with his thighs pressed together, he appears to be being impelled upward out of the rock as though by some magical force (V 353).

25. Nr Piazza Dante, Rome: rock-birth relief found with four other pieces in the Mithraeum of Primus. All had been carefully concealed when the Mithraeum ceased to be used (see also figs 44, 65). Mithras emerging from the rock evokes a long Graeco-Roman iconographic tradition of earth-born deities: C. Bérard, Anodoi (Neuchâtel, 1974).

The multi-layered quality of Mithraic symbolism, which I have already stressed, reappears in the case of the rock: represented and understood not only as the kosmos but also as the earth, on many images it is encircled by a serpent (p. 100), a creature associated with the earth (figs 26, 28). Another exploit of Mithras known to us is the so-called water-miracle or miracle of the rock (pp. 71–4). This is sometimes adumbrated in representations of the rock-birth: one at Romula in Dacia (Reşca, Romania) served as a water-spout (V 2170, fig. 27; see also p. 72). Among the elementary necessities – which thus also symbolised life – promised and bestowed by Mithras is the water that he caused to flow from the rock. Just as the god himself gives life, so too does the rock: the upper rim of the rock is decorated with flowers on a relief from Bingium (Bingen) in Germania Superior (V 1240, fig. 28).

26. *Poetovio/Ptuj: rock-birth statue from Mithraeum I (V 1492). The base bears a dedication* Naturae dei, *'To the god's birth'. This is an uncommon sense of* natura, *perhaps translated from the Greek* genesis *(cf. V 793, Emerita, Lusitania:* aram genesis invicti Mithrae).

27. *Romula/Reşca, Romania: rock-birth statue. The hole is 9 cm in diameter.*

28. Bingium/Bingen: rock-birth relief. Euboulus describes Zoroaster's first cave in Persia, dedicated to Mithras, as 'flower-strewn and furnished with springs' (ap. Porphyry, De antr. nymph. 6) (see also fig. 45).

The significance of the rock-birth for the later events of the myth is emphasised by the fact that on several monuments Mithras is attended at his birth by the most important of the subsidiary figures that occur regularly on the bull-slaying reliefs. I have already mentioned the serpent; the dog, serpent and raven appear on an important relief from Augusta Treverorum (Trier) in Gallia Belgica (V 985, fig. 29; see also p. 84). The two

29. Altbachtal, Augusta Treverorum/Trier: rock-birth relief within an aedicola. The infant god is presented proleptically as 'maker of everything, and Father' (Euboulus, see fig. 28), and supports, or turns, the half-zodiac containing the spring and summer signs, Aries to Virgo. In the spandrels are the wind-gods (cf. fig. 20).

torch-bearers are also often to be found at the rock-birth. Sometimes they just stand there (fig. 59), but sometimes they help Mithras – on a relief from Poetovio, it looks as though they were carefully lifting him out of the rock (V 1593, fig. 30; see p. 70). There are, incidentally, no grounds for calling these two figures 'shepherds', in the wake of the Christian nativity story.[81]

30. Poetovio/Ptuj: rock-birth relief from Mithraeum III (mid-third cen.). Saturnus is being crowned by Victoria.

If the torch-bearers might attend Mithras' birth, and even assist at it, then what of their 'birth' too? That thought may have produced the representation of a triple tree-birth in the mithraeum at Dieburg, Germania Superior (fig. 31). On the other hand, one may well wonder what Mithras' head in a tree might signify.

31. Dieburg: panel from r. jamb of the complex relief (V 1247. 10): tree with three branches each ending in a head in a phrygian cap. The only close parallel occurs on the complex relief from Rückingen (V 1137. 3b), though elsewhere a single bust emerges from a tree (e.g. figs. 16, 33, cf. V 1510. 2). In two other scenes, Mithras is approaching a tree, looking up (V 1292. 2; 1958. 2). The motifs at Dieburg and Rückingen may therefore represent the 'real' or esoteric meaning (whatever that was claimed to be) of an element of the cult myth.

There sometimes occurs on the Rock-birth a reclining divinity who is to all appearances fast asleep (figs 16, 30). His head is generally covered, and is pillowed on his arm. In the corpus of Graeco-Roman myth there were many traditions concerning Saturn sleeping and dreaming, a deity from early times often equated with the Greek Kronos. In his dreams, the god pondered the world-order of the future. We may guess that, for Mithraists, the birth of their god was the most important of these prophetic dreams.

I have mentioned several times that the cult of Mithras was open to a variety of contemporary religious and philosophical influences. Whereas in relation to the Bull-slaying we are unable to grasp the significance of major differences in treatment, this is not the case with many of the by-scenes, in particular the Rock-birth.

Although Mithras is usually represented as a youth when he rises out of the rock, the relief from Augusta Treverorum (Trier), which I have already mentioned (p. 68, fig. 29), shows him as a child. In other words, Mithras manifests his nature and capacities from the very first moment of his existence: already at birth, as a dedication at Rome declares, he is ruler of the world, kosmokrator.[82] With one hand he revolves or supports the planetary circle that spans the kosmos, six of whose signs are represented (p. 84). In the other hand, he holds the world-globe, which, like the four wind-gods in the corners, represents the four cardinal directions of the universe. In this version of the rock-birth, the entire cosmic order is set up already. Analogous compositions are much more common in relation to the bull-slaying (pp. 87–90).

We can discern the influence of Orphic speculation in a Greek inscription from one of the numerous mithraea in Rome, on a statue-base dedicated Διì ʿΗλίῳ Μίθρᾳ Φάνητι, that is to *Deus Sol Mithras Phanes*.[83] Phanes is the embodiment of unlimited light, an Orphic deity who emerged from the cosmic egg. There is also literary evidence for the syncretism of Mithras with Phanes.[84] In this community, therefore, Mithras' identification with the sun-god (p. 146) grounded an allusion to the Orphic-Platonic ideas current among the intellectual élites. Mithras-Phanes is also known to us in icono-graphic form: a relief from Vercovicium (Housesteads) on Hadrian's Wall shows Mithras emerging from the cosmic egg, which is represented both as such and by the shape of the zodiacal ring (fig. 32, cf. fig. 123).[85]

Both complex and straightforward notions thus find a place next to one another in the cult-myths about Mithras' birth, and are partially interwoven – a point that could be made about any ancient cult. In the case of the birth, some elements are invariable, but variants, regional or local idiosyncrasies, are admissible as well. On a number of reliefs the rock is made to resemble an ovoid pine-cone. This thought was pursued further, for example, at Nida, where Mithras, of whom only the bust is visible, is spying out from – that is, probably, being born out of – what may be a pine-tree (fig. 33, cf. fig. 31).

The choice of ideas that were current in a Mithraic congregation depended in many ways upon its priests at any given time. Beyond that, the dedicator of a relief or inscription, possibly even the sculptor, could contribute his own ideas or pick up stimuli from elsewhere. This is the case not merely with the rock-birth but for all aspects of the cult-myth.

32  33

32. *Vercovicium/Housesteads: Rock-birth with Mithras as Phanes (V 860), perhaps the equivalent of the* Mithras Saecularis *in the same mithraeum (V 863–4 = RIB 1599–1600). The zodiacal sequence begins with Aquarius (bottom l.) and ends with Capricorn (r.).*

33. *Nida/Heddernheim: panel from the complex relief from Mithraeum I (V 1083. 1), Mithras ?being born from a tree. At Dura-Europos the figure is represented as a little pink child (V 45). In the Mithraeum at Emerita (Spain), a lion emerges from an acanthus-leaf (V 791). Images such as these seem to allude to an iconographic stereotype known from Anatolia and Syria: E. Will,* Le relief cultuel *(Rome-Paris, 1955), 208.*

WATER-MIRACLE

The theme of the water-miracle is elaborated mainly in the Rhine-Danube area. Mithras is usually represented sitting on a stone and aiming a flexed bow at a rockface, in front of which there kneels a figure. Another figure sometimes grasps Mithras' knees in supplication, or stands behind him with his hand on his shoulder. The scene is particularly striking on the large altar from Poetovio I referred to earlier (fig. 4), where, because of the size of the field available, the sculptor had more space to develop his ideas than is the case with the usual small-scale panel-scenes. Mithras here is aiming his bow at a rockface, from which water will shortly gush forth – a person is standing in front of it ready to catch the water in his cupped hands. On another face of the altar, bow, quiver and dagger are separately represented (fig. 5), the last alluding, as so often elsewhere, to the god's greatest exploit. We may note that the figures who are generally shown taking part in this scene with Mithras are clothed just like the god. They must be the torch-bearers, present here just as they are at the rock-birth and the killing of the bull. This scene can thus be connected with one of the lines in the mithraeum under S. Prisca in Rome, which is addressed to a spring enclosed in the rock: 'You who have fed the twin brothers with nectar'.[86] The spring is Mithras; the twins to whom he has given heavenly nourishment are the torch-bearers.

Apart from the cult-meal, the water-miracle offers the clearest parallel with Christianity, spreading through the Empire at the same period as the mysteries of Mithras. The thinking that underlies these features of each cult is naturally rooted in the same traditions. The water-miracle is one of the wide-spread myths that originate from regions plagued by drought, and where the prosperity of humans and nature depends upon rain. Each in his own manner, Mithras and Christ embody water, initially as a concrete necessity, and then, very soon, as a symbol. Christ is referred to in the New Testament as the water of life. Many Christian sarcophagi depict the miracle of Moses striking the rock with his staff and causing water to flow (Exodus 17.3–6), as a symbol of immortality.

Together with his son, a Mithraist at Aquincum (Budapest) dedicated an elaborate altar decorated with symbolic motifs. Fig. 34 is a detail from the front of the tall fascia, above the abacus with the dedication D(eo) I(nvicto) M(ithrae). The two torch-bearers are represented in their usual position at the bull-slaying or the rock-birth. Between them here, occupying the place usually taken by Mithras, is a large krater. It must represent the water that was so important both for the cult and in real life – probably in fact symbolising Mithras himself, the ever-flowing spring, fons perennis, as a votive altar from Poetovio acclaims him (V 1533).

Just as Mithras as sun-god could in a sense be brought into the mithraeum by means of perforated altars (p. 126), so some congregations brought Mithras in as bestower of water. At Romula in Dacia was found a damaged Rock-birth, lacking the god's head and neck (fig. 27). His hands, holding the dagger and torch, are resting upon the rock, represented as a stylised heap of boulders. Just below Mithras' trunk, a navel has been cut into one of these boulders, a play on the notion of the *umbilicus terrae*, the common ancient idea of an actual spot that is the centre of the earth's surface. Underneath the navel is a circular aperture. The back of the statue has been left rough and evidently stood against a wall, from which a water-pipe could have been let into the aperture. The thought of Mithras as bestower of water could thus be realised concretely.

34. *Aquincum/Budapest: fascia of altar of C. Aelius Anicetus and his son from Mithraeum III (V 1765). Three large kraters, coloured white in imitation of marble, were painted on the dado on either side of the entrance of the Mithraeum of the* Castra Peregrinorum *in Rome. In each case, a pair of doves sits on the rim. Doves were renowned as creatures pure, chaste and monogamous.*

Apart from such iconic representations, the importance of water for all manner of ritual purposes is revealed by the water-basins and cisterns, by the representations of Oceanus, and also by the evident desire to locate temples in the vicinity of a river or a spring. Water-basins were clearly part of the basic equipment of all mithraea. Two examples have been found at Koenigshoffen/Strasbourg. One of them is fitted with projections so that it could be tilted, and has clear traces of mineral-sediment (V 1368). It may have been used to hold red paint when the temple was redecorated, and then bricked up in the wall. At Carnuntum in Pannonia Superior, a large shell carved out of sandstone was used as a water-basin (V 1691).

Mithraeum I at Poetovio had access to a spring a little way off, and two Mithraists put up an altar there with the inscription mentioned earlier, *fonti perenni*, 'To the ever-gushing spring' (p. 72). When the community later decided to build another mithraeum, the spot chosen was on the site of the spring, so that it and the altar could be incorporated into the new building.[87] The spring itself was retained by means of marble revetting, and a covered drain led from it to the outside. Worshippers threw coins into the basin, and 80 coins, mostly from the first half of the fourth century AD, were found there.

Both at Mackwiller (Gallia Belgica) (V 1329) and probably at Paraćin in Upper Moesia (Morava valley, Serbia), the followers of Mithras built their shrine by a spring reverenced by the local population. Probably in the fourth century AD, Mithraists at Bijelo Polje (Bosnia) rather clumsily fashioned a revetment slab for a spring near their temple. In the middle of the slab is depicted rather crudely a cauldron-like vessel, out of which there rise two streams that flow away one to each side (V 1891; fig. 35). Water and vessel are depicted far more convincingly by the sculptor of a relief at Bononia in Italy (Bologna) (V 694, fig. 61). A krater might be substituted in the mithraeum for a spring, and hence, as a symbol of water, is to be found on numerous reliefs (figs 9, 15, 58, 85). The rôle of the serpent in the mysteries should therefore perhaps be seen in relation to that of water.

35. *Bijelo Polje, nr Mostar, Bosnia: revetment slab depicting streams emerging from a vessel. A stray find re-used, perhaps Mithraic.*

HUNTING THE BULL

Although the bull-slaying is the climax and finale of Mithras' pursuit of the bull, it was preceded by a protracted struggle, since god and bull are almost evenly matched. The god could accomplish his redemptive deed only after a bitter struggle requiring the utmost exertion. That is why the different phases of his pursuit of the bull are carefully depicted in the dense iconography of the cult-images of the Rhine-Danube area. The great cult-relief from Neuenheim/ Heidelberg (fig. 16) illustrates it altogether in four panels, which are to be read from top to bottom. First one sees the bull grazing peacefully (fig. 36), before he is captured and carried off by Mithras. There was, however, no canonic iconography for the depiction of these events. Whereas at Neuen-heim the bull is grazing, at Dieburg (V 1247) he first appears lying inside a temple, from which Mithras has then to drag him (fig. 37, cf. 57). In either case, it is not so much that the hunt is narrated for its own sake, as that the god's prowess is emphasised. At Neuenheim, Mithras resembles a shepherd carrying a sheep on his shoulders: the point here is less figural realism than conveying the imaginative conviction of the god's extraordinary strength. Statius also gives us an idea of Mithras' strength when he describes him forcing the bull's stubbornly renitent horns (p. 22). At Vindovala (Rudchester) on Hadrian's Wall was found an altar which virtually illustrates these lines: Mithras is conducting the bull by the horns (fig. 38).

36. *Neuenheim/Heidelberg: r. jamb of the complex relief (V 1283. 11–14, cf. fig. 16). Hunting the bull.*

37. *Dieburg: complex relief, obverse, top panel, central scene (V 1247. 6). The bull, his tail proleptically ending in ears of wheat, lies in a temple, i.e. 'heaven' (cf. figs 29, 112). The significance of the figures in the pediment is unclear.*

38. *Vindovala/Rudchester: base of altar of L. Sentius Castius, with Mithras leading the bull. The shaft carries the inscription DEO, 'To the god', within a wreath, framed by two victory palms (cf. Henig, RRB, 100 fig. 39).*

But this is by no means the end of the chase, for the bull evidently managed to escape again. In the next scene at Neuenheim, one can see the god hanging on to the bull with his arms round its neck and being carried off at a gallop (fig. 36). The sculptor has tried to give an impression of the sheer speed of it all by making Mithras appear almost to be flying horizontally over the bull's back.

It may be that the scenes in which Mithras is shown riding on the bull belong to the same phase of the conflict. The god has managed to bring the now weary beast under his control (figs 13, 40, 57). This scene was especially popular among Mithraists on the lower Danube: of around forty representations in total, more than three-quarters come from the area of Dacia, Moesia and Thracia (Romania and Bulgaria). The cult of the 'Thracian Rider-god', an indigenous deity popular in this area and often depicted on votive reliefs, must have been a factor here: he is sometimes represented with a radiate crown and killing a bull with a lance,[88] and the two cults show a good deal of mutual influence in other respects. A relief-fragment from Callatis in Moesia Inferior (Gànt la Mangalia, Romania) offers a pleasing detail (fig. 39). It shows Mithras keeping his seat by grasping the bull's left horn with one hand, while triumphantly waving his phrygian cap with the other. The bull-riding must remind us of a passage of Porphyry: '[Mithras] also rides on a bull, Taurus being assigned to Venus. As a creator and lord of genesis, Mithras is placed in the region of the celestial equator' (*De antr. nymph.* 24, tr. Arethusa). Images such as these could evidently always be interpreted in many different ways.

39. *Callatis/Gànt la Mangalia: lower r. corner of a fragmentary relief, with Oceanus reclining (c.) and Mithras (r.) riding the bull (compare V 2107). Except for V 640 (Nersae), the Bull-riding in this form occurs only on Danubian reliefs, mainly from Dacia and the two Moesias.*

Once the bull's strength has finally been exhausted, Mithras can over-
whelm him and drag him away. The representations of this divine exploit
are fairly standardised. Several monuments, some with accompanying
inscriptions, confirm that at least in this case there existed a standard
iconography, with a specific terminology. Mithras lays the bull's hind-legs
over his shoulders and hauls the animal into the cave. The relief-fragment
illustrated here (fig. 40; cf. figs 57, 76), which was found at Singidunum in
Moesia Superior (Belgrade, Yugoslavia), and dedicated by one Jer(. . .)
Valentinu[s, depicts the exploit in a few summary lines.[89] The thrashing of
the bull's tail on a relief from Nida shows that the bull is still alive (V 1083.
3, fig. 41), but he has already been overcome by the Invincible one.[90] The
feat of hauling the bull was evidently of special importance as proof of the
god's might, since it receives individual commemoration in several mithraea. Such representations are more widespread than the Bull-riding, but
are still uncommon in Rome and Italy. On the other hand, one of the
dipinte at S. Prisca at Rome acclaims Mithras carrying the young bull on his
golden shoulders.[91] The exploit is given a title at Poetovio in Pannonia
Superior (Ptuj), *Transitus*, denoting the transition or alteration which the
bull, or Mithras, or both, have to go through before the central act of killing
can take place inside the cave (V 1494, fig. 42).

40. *Singidunum/Belgrade: fragmentary
Danubian relief showing Mithras riding
the bull (r.) and Mithras taurophorus (l.).*

41. *Nida/Heddernheim, Mithraeum I:
detail of Mithras taurophorus, to r. of
the scene shown in fig. 33. The bull's tail
ends proleptically in three ears of wheat.*

This 'bull-hauling' god evoked a good deal of mockery from Christians,
mockery that suggests not merely the apologists' zeal and the level of their
attacks, but also how widely known this very act of Mithras was. In the third
century AD, the poet Commodianus composed an acrostic on the name
INVICTVS, a poem in which the initial letters of each line, when read

42. *Poetovio/Ptuj, Mithraeum I: Mithras dragging the bull, dedicated* Transitu(i), *'To the removal/transition'* (cf. V 1497).

downwards, yield Mithras' epithet. He compares the god with Cacus, the notorious son of Vulcan, who stole the cattle of Hercules while the latter was sleeping off a carouse:

> If indeed a god, Invictus was rock-born;
> Now which came first? Here rock has
> Vanquished god: for who created it?
> If a god, by theft he could not live; yet
> Cattle-thief is the name he goes by.
> Terraneous he was born, a monster;
> Vulcan's son he's like, old Cacus, who
> Stole another's beasts, hid them in a cave.[92]

SLAYING THE BULL

Combats with animals are among the most prominent features of ancient myth: humans, heroes and gods all fight against them. The bull is often a focal-point of myths, in Egypt, Crete and Greece. Since very early times it has been correlated with fertility. The very fact that Europè 'sits' on the bull can surely be taken as a token of the animal's dominant rôle in myth.

Of all Mithras' heroic feats, the slaying of the bull is the grandest, and thus the central, achievement. It is not just that it is the image that is most commonly found: it was so canonical that it could not fail to be present in any mithraeum. There are of course many variations in detail, but essentially the same subject is always repeated.

Beneath the arching roof of the cave, Mithras, with an easy grace and imbued with youthful vigour, forces the mighty beast to the ground, kneeling in triumph with his left knee on the animal's back or flank, and constraining its rump with his almost fully extended right leg. Grasping the animal's nostrils with his left hand and so pulling its head upwards to reduce its strength – this is very well shown by the fragment, probably from Salona in Dalmatia (nr. Split, Croatia), illustrated in fig. 43 – the god plunges the dagger into its neck with his right hand. The animal's throat rattles, the tail jerks up: it dies. Victory is what characterises the god; his one unvarying epithet is *Invictus*. At Rome there is a statue (V 352, fig. 44) which we may take as typical of free-standing images: it conveys the impression that the bull has been overcome not so much by sheer strength as by a kind of psychic superiority.

43. *Probably Salona/Split or neighbourhood: fragmentary relief, with bull's head (V 1868). The model for the Mithraic bull-killing scene was probably the type of winged Nike (Victory) killing the bull, which became a fashionable image once again in the reign of Trajan.*

The killing of the bull took place in a cave, and most sculptors depict the event as taking place there (for example, figs 18, 50–2, 56, 85). In the mithraeum, it was reproduced for the community through re-telling the narrative and contemplation of the cult-image. Hence on some images, such as that at Jajce in Dalmatia (Bosnia), the sacrifice of the bull by Mithras takes place in a temple: one can see the roof, decorated with leaf-ornament, and the two columns supporting it (fig. 45; cf. fig. 15, with p. 52). The leaf-crown, which sometimes surrounds the scene (figs 13, 14, 59), has here become the decoration of the temple pediment.

The killing of the bull has nothing to do with mere slaughter or destruction, rather with transfiguration and transformation. The transformation is often

44. *Nr Piazza Dante, Rome: free-standing statue from the Mithraeum of Primus (see figs 25, 65). Due to its greater wealth, and the presence of numerous craft-workshops working in the tradition of high art, there are many more free-standing Mithraic statues in (central) Italy than in the provinces, where, except in Roman* coloniae, *statues are unusual items.*

depicted, namely in the cases in which corn-ears or a cluster of grapes are shown beneath the wound on the bull's neck, or the tail ends in one or more ears of corn (figs 3, 16, 51, 52, 85). On a number of reliefs from Italy and elsewhere, a tree is placed on either side of the bull, or in his vicinity (fig. 52; cf. figs 16, 50). He is surrounded by a green leaf-crown on the relief from Nida illustrated above (figs 13–14), while at Siscia in Pannonia Superior (Sisak, Croatia) the wreath is made of corn-ears (V 1475). We can explain why the dog, serpent and scorpion are so eagerly pushing their way towards the bull (pp. 98–100) by assuming that the dying beast is emitting some sort of magical force. This force was imagined to reside in the animal's blood, hide, seed, often too in the tail, as is shown by the corn-ears that shoot up from it. We may also note the cases in which the torch-bearer standing on the left, generally Cautopates (p. 97), grasps the tail, in order to have a share in its magical power. Since Cautopates in such cases symbolises death, he needs the power to find new life, now symbolised by Cautes.

45. Jajce, Bosnia: cult-relief carved into the living rock (V 1902). Another example has recently been found in a cave at Doliche/Dülük in Commagene. Traces of pigment survive on this relief. There was evidently no fixed tradition about the colours to be used on Mithraic reliefs: e.g. the bull here is black, but at Marino (front dust-jacket) and Capua (V 181) in Italy, white; in the Barberini Mithraeum, light brown (390, cf. 386); on a stucco group now in Frankfurt, but also from Rome, reddish-brown (430). Mithras' tunic at Jajce is blue, at Marino red; his cloak red here, at Marino blue; in the Barberini Mithraeum, tunic and trousers (anaxyrides) are green.

What is at issue here then is not a drama of the destruction of life, but life being reborn out of death. The bull is sacrificed so that new life may be produced, life brought by Mithras, god of light, the Sun, a god who is indeed almighty. This interpretation of the slaying of the bull as a sacrifice is supported by those cult-images on which the bull is adorned with a dorsal band, the Roman dorsuale, which is sometimes decorated with embroidery (figs 14, 52). This manner of representing the bull was taken over into the cult of Mithras from contemporary images of public sacrifice, and the same is true of other details, such as the colour white used for the bull when painted on wall-frescoes (e.g. at Capua in Italy, V 181). Descriptions of sacrifices had always stressed the type and beauty of the sacrificial animals. Whereas in representations of Republican date the animals stand quietly beside the altar, from the Augustan period it was the moment of death that was highlighted. The drama of this ritual moment could evoke powerful emotions. To that extent, the Mithraic image of the slaying of the bull was fully in keeping with the style of the period.[93]

The geste of Sol Invictus Mithras is one that brings about creation and deliverance. This is the core of all sun- and vegetation-myths, the very pith of this as well as of all other ancient mystery-cults. They revolve around the central problem of life, that confronts human beings year by year in the rhythms of nature. The being who can set this rhythm into motion and control it guarantees in equal measure earthly and heavenly salvation. His is a revolutionary cosmic deed. For his followers, Mithras was one such creator-god, who awakes nature to new life and at the same time creates the kosmos.

Creation arises from the death of the bull, who, as a symbol of the Moon, embodies death and rebirth. Porphyry, whom I have already cited on several occasions, has this to say about Luna in relation to the cult of Mithras: 'The Moon is also known as a bull and Taurus is its "exaltation" ' (*De antr. nymph.* 18, tr. Arethusa). On the Mithraic cult-image, Luna is depicted as often as Sol: her bust, with its characteristic crescent, is placed in the top right-hand corner of the scene (figs 3, 16, 17, 45, 47 etc.). There is a close relationship in Graeco-Roman mythology between Moon and bull; the Moon's striking crescent, reminiscent of a bull's horns, was known as the *cornua lunae*, the 'Moon's horns'. On those Mithraic reliefs on which the bust of Luna is substituted, by analogy with Sol's quadriga, by Luna in a biga, the latter is generally drawn by oxen (fig. 54). The close relation between bull and Moon is likewise expressed in those Danubian reliefs in which the bull is shown standing in a boat made to resemble the Moon (figs 17, 59).

The dying bull is often represented so as to allude to the lunar crescent. Given that Mithras wrenches back the head, and the tail jerks up in the animal's death-throes, the sculptors were able to fashion its trunk so as to suggest a crescent. On a relief from Durnomagus (Dormagen) in Lower Germany, the bull's back is concave, which also emphasises the strength the god requires to press the animal to the ground with his knee (V 1012, fig. 46, cf. p. 141). The sculptor of a rather artless relief, now at Cluj in Romania but probably from Moesia Inferior, had no compunction in giving his bull a drastic anatomical deformity for the sake of the symbolism (V 2025, fig. 47).[94]

46. *Durnomagus/Dormagen: cult-relief. The bull's body has been made to allude to the Moon. The epic poet Nonnus of Panopolis (fifth cent. AD) relates that the Indian Brahmins, imagined as Graeco-Roman sorcerers, could bring down the Moon, which normally rides the sky 'as an untamed bull' (36. 345–7).*

47. *Unknown provenance, now at Cluj, Romania: cult-relief, influenced by local workshop tradition (cf. figs 56, 57, 66). Frontality, and especially the figures' exaggerated eyes, engage the viewer directly. Note that Mithras is not wearing his phrygian cap.*

The fifth- or sixth-century commentator on Statius known as Lactantius Placidus has the following observation about the two lines from the *Thebais* (1.719–720) I have already cited several times (pp. 22, 42), where the poet describes Mithras overcoming the bull. He writes:

> (Mithras) grips the bull's horns with his two hands. The interpretation of this concerns Luna . . . In these lines (the poet) reveals the secrets of the mysteries of the Sun. For the Sun(-god) sits on the bull and twists his horns, so as to teach Luna by dint of his strength that she is not so great as he, and inferior.[95]

Mithras, as the Sun, overcomes the bull, and thereby also the Moon, from earliest times a symbol of death and restoration to life.

The sacrifice of the bull brings about not merely life on earth but also the creation of the kosmos as a whole: according to Euboulus, as cited by Porphyry, Mithras is at one and the same time 'creator of the universe and father' (*De antr. nymph.* 6). One Mithraist designates his god *kosmokrator* (pp. 70, 143f). This term is taken from astrology and was originally applied to the planets, which were the seven *kosmokratores* ('lords of the kosmos'). But, according to astrological lore, the planets control life on earth through their rotation, and hence *kosmokrator* became a term for the lord of the entire universe. Finally, astral lore and its associated theology (p. 30) considered the Sun to be the first cause of the stars' motions, and the supreme god of the universe. As the Sun, Mithras was also considered ruler of the universe, and that from the very moment of his birth (fig. 29, see also p. 68).

On many of the cult-images, Mithras' cloak flutters out behind him, and on the surviving frescoes is painted blue to symbolise the sky. The seven planets (p. 159) are picked out in the form of golden stars, that begin to glitter the moment the sacrifice is performed. There are also sometimes traces of blue paint on Mithras' tunic. Now and again stars are scattered all over the field (figs 13, 14, 50, 111). The busts of Sun and Moon, and of the wind-gods, and the symbols of the seven planets and zodiacal signs (p. 160) also allude to the event's cosmic dimension.

In place of the ordinary busts of Sol and Luna that survive in their hundreds, on the more ambitious cult-images we sometimes find the Sun's quadriga mounting upwards on the left, and the biga of Luna descending on the right (fig. 54). On one relief from Rome, Sol in his chariot wears only a cloak streaming out behind him (V 415, fig. 48). In his left hand he holds the guide-reins, in his right the whip with which he is urging the horses on; in front of them strides a naked boy, Phosphorus, with a raised torch, thus alluding to Cautes. In the upper right corner, Luna steers her biga downwards (fig. 49). Here again, she is preceded by a naked youth, with a lowered torch, who is Hesperus, alluding to Cautopates.

48  49

48. *Capitoline Hill, Rome: detail of Sol's quadriga from the upper l. spandrel of the cult-relief from 'lo Perso', one of the first mithraea to be rediscovered in the late mediaeval period (all the heads are Renaissance restorations). This relief may have inspired one of the few Renaissance Biblical images to allude to Mithras' bull-killing, King Saul cutting up the oxen at Gibeah (1 Samuel 11.7), on a decorated chimney-breast in the Château d'Écouen (Val d'Oise), c.1550.*
49. *The same: detail of Luna's biga from the upper r. spandrel.*

Occasionally the heads of two (fig. 54) or four (fig. 51) wind-gods are found in the corners of cult-reliefs; and sometimes also representations of the zodiac or its protective deities (figs 54, 55, 116).

Allusions to the seven planets are common; and the number seven plays a considerable rôle in the mysteries. We may recall the seven steps that descend into the main room of several temples (p. 44). Mithras, as creator of the universe, often has seven stars on his outspread cloak, or scattered on the background (figs 15, 50, 51). As well as seven stars, seven burning altars, such as those beneath the serpent on a relief from Rome (V 368, fig. 50), sometimes also allude to the planets (see pp. 86, 153). In this case, the sculptor has also chosen the number of trees and altars above the cave-arch to accord with the number of stars (the seventh altar must be behind the raven). On the basis of such images, we may assume that in many mithraea altars were dedicated to the planetary gods, and that they were lighted to make burnt-offerings. These gods are depicted, as busts or full-length, on several of the more detailed reliefs. Occasionally they seem to be arranged in the order of the days of the week, though no standard sequence is discernible. The series on a bronze plaque from one of the mithraea at Brigetio in Pannonia Superior (Szöny, distr. Komárom, Hungary) runs, left to right: Saturn, Sol, Luna, Mars, Mercury, Jupiter, Venus (V 1727, fig. 51; see also pp. 86, 159). On a relief from Bononia (Bologna), the sculptor has fitted the gods along the upper rim between the busts of Sol and Luna, whose canonical positions he wanted to retain (V 693, fig. 52; see pp. 79, 84). If we read in the same direction, from Sol to Saturn and then up to Luna, we would have the gods of the week in reverse order; if not, the series would begin, exceptionally, on the right with Luna.[96]

50. Nr S. Lucia in Selge, Esquiline Hill, Rome: cult-relief. Two of the stars above the bull's head are modern restorations. Although sequences of seven altars are fairly common (e.g. V 40, 1275, 1818, 2245), the alternation of altars and trees above the cave is rare (e.g. V 45), paralleled at Rome only on the fresco of the Barberini Mithraeum (390), and the (partly lost) monument of Ottavio Zeno from nr S. Maria in Domnica on the Caelian Hill (335), where the altars were separated by swords.

51. Brigetio/Szöny, Hungary: bronze plaque (late Antonine). The arrangement of the planets in the order of the weekdays emphasises the regular passage of the days, thus picking up the allusion to the sequence of seasons in the main scene. Note the long ray connecting Sol with Mithras (see p. 147).

52. Bononia/Bologna (unknown provenance): votive-relief, with the planets in the reverse order of the weekdays. If not purely contingent, the reverse order may be connected with the astrological system of the decans. Note the scorpion (l.) and bull's head (r.) beside the torch-bearers: the zodiacal signs Taurus and Scorpius are associated in agricultural calendars with the beginning of summer and winter (e.g. Varro Rust. 1.28). These symbols, which appear on a number of other reliefs (see fig. 62), have stimulated much of the speculation that the Mithraic relief must be in fact a 'star-map'.

Atlas sometimes appears on the reliefs, sustaining on his shoulders the heavy weight of the sky. When the figure is clothed in the garments and phrygian cap of Mithras, as in one of the panels at Neuenheim (fig. 53), we may take it that he is Mithras himself, supporting the sphere in his rôle as *kosmokrator* (p. 70).

The evidence for the cult of Mithras contains numerous astronomical symbols. Scarcely less numerous are the modern attempts to explain them in detail. But this cannot be done without making assumptions that are themselves highly speculative.[97]

The zodiac sometimes appears above the arc of the cave. Reinhold Merkelbach has rightly emphasised that the zodiac was the 'circle of the be-souled beings', that is, the planets.[98] The planets follow regular courses, from which it was deduced that they must be fully conscious, and therefore possess souls. This circle was divided into twelve sections, each marked by one of the constellations of the fixed heavens standing behind it. The representation of the zodiac means, therefore, that with the sacrifice of the bull there came into being the ecliptic, the path along which the planets move around the earth. This is noticeable particularly in those reliefs on which the stereotyped signs of the zodiac are set in a circle all round the bull-slaying scene, so that the act takes place within the zodiac. In such cases, the zodiac replaces the cave, the usual scene of the event, as an image of the kosmos.

53. Neuenheim/Heidelberg: panel from l. jamb (V 1283. 7), Mithras-Atlas. The only other comparable scene occurs at Osterburken (V 1292. 4b). In each case, the universe bears the circles marking its apparent eastward and westward motions.

We can see such a circle on a marble relief from Londinium (London) in Britain: within it, Mithras kills the bull, accompanied by the torch-bearers (here in the less common arrangement with Cautes on the left, Cautopates on the right, p. 96); dog and scorpion can be recognised, while the snake and the raven are broken off, though traces of them remain (V 810, fig. 54). In examples such as these, Mithras is indeed in the middle of the universe, but he does not function as mediator between two opposed worlds, as Cumont argued (p. xix). In the upper corners of the relief, Sol is driving up into heaven with his quadriga and horses, Luna downwards on the other side, with her biga and oxen. At the bottom there are two wind-gods with ruffled hair and wings at their partings. On the circular band, the sphere of the heavens, reading anti-clockwise and starting from above Mithras' head, are represented: Cancer, Leo, Virgo, Libra, Scorpius, Sagittarius, Capricorn, Aquarius, Pisces, Aries, Taurus, Gemini. The dedicator's inscription is distributed over four different vacant spaces on the relief, beginning with the left-centre: *Ulpi/us / Silva/nus // emeri/tus / leg(ionis) / II Aug(ustae) / votum / solvit // fac/tus // Arau/sione* – he was a soldier, now released from service, who had been recruited in Arausio, the modern Orange in Provence (*factus Arausione*) (RIB 3).

54. *Walbrook, London: cult-relief within the zodiacal circle. The signs are so positioned that Leo, the astrological 'house' of the Sun, is leaping up towards Sol, and Taurus, the 'exaltation' of the Moon, is by Luna. The conventional divide between spring and summer falls directly above Mithras' cap; cf. the similar design of a relief from Siscia/Sisak, Croatia (V 1472).*

A whole variety of symbols is assembled, in a manner reminiscent almost of a still-life, on a relief from Sidon in Syria (Lebanon); the message of course remains unaltered (V 75, fig. 55). The relief is of Parian marble. As usual Mithras is at the centre; the raven, dog, serpent and scorpion are present, though not the torch-bearers. The god's cloak carries stars (p. 85), and there is also a star on the point of his phrygian cap. In the corners, one notes the youthful busts of the Seasons in tondi, and near them their various appropriate symbols. The sequence starts at top-left with Spring, who wears a leaf-chaplet, and whose symbol is a basket of flowers; then, reading clockwise: Summer, wearing a crown of corn-ears (sheaf); Autumn, wearing a crown of leaves (fruit-basket); and Winter, wearing a cap (duck). The positions of the busts of Luna (left) and Sol (right), also in tondi, are among the few variations from the norm here. The signs of the zodiac must be read counter-clockwise; beginning above Mithras' head they are: Taurus, Gemini, Cancer, Leo, Virgo, Libra, Scorpius (which belongs both to the zodiac and to the bull-slaying scene), Sagittarius, Capricorn, Aquarius, Pisces,

Aries. Beneath Summer, the designer has inserted an eagle standing on a thunderbolt, symbolising Jupiter.

Mithras had performed an act which could be reproduced by human beings: a person who committed himself to the god partook also of his strength. Mithras is *invictus*, and through him men would be so likewise, at any rate in the sense of being able to obtain visions anticipating what awaits the soul after death. This aspect of invincibility was manifested concretely in the stone of the monuments, and we can scarcely doubt that it would initially have been more appealing to a soldier than to an administrative official. But even the latter could make invincibility meaningful to himself, albeit perhaps in a slightly less concrete form, that is, primarily in relation to the condition of the soul.

55. *Sidon, Lebanon: cult-relief. The busts of Sol and Luna are reversed (as at Dura-Europos: V 37), as is the order of the signs of the zodiac. This made it possible to place Aries, the 'exaltation' of the Sun, facing Sol, and Taurus facing Luna. The same association is found on a relief from Mauls in Noricum (V 1400).*

SOME UNUSUAL RELIEFS

Simple as it is, a cult-relief from Sankt Andrä in Noricum (Austria) stands out for its quirkiness. The scene itself is perfectly ordinary: what is remarkable about the monument is its unusually awkward execution (V 1423, fig. 56). Sol and Luna are shown without attributes, and can only be identified by their normative positions, Sol on the left, Luna on the right, and the treatment of Luna's hair. Mithras' left hand, which is outsize by comparison with the bull's head, has been thoroughly mismanaged, as has the giant dagger; equally peculiar are the four round stone bumps on the hem of Mithras' fluttering cloak, which are presumably to be understood as stars – no doubt they were highlighted in paint. The appearance of the torch-bearers is almost military, both being dressed in short-skirted tunics under a cloak – the round fibula is clearly visible on Cautopates' (l.) right shoulder – and they look almost as though they were standing on sentry-duty: Cautopates seems to be holding his downward-turned torch as though he were on parade. This hint of a military character is confirmed by the inscription, which tells us that a certain Verus dedicated it to Mithras for the benefit of the soldiers of an auxiliary unit.[99]

56. *Skt Andrä, in the Tullner Feld by Klosterneuburg, Lower Austria: votive relief. See on fig. 47. This type of frame is typical of the middle Danube region, centred on Upper Pannonia, but extending into Dalmatia and Noricum, as in this case.*

It was especially common in Dacia to dedicate small plaque-like reliefs (p. 56). The sculptors always tried to crowd as much information as possible onto these diminutive surfaces. Fig. 57 shows a relief from Romula in Dacia whose total dimensions are 35 × 24 cm (14 × 10 in). The upper register measures 7 cm, the lower 6, leaving just under 20 (7 in) for the main scene (cf. p. 98). The god kneels on the bull, Sol, Luna and the torch-bearers are visible, dog and serpent rather sketchy, no scorpion. One can see Sol and Luna immediately to the left and right of Mithras' head; the free corners are occupied by the raven (r.), whose rôle as a link between Sol and Mithras (p. 98) has been lost by putting him here; and, on the other side, the Rock-birth, which in this type of relief is generally on the main part of the relief.

In the upper register, we see the god hauling the bull along, riding on it, the 'Water-miracle' (p. 71) – a scene in which aesthetic considerations have led to the right-hand figure being elongated, so that, for all that he is kneeling, he is as tall as Mithras who is standing – ; and the bull in the temple. The bottom register contains the sequence: Sol's obeisance, feast-scene, ascension to heaven, and Oceanus (pp. 149–53).

57. Romula/Reşca, Dacia: Danubian-type stele relief (V 2171). These little-studied reliefs have rightly been seen as a 'humble reflection of the triumphal art of the Empire'.

There is a more or less standard range of frames for Mithraic reliefs. But the designers – dedicators or sculptors – kept trying to develop new shapes, in part or in whole. One original type, not limited geographically to one area, is the tondo, a design which, being already circular, locates the bull-slaying in the heavenly sphere. From Salona in Dalmatia (nr Split, Croatia) there comes a marble relief measuring just 22 cm (9 in) across (fig. 58; see pp. 74, 100). Mithras and bull, raven, torch-bearers, dog, snake and scorpion are all in their usual places.[100] Sol and Luna are located in the band surrounding the scene. Between them, one can make out a reclining figure, who, given the other subjects, can be identified as Oceanus. The sculptor, presumably at the instance of the dedicant, has modelled various sea-creatures, which have nothing to do with Mithras, but rather with the immediate vicinity of Salona, which was a port. Beneath Sol, we can see a shrimp and a lobster, beneath Luna a crocodile and a dolphin. At the very bottom stands a krater, approached by two serpents.

58. *Salona/Split, Croatia: votive-relief in tondo form (V 1861). Note the torch-bearers' unusual heroic nudity.*

A rather odd relief has come to light at Biljanovac in Moesia Superior (nr Kumanovo, Macedonia). The type of bull-slaying scene within a circular relief has here been combined with the upright form with three registers usual in the Danube area (e.g. figs 17, 111). The marble plaque was found broken into 25 fragments, though fortunately hardly any are missing (fig. 59; see also pp. 79, 82, 110, 125). The central scene, framed by a circular leaf-crown, shows Mithras killing the bull, with the two torch-bearers, all standing on a horizontal base. The representation of the serpent is interesting, since its writhing coils bind the main scene to the lower register. The upper register is complete except for Sol, who is missing on the left. Proceeding left to right, one first sees the Water-miracle. Mithras sits on a stone, a figure stands in front of him, another behind. After that comes the bull in a boat, and four uncertain divinities, perhaps Mercury, Jupiter, Juno and Mars. Then come two people watching Mithras being born from the rock, then the Rock-birth itself, and the bust of Luna. Only four scenes of the lower register survive. From the left they are: Mithras riding the bull; Sol's obeisance; the feast-scene; the ascension. Oceanus, who often appears in connection with this last scene, is squeezed into the spandrel above (p. 152).

59. *Biljanovac, Macedonia: open-work votive-relief (V 2202). A relief such as this was probably illuminated from behind at particular ritual moments. One of the by-scenes, the two figures to the right of the group of four deities, occurs nowhere else. Though they usually chose to illustrate standard moments from the sacred narrative, the patrons who commissioned these monuments were free to select any they wished or that appealed to them. At Hawarti (Syria) we even find 'demons'.*

A relief from the area of the lower Danube shows the god after the killing of the bull (fig. 60).[101] Once again, the gigantic boulders locate the event in a cave. Mithras is almost naked – an allusion to Attis (p. 156) – and wears only his phrygian cap, his cloak and a breech-clout. The dagger is sticking into the bull's shoulder, and Mithras' left hand is still grasping its nostrils. His right arm is already flung out in triumph. The other figures are all as usual, though there are no torch-bearers.

60. *Unknown provenance, now in the Louvre, Paris: votive-relief from the Lower Danube (V 2196). Mithras' heroic nudity, and his gesture, are paralleled on a relief from Gaganica in Thrace (V 2327). The god is also represented naked on a plaque from Italy (201), and at Lopodunum, Upper Germany (1275). Nike (Victory) is often shown in the triumphalist stance, with her hand flung out.*

THE TORCH-BEARERS[102]

The torch-bearers are, however, seldom absent from the cult-reliefs. They stand on either side of the bull, apparently relaxed, their legs often crossed (figs 3, 15–17, 24, 50–2 and passim). They wear oriental garments just like Mithras. No satisfactory etymology of the names Cautes and Cautopates has yet been offered, but it is certain which name applied to which: Cautes holds his torch up, Cautopates down. That it was possible to represent them sometimes simply by their phrygian caps shows that the Mithraists took their presence for granted (p. 49; fig. 9).

The two torch-bearers are often interpreted as symbols of light, the one for the Sun rising in the morning, the other for the Sun setting in the evening. In company with Mithras himself, who stands between them, they stand for the three cardinal positions of the Sun, morning, noon-day and evening. At Jajce in Dalmatia (Bosnia) little triangular niches for lamps were cut into the rock above the torch-bearers' heads (fig. 45), to give the effect of a star over their caps. T. Martialius Candidus dedicated a pair of altars of the same size at Stockstadt in Germania Superior (on the

Main-*limes*) with similar inscriptions. The only difference is in the deities they invoke: the first lines read *D(eo) Oc(cidenti)* and *D(eo) O(rienti)* (*CIL* XIII 11791a, b = V 1214–15). The frequent occurrence of such parallelisms on votive-altars, together with the fact that they were found near the podia, supports the interpretation of the divinities 'Oriens' and 'Occidens' ('East' and 'West') as Cautes and Cautopates, worshipped as the rising and setting Sun. A similar connection was seen by Senilius Carantinus at Nida, in dedicating his rock-birth stele with the torch-bearers on either side (V 1127, fig. 24). The inscription on one face, *C(a)elum*, Heaven, into which the Sun rises, refers to Cautes, that on the other, *Oceanum*, Ocean, into which it disappears, to Cautopates.

Such an explanation may well suit those reliefs, about fifty of them, in which the sequence runs, from left to right, Cautes→Mithras→Cautopates. In these cases, Cautes is beneath the image of Sol, Cautopates beneath Luna (figs 47, 50, 54, 66). The connection between one torch-bearer and the Sun or Moon may be emphasised on occasional pieces, such as the plaque, now in Bologna, which shows Cautopates with Luna (fig. 61; see p. 74). The rather odd relief-panel from Dieburg, mentioned earlier (fig. 31), which shows a tree with three branches, each of which ends in a head wearing a phrygian cap, way well be explained with reference to this three-fold manifestation of Light, at first appearance, at zenith, and at occultation. This might be the worship of the 'three-fold Mithras' ('ο τριπλάσιος Μίθρας) alluded to by the sixth-century pseudonymous Christian author 'Dionysius the Areopagite' (*Epist.* 7).

61. *Unknown provenance, now in Bologna: uninscribed votive-relief of Cautopates with the crescent Moon (V 694). At his feet, an apparently dead bull (l.) and a clump of reeds, of the type often associated with fresh-water divinities. Below the Moon, an upturned hydria, with water gushing forth. This symbolism seems to confirm the links between Cautopates and night (he is elsewhere associated with the owl) and the fecundity released by the bull's death: the Moon 'nourishes the happy seeds with her wet fires' (Apul. Met. 11.2.3). Cautopates is shown with a sickle and ears of corn on a relief at Rome (V 532); and with a dolphin on statues from North Africa and Spain (124; 773).*

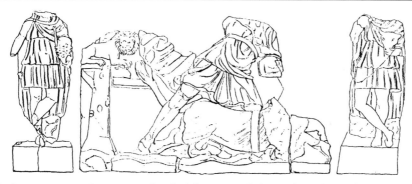

62. *Sarmizegetusa, Romania: cult-relief, later extended to include the torch-bearers. The association between Cautes and the zodiacal sign Taurus, and Cautopates and Scorpius, is found twice at Rome, at Bologna (fig. 52), and three times in Dacia/Moesia Inferior, confirming that esoteric speculation could travel widely within the mysteries. Behind the tree on the central relief is a lion, a common solar symbol, holding down a ram's head.*

A large tree visible on the left margin of a large cult-image at Sarmi-zegetusa in Dacia shows that the torch-bearers were omitted from the initial design (V 2084, fig. 62). When they were later attached to either side, the elbow of the right-hand figure (Cautes) had to be partly removed to make enough room for it to fit between the relief and the wall (V 2122, 2120). We should also note their attributes here: Cautopates holds a scorpion by the tail, its claws resting on his shoulder; Cautes carries a bull's head (cf. fig. 52). Cautes might here symbolise the half-year in which the day is longer than the night (taking the head as a cipher for Taurus), and inversely Cautopates the other half-year. Aries and Libra would have been more appropriate ciphers for the beginning of the two periods, but the signs next following were probably preferred because they were familiar in the cult.[103]

But in most cases (around 240 of them), this relation between the torch-bearers and Sol and Luna does not hold good. Quite apart from the local variations that are so common, therefore, there are two quite distinct ways of representing the torch-bearers, which require appropriately different explanations. On these reliefs, Cautopates is to the left of the bull-slaying, and Cautes to the right (figs 15, 16, 45, 51, 52, 56, 111, 113). We should perhaps interpret Cautopates here as a symbol of death,[104] signified by the downward-pointing torch and the fact that, sometimes at least, he seems to be grieving, with an air recalling that of grave-guardians in antiquity. In other mystery cults too, the light that fails and is extinguished was under-stood as a symbol of death and decay. Cautes, on the other hand, with his raised torch, stands for joy and new life. At Tîrguşor in Moesia Inferior (Romania), he is shown with the torch and a pine-cone, the symbol of rebirth (V 2306). The torch-bearers appear in their ordinary attitude on the lateral faces of the altar dedicated by the Tetrarchs at Carnuntum to D(eo) S(oli) I(nvicto) M(ithrae) as protector of the Empire (p. 28). Whereas Cautopates has just his lowered torch, Cautes holds his torch up in his right hand, and grasps a sheaf of corn-ears in his left (fig. 63). Cautes is thus associated with fertility, growth and life, symbolised by the corn-ears (p. 81). This passage from lower (Cautopates) to higher (Cautes) is depicted metaphrastically on the large relief from Neuenheim in Germania Superior (fig. 16). Again, Mithras stands in between them: it is his act which guarantees life, it is he who leads the way from death to new life. There are many examples of reliefs in which both torch-bearers raise their torches, such as the relief from Romula in Dacia cited earlier (fig. 57). Are Cautes and Cautopates both symbols of hope in such cases, or is Cautes represented twice? There are too many instances for us to suppose that the sculptor has simply made a mistake.[105] We have to accept that many images will not yield up their meaning to us. It was obvious to people in antiquity that the interpretations suggested here were not mutually exclusive.

63. Carnuntum/Bad Deutsch-Altenburg: l. lateral face of the tetrarchs' votive altar recording their repair of Mithraeum III (V 1697). Cautes holding his torch up in his r.h., and ears of wheat down in his l. Cautes is elsewhere associated with the cock, the 'Persian' bird of the sun and morning, and with the pine-cone, a generalised symbol of fertility.

ANIMALS

The standard position for the raven is near Sol. In Greek mythology, the raven is a messenger, κόραξ κῆρυξ, indeed the messenger of Apollo, a sun-god. Should we take it that in the cult of Mithras, by metalepsis, the raven was also Sol's messenger to Mithras? One of the rays from Sol's radiate crown is sometimes greatly elongated so as to strike Mithras (fig. 106); and sometimes the latter apparently turns his head back up towards Sol (figs 15–18, 50, 52, 58). It is in fact much more common for the god's head to face forward, so that his gaze is directed toward the spectator, looking as it were into the congregation (figs 3, 13, 45, 47, 51, 55–7, 66). It has been suggested that Mithras is rather turning his head away from the dying bull, because he is putting it to death against his will: this explanation seems to me the least convincing of all. Is Mithras' head turned up so that he can listen to a message, albeit one whose purport is quite unknown to us? Or rather just to express the idea of a relation between Sol and Mithras? We can do no more than throw up questions.

No less thorny is the problem of how to take the dog, scorpion and snake, and also the lion, who occasionally belongs with them (figs 15, 16, 51, 85; cf. 74, 75). We should probably assume in all four cases that they are not there to hinder the god's act but to partake of the bull's life-force. The scorpion grabs its testicles, the dog and the serpent lick the blood from the wound in its neck, so that they all may absorb its life-giving power.

The sculptors had most difficulty in getting the scorpion right: the creature is not always as convincingly represented as it is on a fragmentary relief dedicated by a Roman equestrian official, a v(ir) p(erfectissimus), at Axiopolis in Moesia Inferior (Hinag, Romania) (fig. 64; cf. 50). Often it is only recognisable as a sort of bulge at the appropriate spot. The dog's intent is clear on many reliefs, such as one from Rome illustrated in fig. 65 (V 435), where the dog is protruding its tongue to lick up the blood.

64. Axiopolis/Hinag, Romania: fragment of a cult-relief, showing the scorpion at the bull's testicles (V 2279). The significance of the scorpion is disputed. On a painted relief from S. Stefano Rotondo in Rome, it is black, which might suggest a malevolent creature. On the other hand, the black scorpion was believed to be especially characteristic of Persia, and scorpions in general were thought of, like snakes, as earth-born. At Capua, however, the scorpion is yellow (V 181, cf. 386), at Marino reddish-brown (dust-jacket).

65. Nr Piazza Dante, Rome: detail of cult-relief from Mithraeum of Primus (cf. figs 25, 44), the dog leaping to lick the bull's blood. In view of the feats of Indian and Karmanian hunting dogs, which include running bulls down, we should perhaps take it that in myth the dog helped Mithras to track the bull (cf. the hunting hound with Cautes, V 80). But in the religious context this fact had no significance, which is why the dog is often, as in this case, rather weedy-looking.

For the serpent's rôle in this sacrificial drama, however, there is an explanation that takes us further.[106] In Greek traditional lore, the snake could be understood as a chthonic creature, that is, as a symbol of the earth that, once soaked with the bull's blood, will give forth its fruits. The transmission of the force that emanates from the bull is particularly striking on a relief from Sia' near Kanatha on the Jebel Hauran (Syria Phoenice) (fig. 66). Mithras is kneeling on the bull; his hair, under the phrygian cap, is finished so as to suggest a radiate crown, whereas the bull's horns form a lunar crescent. The tiny, only partly preserved, figures of Cautes (l.) and Cautopates (r.) are in their less common positions (p. 96). The busts of Sol and Luna, the raven, dog and the scorpion, are all in their ordinary places; but whereas the scorpion as usual grabs the testicles, the snake is sucking semen out of the bull's pizzle so as to absorb its force and fertility.

Apart from being identified as a chthonic creature, the snake also has a close association with water. Water's life-giving power, as it comes tumbling out of fissures in the earth, and rocks, could easily be imagined in the form of a creature naturally earth-bound. And this benedict power, a power that emanates from the depths of the earth, was the serpent. For that reason snakes became protective spirits of springs and fountains. On some reliefs there appears, in contrast to the ordinary representation of the serpent reaching up to the wound, a collocation of krater and snake, the depiction of which makes clear that the snake is making for the vessel in order to drink from it (figs 58, 75, 85; cf. 15, 16).

Snakes are also frequently represented on the lateral faces of votive-altars. The Mithraists' preference for water-vessels decorated with appliqué serpents is understandable once we think of the close relationship of snakes to water and water-containers. To be sure, such kraters were very popular in other cults too, such as that of Sabazius, so that one cannot infer the existence of a mithraeum simply on the basis of finds of this kind. But a good number have indeed been found in what are undoubtedly Mithraic temples (p. 119).

66. Siā, Jebel Hauran, Syria: cult-relief from the forecourt of the temple of Dusares (V 88 with fig. 244: third cent.). The bull is the humped form typical of the ancient NE, and found in other reliefs from the region, e.g. V 75, 76 (Sidon): another example of local diversity. Three other reliefs, probably by the same sculptor, are known from Siā, all with the Latin dedication D(eo) I(nvicto) S(oli).

The Bull-slaying gives us an insight into the importance of the language of images for the mysteries. Mithraic religious experience was captured in shorthand as it were, a shorthand that, compressed into symbolic format, commuted the whole myth, the entire cult-legend, into a single image. The cult-relief depicted a unique event, which yet symbolised all of creation. Out of the death of the bull new life burgeons; and this new life, which is true, real life, is owed to Mithras alone.

CHAPTER 9

Ritual

INITIATION

The late tenth-century encyclopaedia known as the *Suda* notes under the lemma 'Mithras': 'no one was permitted to be initiated into them (the mysteries of Mithras), until he should show himself holy and steadfast by undergoing several graduated tests' (3: 394, M 1045 Adler). Towards the end of the fourth century, Gregory of Nazianzen refers in general terms to the 'tests in the mysteries of Mithras' (*Or.* 4. 70). Before any person could be accepted into any group of *mystai*, he or she had to undergo the initiation rituals. Before the actual initiation there came a period of instruction; in the cult of Mithras one had to apply for this to the *pater*, Father, of the community. Tertullian suggests this (*Apol.* 8.7; *Ad nat.* 1.7.23), but gives no details.

Rather oddly, initiation is one of the aspects of the mysteries of Mithras the literary sources do mention, albeit that initiation was without a doubt one of the cult's real secrets. For that very reason, we can discount the reports of the (mainly Christian) sources, the fancifulness of whose accounts of the supposed tests of courage grows with their date of composition. 'Nonnus', the pseudonymous early-sixth-century author of a commentary on Gregory's first four *Orations*, speaks of eighty tests, at first easy, then gradually more difficult, in the course of which the initiand had to swim for many days, was hurled into a bonfire, compelled to fast and live as a hermit (Migne, PG 36: 989). Cosmas of Jerusalem (eighth century AD) claims to know further details: 'for example, first the initiands were made to starve for fifty days; then, if they endured steadfastly, they were abraded for two days, and afterwards thrown into snow for twenty' (Migne, PG 38: 506).

Over against such fancies, we can set a series of frescoes from the mithraeum at Capua Vetere in Italy, five of whose panels have been interpreted as depictions of an initiation ceremony. Whether the rituals represented in the frescoes are those carried out for normal initiates or for the seven grades of priests (pp. 131–8) is undecidable.

The first panel shows us an assistant mystagogue dressed in a short white tunic guiding the initiand, whose naked body is rendered in red ochre, and whose eyes are covered by a white blindfold (V 187). This recalls the remark of Ambrosiaster (the name now given to an anonymous fourth-century commentator on the Epistles of Paul) that *in spelaeo velatis oculis illuduntur*, 'they are deceived in the cave when they have their eyes blindfolded'.[107] In the next panel, there are three figures in a dramatic group. The mystagogue, in a billowing cloak edged in red, and wearing a phrygian cap, stands on the left; in his outstretched left hand he is extending a stick-like object, perhaps a sword, towards the initiand. The latter's eyes are still blindfolded, and he is kneeling: his arms appear to be tied behind him (V 188). Ambrosiaster describes, in the passage just cited, how the initiand's hands were tied with chicken's guts, which were then cut through by a man calling himself his 'liberator'.[108] Behind the initiand stands the assistant mystagogue, who seems to be keeping a firm grip on him.

In the third panel, the initiand is again kneeling on one knee, with his hands tied behind him. The sword seems to be lying beside him on the ground, which may mean that he has successfully passed the first test. At any rate, he is no longer blindfolded. The assistant mystagogue is again standing behind him, this time setting a crown on his head (V 191). This may be an illustration of the crown-ritual described by Tertullian, *De cor.* 15 (pp. 134–5). The next panel shows the initiand on his knees; the assistant mystagogue holds him by the shoulders and seems to be putting his foot on his calves, as though he were trying to prevent him from rising. The mystagogue, in a red cloak, is approaching the initiand and with his staff indicating an object lying on the ground (V 194). In the fifth and last panel, we see the initiand stretched out on the ground as though he were dead. At his head and feet are the same two persons as before (V 193). Modern interpreters have seen here a kind of symbolic execution, taking it as a test, albeit not a life-threatening test, of courage.

There is no point in speculating too much about the meaning of these initiation rituals, or supposing for example that the initiand might have been rendered somnolent by drugs. There are no contemporary interpretations of the paintings; and they are anyway now so damaged and defaced that they cannot be illustrated here in black and white.[109] But we do have a prayer uttered by an initiand into the mysteries of Isis, recited after he has returned from a death-like slumber, and which can help us to understand analogous rituals:

I came to the boundary of death and, having trodden the threshold of Proserpina, I travelled through all the elements and returned. In the middle of the night I saw the sun flashing with bright light. I came face to face with the gods below and the gods above and paid reverence to them from close at hand.

(Apuleius, *Met.* 11.23, tr. J.A. Hanson)

Such were the experiences of initiands after, or even during, the ceremonies, experiences denied to non-initiates. To behold the Sun at midnight: that was the singularity, for of course anyone could see it by day. The initiand was supposed to attain knowledge, by virtue of which he might succeed in gazing upon the divine.

It is therefore intelligible that initiation was understood as a kind of rebirth. An unknown person scratched a graffito (fig. 67) into the side-wall

67. S. Prisca, Rome: graffito on the outer face of the l. wall of the cult-niche (V 498 = AE 1980: 60), recording the precise time and date of a 'birth'. Both a conventional and an astrological date are given.

of the cult-niche of the mithraeum beneath S. Prisca in Rome: 'Born at first light when the Emperors (Septimius) Severus and Antonius (Caracalla) were consuls, on the 12 day before the first of December, the day of Saturn, the 18 of the Moon'.[110] That was 20 November AD 202. By analogy with the Sun's birth at sunrise, the initiand is also 'born' through initiation into the mysteries.

Final admission into the community was concluded by a handshake (δεξίωσις) with the *pater*, just as Mithras and Sol had shaken one another's hand (p. 151). The initiates of Mithras were for that reason called *syndexioi*, those 'united by the handshake', the term used, as we saw, by Proficentius in his poem (p. 42).[111] According to the Christian apologist Firmicus Maternus, the followers of Mithras were the 'initiates of the theft of the bull, united by the handshake of the illustrious Father' (*Err. prof. rel.* 5.2).

The overt purpose of initiation was to enable one to obtain salvation. But we should not on that account neglect its effects upon the earthly community, particularly in relation to the sense of mutual belonging. Modern sociological studies have made plain how widespread is the need to belong, and in antiquity the case was no different. Early in the second century AD Epictetus described the terrible loneliness which can come over a person in the midst of daily life (3.13.1–3), and since then his words have lost none of their truth. Religious associations, and specifically that of Mithras, fulfilled an important function here. The individual passed tests of courage, got to know rituals and secrets, 'mysteries', and so became a member of a select group, whose values he accepted just as the group accepted him. Some of the rituals were strange and contained primitive elements, but they were submitted to, with all their emotional freight, in the context of a community: the initiand confronted the unwonted in a social context. Because mithraea remained face-to-face places of worship, this social experience may well have been more intense in the cult of Mithras than in other mystery associations. The very fact that the cult, despite its success, continued over two centuries to build the same small temples rather than large complexes indicates that the instinct to remain small was part of the cult's essence, and also of its ability to attract new members.

PRAYER

A document in Greek belonging to a mystery context has come down to us among the recipes of the so-called Paris magical codex, which to judge from the hand must have been written about AD 300. It is an *apothanatismos*, an 'Immortaliser': these were Egyptian prayer-texts to be recited by the initiand, on completion of the initiatory tests, when he was received into the community. The evidence for the cult of Mithras in Egypt is indeed limited, but there certainly was a temple in Alexandria. Doubts have been expressed about the authenticity of the text, but probably wrongly.[112] I emphasised at the beginning that we must allow that there were many local variations in the cult of Mithras (p. 16), and the point holds good for this text too. It is, however, sufficiently instructive to stand proxy for a great deal of evidence now lost to us.

After a brief introduction, which mentions Sol Mithras, the main part of the document contains the initiand's seven prayers, interspersed with detailed instructions given by a priest. The first prayer seeks, and describes, a meditative immersion in the essence of the four elements, fire, water, earth and air (487–537). The initiand, like an eagle, leaves the earth far beneath him: he is to take three breaths as deep as possible, and then he will breathe in the divine spirit and feel himself lifted up into the air. He will leave behind his earthly matter and rise to the planetary spheres, to behold with his spiritual eye the immortal source of all (538–47). The final result of the meditative exercises is that the soul becomes a soul-star: 'I am a star' cries the Mithraist (574–5). The initiand then sees the Sun's disk unfolding, and a shower of stars falling from it; the sun-god's outer garment is revealed. The third long prayer, to be recited with the eyes closed, begins with the three times seven appellations of the Sun's disk (590–604). When the initiand opens his eyes again, he sees the doors to the world of the gods opening, and there appears Helios, as a young god transfigured, the god of gods, youthful, beautiful, with lambent hair, arrayed in a white robe under a short red cloak, and wearing a flaming crown (634–7). After further prayers to the seven virgin goddesses of Fate, and the seven guardians of the axes of the kosmos (661–92), syncretistic figures whose meaning is unclear to us, the initiand finally beholds the Highest descending, a gigantic, youthful, golden-haired god, wearing a white tunic, and golden crown and trousers, who holds in his right hand the golden shoulder of a young bull (696–704). This highest god is evidently the ultimate form of the sun-god, pictured as Mithras. The initiand beholds him finally face to face.

The 'names' and terms woven into this prayer-text were among the secrets that it was the purpose of initiation to reveal. The utterances are all more than mere words, they constitute the very substance of what was to be imparted. To grasp the force of the following brief examples, it should be stressed that in Greek there are seven vowels, which are conventionally represented as: a, e, long ê, i, o, y and long ô. 'Names' such as the following cannot and could not be understood, nor can they be translated; but they were without any doubt uttered with fervour by the initiand: *pitêtmi meôy enarth phyrkechô psyridariô tyrê philba* (564–5).

Equally untranslatable are the numerous magical vowel-combinations, the *voces mysticae*, long strings of vowels such as *êeô oêeô iôô oê êeô êeô oê êô iôô oêêe ôêe ôoê iê* and so on (610–12). The vowels were combined in such a way that they formed no known word and gave no immediate sense. If they were to be effective, they had to be recited in a specified sequence. The planets, the seven deathless gods, were invoked in a state of ecstasy like this, and equated with the seven vowels, though there was no generally-recognised connection between individual planets and the sounds. The initiand ascended higher and higher up the ladder of the planets into the sphere of the fixed stars with the aid of these varied vowel-sequences, sometimes spoken naturally, sometimes intoned.

This vowel-planet ladder is depicted in visible form on a gem (fig. 68), though unfortunately it cannot be definitely associated with the cult of Mithras.[113] Such sequences were able to evoke a psycho-cerebral state of excitement by phonaesthetic means. In combination with light-effects (pp. 120–30), and repeated alternation between recited prayers, violent noises and utter silence, they served to induce the voluntary production of interesting psychic states.

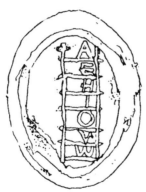

68. *Heliotrope gem with the Greek vowels arranged in a ladder: 'in Egypt, the priests, when singing hymns in praise of the gods, employ the seven vowels, which they utter in due succession' (Demetr., De elocut. 71). The signs are 'positive' (not reversed, as would be the case if this were a seal-ring gem). On the obv., an eagle standing on an arrow.*

The initiand learned the meaning of those terms that were deliberately used in the cult because they were unknown to the world outside. One example is *nama*, which meant roughly 'Hail . . .!' or 'Honour to . . .' (pp. 8, 133). These were words whose allure lay in the fact that they had been taken over from foreign tongues and preserved in their original form. Initiation involved not merely the setting forth of facts or the imitation of deeds, but also modes of utterance. We can glimpse in the complex relationship between special languages and new cognitive experience something of the rôle played by initiation into the mysteries.

In the 'Mithras liturgy', prayers alternate with ritual silence. Extended whistling and tongue-clicking (561–2; 579–80) succeed godly obmutescence. Both are animal noises, which can both protect one against the gods and summon them up. And when the priest warns the initiand that he will hear a mighty crash of thunder which will shock him (572–4), this will have been an actual noise. The initiand himself is told to give a long bellow, on one occasion as loud as a horn (657–8); Ambrosiaster says that the Mithraists roared like lions.[114] The *mystes* is also instructed to bellow until he has no breath left, even perhaps to the point of exhaustion, almost to fainting, 'belabouring his chest', before he sees the goddesses of Fate and the seven guardians of the axes of the kosmos (657–9). All this is raised to a still higher pitch at the final vision of the sun-god (704–8; 711–12).

THE RITUAL MEAL[115]

The Samaritan Justin Martyr, who had long lived in a pagan world before turning to Christianity, expresses surprise at the similarity between the Christian Eucharist and the Mithraic ritual meal. He first describes the Eucharist, in which bread and wine are not received as ordinary food and drink: Jesus took on flesh and blood by the Word of God to save humankind. Nourishment, that which feeds the flesh and blood of the faithful, is consecrated through the prayer of the Eucharist, and thereby becomes Flesh and Blood of the incarnate Word, as we can read in the Gospels. After citing the prayer of consecration, 'This is my Body which is given for you: Do this in remembrance of me' and, 'this is my Blood of the New Testament', Justin explains that the wicked demons have introduced a similar ceremony into the mysteries of Mithras (*1Apol.* 66). Justin is familiar with the analogous Mithraic ritual, both the actions and the spoken formulae, and sees very close parallels not merely between the material components of the two ritual meals but even between the linguistic formulations which accompanied the consecrated nourishment.

Around a half-century later, Tertullian, writing in Carthage in North Africa *c.* AD 200, and who knew a great deal about the cult of Mithras, maintained among other things that the devil had imitated the celebration of the Sacraments in the mysteries. In saying this, he was thinking primarily of the ritual meal. The Mithraists performed in the meal a semblance of the resurrection (*imaginem resurrectionis*).[116] Tertullian saw in the mysteries of Mithras, as in Christian initiatory rituals, a way of speaking about eternal life.

The Mithraists evidently believed that they were reborn through the consumption of bread and wine. The food was of course not simply actual or literal food, but also food in the metaphorical sense, which nourished souls after death: the meal was the guarantee of their ascension into the undying light.

In the case of these analogies, there can be no question of imitation in either direction. The offering of bread and wine is known in virtually all ancient cultures, and the meal as a means of binding the faithful together and uniting them to the deity was a feature common to many religions.[117] It represented one of the oldest means of manifesting unification with the spiritual, and the appropriation of spiritual qualities. And if the Mithraists' meal could be seen by Christians as a distorted copy of Christian mysteries, indicating a close similarity with Christianity, that was because such offerings were made in the same manner in the cult of Mithras and in Christianity, perhaps even to the accompaniment of the same words of consecration.

The most striking representation of this Mithraic meal is that from Konjic in Dalmatia (Bosnia-Hercegovina). Columns on either side of the relief indicate that the event depicted is to be understood as taking place in an enclosed space, a *spelaeum* (fig. 69). We see in the centre of the field a *pater* and a *heliodromus*, priests of the two highest grades (p. 137), sitting down to

69. Konjic, Bosnia-Hercegovina: rev. of cult-relief (V 1896. 3), the Mithraic ritual meal (probably fourth century). It is not clear whether the two inner figures represent the torchbearers, who elsewhere offer the main celebrants a rhyton (e.g. V 641 rev.; cf. figs 71, 76), or are to be understood as other grade-representatives: the crucial r.h. figure has been defaced. Note the symbolic lion to the l. of the table, who is present on other feast-scenes (e.g. fig. 76). This relief is important evidence for the view that the members of the grades sometimes wore masks.

a meal. On the table in front of them is spread a bull's hide, the symbol of Mithras' victory which the meal celebrates – a victory which also promises success to his followers. These two figures are almost a head taller than the others, and are the most important persons present. As the representatives of Mithras and Sol, they recline against cushions on a *triclinium*, a dining-couch. As usual, they support themselves on their left arms; their right hands are raised in a gesture of blessing. They are apparently speaking sacred formulae over the offerings on the small circular table in front of them. This table, to which the viewer's attention is deliberately drawn, is viewed from above, in defiance of the rules of perspective. On it there lie small round loaves or bread-rolls, scored with a cross so that they could be broken open more easily at the fissure. To left and right stand lesser priests as servants: a Raven and a Lion are clearly recognisable. This earthly meal is a ritual reproduction of the celebration of his victory which Mithras performed with the sun-god before their joint ascension in the Sun's chariot, a scene repeatedly depicted on reliefs, especially in the Danubian provinces (figs 17, 57, 59, 111; see p. 152).

The significance attributed in the mysteries to grain and wine, the two most important basic foodstuffs in the ancient world, can easily be seen in the cult-legend. As I described earlier (p. 81), Mithras kills the bull that he has overcome, and at that point an extraordinary transformation occurs: ears of wheat grow out of its tail, and grapes burgeon from the blood at the knife-wound. That is why the table is covered with the bull's hide. On a relief from Lopodunum in Germania Superior (Ladenburg, now a suburb of Heidelberg) the couch on which Mithras and Sol are reclining is covered by the bull's hide, and each has a drinking-horn (*rhyton*) in his hand (fig. 70).[118] A bunch of grapes and two striated rolls are lying on the table. The scene takes place inside a cave, an image for the mithraeum and the kosmos alike.

The ritual meal takes a similar form on the double-sided relief from Rückingen, on the Wetterau-*limes* in Upper Germany, though the heads of all the figures have been deliberately defaced (V 1137, fig. 71). Here again, the table is covered with the bull's hide. The sun-god, who has removed his radiate crown, holds a *rhyton* high in his right hand, while Mithras reaches his towards one of the two torch-bearers. It is significant that both Sol and Mithras are touching the bull here: Sol is holding the tail, the end of which has turned into ears of grain, while Mithras has one hand on the hide. Both seek to partake of the dead bull's magical life-force.

On the large cult-relief from Nida (Heddernheim/Frankfurt), Mithras and Sol are both standing behind the bull's enormous cadaver, now looking rather the worse for wear after being overcome by the god (V 1083, fig. 72).

70. *Lopodunum/Ladenburg by Heidelberg: relief with feast-scene. The odd detail that the table's legs are constructed of the bull's lower legs may refer to a narrative detail in the cult myth: that is how the first common table was made. The disk on a stand behind Sol's raised hand was presumably painted to resemble the solar-crown.*

71. *Rückingen: rev. of double-sided cult-relief, feast-scene. Mithras and Sol are represented behind rather than on the klinè (cf. fig. 70) in order to stress the symbolic importance of the bull's hide and the death it betokens. The sword and solar-crown 'trophy' (cf. fig. 72) summarize the section of the cult myth describing the death of the bull and the 'obeisance' of Sol.*

72. Nida/Heddernheim: rev. of complex relief from Mithraeum I, feast-scene. In this example, the significance of the bull's death is suggested by representing it unflayed, so that the place of the table has to be taken by the attendants with their baskets (which only occur here). The usual rhyta, vessels specifically for wine, are substituted by grapes, perhaps again an allusion to the first feast (cf. V 1528).

Mithras is holding the *rhyton* in his right hand, and taking a grape from the bunch offered him by Sol; in between them stand the dagger and the radiate crown that Sol has taken off. On either side, two servants, here dressed and posed like the two torch-bearers, are holding bowls or baskets which seem to contain small bread-rolls. This relief is one of those worked on both faces, and which could be reversed: in this particular case, the frame remained static and the inner panel was pivoted on its axis. Here, as at Rückingen, the two most important scenes, the slaying of the bull and the feast, were made visible at suitable moments during the course of the ritual. What we might understand one-sidedly as a mere act of slaughter thus takes on a new and different significance. Slaughter and feast together effect the salvation of the faithful.

It is especially these Rhineland monuments which stress the feast-scene, by depicting it large-scale and in considerable detail. On the Danubian reliefs with three registers, it generally appears as the centre scene on the bottom register. Even though these panels are so small, often just 5 cm (2 in) square, the rectangular shape of the dining-couch on which Mithras and Sol recline can still be made out (figs 17, 57, 59, 111). In the ritual meal, Mithras' victory over the bull was celebrated and reproduced. There can be no doubt that the Christian apologists were quite right about its importance for the cult of Mithras as a whole. The very configuration of the mithraeum proves it, for the main chamber is designed as a sort of dining-room: it resembles a *triclinium*, with its three dining-couches arranged around a table. On some of the podia the cill is preserved, where food and drink could be set down. But in the mithraeum one of the three sides is always occupied by the cult-image of Mithras. The god himself is the host.

The ritual meal was probably simply a component of regular common meals. Such meals have always been an essential part of religious assembly: eating and drinking together creates community and renders visible the fact that those who take part are members of one and the same group.[119] The table-ware used at these meals was decorated with appropriate religious motifs, depending on the financial resources of the congregation (p. 116).

CHAPTER 10

Utensils

Prominent among the numerous smaller finds from mithraea are pottery and objects used for illumination, which I shall discuss in this chapter (there are too many objects of other kinds to discuss in a book of the present scope). By no means all of them were made especially for the cult, though their ornamentation must often have seemed fitting to Mithraists. I may here just pick out one example, an iron key with a fitted bronze handle from Nida in Upper Germany (fig. 73). The handle ends, as is often the case with ancient keys, in a lion's head. Because of the lion's rôle in the mysteries (pp. 135, 163), even a familiar object like this could take on new meaning: Mithraists could open up their own world with it.

73. Nida/Heddernheim: iron key with lion's-head handle from Mithraeum III. The lion-headed god himself often holds one or more keys (e.g. V 312, 314). Another example of serendipity might be the infusor (?wine strainer) and its container from the Walbrook Mithraeum in London (Henig, RRB, 106, figs 43 a, b), with vaguely Dionysiac decoration which resembles the hunt of Mithras.

POTTERY

The great quantities of pottery for eating and drinking, as well as a mass of other finds in mithraea, support the inference that the ritual meal was indeed part of a regularly-held banquet (pp. 109–13). In other words, Mithraists did not just receive bread and wine or water, as the literary sources seem to suggest, but were in addition served actual meals.

Among the evidence that points to this conclusion are the finds of bones, which, like many other aspects of the cult, reveal local differences, while at the same time representing a wide variety of animals, cattle, pigs, sheep, lambs, goats, poultry (e.g. geese, chickens), fish. From time to time egg-shells and shell-fish turn up. There are two price-lists from Dura-Europos, which were scratched into the wall-plaster of the mithraeum: the main items in them are the outgoings for meat, wine and *garum* sauce (V 64, 65). At Lentia in Noricum (Linz), uniquely, the remains of fruit, berries and nuts were recovered (V 1421), weighing in all 4.21 kg (> 9 lb); of these no less than 3.92 kg (> 8½ lb) were cherries. Grapes, plums, various different (wild) varieties of damson and cherry, apples (crab- as well as cultivated) and walnuts have all been identified.[120] It is undecidable whether the predominance of cherries reveals a special preference for them among local Mithraists, or is evidence for otherwise unknown ritual practices.

Most of these foodstuffs will have been to eat, since in many temples their remains have been found in 'ritual pits'. These are holes dug into the floor, partly revetted with wood or brick and originally covered by boards. Such a receptacle was found in the centre aisle of Mithraeum III at Nida, between the two podia. It measures 100 × 50 cm, and is 79 cm deep (40 × 20 × 31 in); and on discovery was filled to the brim with animal bones, mainly of ruminants.[121] The Mithraists deposited in these cavities the remains of extensive meals which they did not want to bury in the normal public refuse-pits. Some of the animals, or parts of them – we can hardly imagine most Mithraic congregations sacrificing or consuming an entire bull, for example – could have been victims sacrificed at public festivals before being bought and eaten by the Mithraists. This would explain why the bones were preserved in the temple.

The meals seem sometimes at least to have been prepared in the mithraea themselves. At Lentia, again, a small kitchen was found in the complex (V 1414), and in the ante-room at Brocolitia (Carrawburgh) on Hadrian's Wall, there was a hearth with charcoal and ashes. Elsewhere sacrificial knives of iron, and whetstones to sharpen them with, have been found; also pots and pans, lids and cooking-spoons – though it is also possible that the food might have been brought into the temples from neighbouring houses in utensils of this kind. Finally, as I have mentioned, an amazing quantity and variety of pottery for eating and drinking have come to light in many of the mithraea which have been carefully excavated: cups and jugs, as well as smaller bowls, basins, plates and mortaria too, which were used to prepare the food. In the ante-room of the mithraeum at Koenigshoffen/Strasbourg, most of the sherds of broken plates and bowls lay on the floor near the entrance to the mithraeum proper. They probably stood here on wooden racks, from which one could take the crockery one required before entering the main room.

Mithraic pottery for eating and drinking was of variable quality, from plain coarse-ware to carefully-decorated pieces, depending upon the financial circumstances of the congregation or owner/founder. The motifs found on the better examples repeat the whole range of images and symbols that we have seen on the reliefs.

The decoration of a terra-sigillata sherd from Ittenwiller in Germania Superior, for example, allows us to recognise it as Mithraic (fig. 74). By itself, the snake would not be decisive, but the lion, and above all the figure dressed as a lion, confirm the item as a sherd from a Mithraic cult-vessel.[122] This lion-headed figure reminds us of the relief from Konjic in Dalmatia (fig. 69), where we find individuals attending the ritual meal similarly disguised. Cult-vessels of this kind repeatedly affirm their relation to the content of the rituals. The point is made still more clearly by a bowl, likewise of terra sigillata, from Augusta Treverorum (Trier) in Gallia Belgica, which represents the feast-scene (V 988, fig. 75). Mithras, in his phrygian cap, sits on the left, Sol, in his radiate crown, on the right; in front of them, a table with rolls and a plate. Sol is lifting his *rhyton*, while a torch-bearer is giving one to Mithras. The other torch-bearer is bringing some food. Underneath, a lion couchant; below that, a serpent drinking out of a krater, and, on either side, a cock (l.) and a raven (r.). This highly decorated bowl may have been a votive, intended to adorn the mithraeum.

One of the very finest pieces to have come down to us is an Italian red-ware bowl from the site of Lanuvium (Lanúvio) in Latium whose interior is shown in fig. 76 in a line-drawing (V 207). By turning the dish, one could view *seriatim* two of the exploits which demonstrate Mithras' might: Mithras dragging the bull, and then the slaying of the bull, the centre-piece of all cult-images. We may surmise that this might is to pass into the initiate by way of the liquid that the bowl once held, presumably wine. In this connection, we may also cite two sherds of another cult-vessel, from Mogontiacum (Mainz) in Germania Superior, showing Mithras in his phrygian cap and surrounded by six (originally surely seven) stars. This must be Mithras as kosmokrator driving or pursuing the bull, whose rump survives (fig. 77).[123]

74. *Ittenwiller: terra-sigillata sherd, with a standing figure apparently disguised as a lion. A similar figure has now been found on another terra-sigillata bowl, probably also from the potteries at Ittenwiller (potter: Verecundus), in the mithraeum at Biesheim (dép. Haut-Rhin), a little higher up the Rhine. A third similar figure apparently wearing a lion's mask has now been discovered in the mithraeum at Bornheim/Sechtem nr Bonn.*

75. *Augusta Treverorum/Trier: terra-sigillata bowl found in the Roman cemetery of St Matthias. The deeper or allegorical meaning of the feast seems to be represented below the naturalistic representation. The finds of animal bones in mithraea indicate that the food was by no means simply symbolic. The small wooden mithraeum at Künzing in Raetia has produced 19,000 animal bones (35 kg), 50 per cent of which were piglets under 6 mths, and 18 per cent each of sheep/goat and chickens (virtually no cattle); the bones are from complete skeletons: they were sacrificed on the spot. At the tiny temple at Wiesloch in Upper Germany, the bones of cattle, pigs, sheep/goat and horses were found.*

76. *Lanuvium/Lanúvio, nr Velletri: red-ware bowl with moulded interior decoration, showing the Transitus, and Mithras slaying the bull. Fragments of similar bowls were found on the same site. Another specially-commissioned vessel is the barbotine vase, dedicated Deo invicto Mithrae by the potter Martinus, found in the Pons Aeni Mithraeum on the Inn nr Rosenheim, Raetia.*

77. Mogontiacum/Mainz: sherd of a Mithraic cult-vessel, figures in red: a stray find near the outer perimeter of the legionary camp. If the figure is Mithras, the scene will allude to the theme of Mithras' 'theft' of the bull (p. 78). This theme must have been an important motive for assimilating Mithras and Mercury (fig. 115).

The most complete representation of the bull-slaying, with several accompanying figures, occurs on a barbotine vase from Lezoux in Aquitania (fig. 78). The vase carries several motifs, the most prominent of which is Mithras and the bull, with the snake and scorpion. The god's billowing cloak is decorated with a large rosette, and the whole, as in the case of the other figures, framed by barbotine whorls and beads. The illustration also shows a blob below the torch-bearer, which is the dog that has been put on in the wrong place; the vase in fact has three of these torch-bearers, all with raised torch. In combination with two appliqués of a seated goddess with cornucopiae, Abundantia, the images emphasise the abundance of life that stems from Mithras' act. What, apart from the sheer number of appliqués, distinguishes this find from others is the fact that two of the moulds for making the appliqués were found close beside it, namely the one illustrated in fig. 79, which is for the main scene, and a fragmentary one for the torch-bearers.

78. Lezoux, dép. Puy-de-Dôme: barbotine vase (fragmentary) (V 908 C 1). Note the rosette in the centre of Mithras' cloak, recalling the two rosettes on the feast-scene from Ladenburg (fig. 70). If the rose has any significance other than decorative, it might denote its flowering season, May or June (depending upon the region), which was also significant in the mysteries (figs 29, 54); or it might simply denote the notion of feasting, through allusion to the use of roses in crowns. An allusion to the Rosalia, the popular feast of the dead, is less likely.

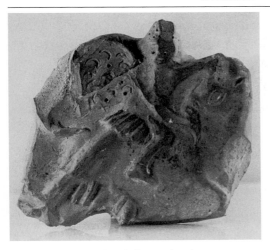

79. The same: clay mould for the appliqué of Mithras (V 908c 2).

Scenes from the full-sized cult-images are repeatedly found on individual vases. In this context, Mithraists seem to have favoured representations of animals: snakes writhe round the handles and the body of a terracotta wine-mixing bowl, a krater, from Taunum (Friedberg) in Germania Superior (fig. 80). In fact, vessels with snakes applied to the handles or the rim enjoyed great popularity among Mithraists, perhaps because of the snake's rôle as a symbol of fertility in the bull-slaying scene. The creature occurs much more frequently than any other, particularly on drinking-vessels; among other considerations, it was very common as an ornament on all vessels of this type, which made it easier for Mithraists to purchase them than the krater in fig. 80, which was probably specially commissioned. For here, in addition to the serpents, there are a scorpion, also familiar from the cult-images, and an object that looks like a ladder. Given the seven-runged ladder on the floor of the Mithraeum of Felicissimus at Ostia (fig. 9), which is a symbol of the seven priestly grades, we may speculate that this krater was a votive given by a priest of the third grade, a *Miles* (p. 134).[124]

80. Taunum/Friedberg: krater from the Mithraeum (V 1061, fragmentary: re-stored). Apart from the snakes on the handles, the vessel is unique in being decorated also with a scorpion and a summary ladder.

The *Spruchbecher* from Augusta Treverorum (Trier) were also especially commissioned. Here it is not the shape, or the decoration, which is out of the ordinary, but the slogans, from which these vessels get their name. In the place where the toasts are usually found, for example: *vivamus, reple me* – 'Life's the thing: another bumper!' – we find on the example in fig. 81 a dedication to Mithras, *Deo Inv[icto*.[125]

81. Augusta Treverorum/Trier: Spruchbecher from the temple area of the Altbachtal, not directly associated with the mithraeum there. A coarse-ware vase from a recently-discovered mithraeum at Forum Claudii Vallensium/ Martigny (Switzerland) carries a dedication in Greek: 'I, Theodoros, have dedicated (this vase) to the God Helios.'

Vessels of this sort were dedicated by individual Mithraists just like reliefs or altars, and could be the subject of a vow. For example a man named Tertius, son of Rusticus, dedicated ten terra-sigillata vases to Mithras the invincible god, thus gladly fulfilling his vow; the remains of two of them have been found, carrying what is evidently an identical text.[126]

The bulk of the finds in well-excavated mithraea consists of ordinary ceramic ware, either undecorated or with banal figural decoration, of the kind also encountered in legionary camps. Some terra-sigillata bowl-fragments from Immurium in Noricum (Moosham nr Salzburg in Austria) bear representations of hares, trees, a wild-boar, dancers and archers.[127] Two pieces from Carnuntum in Pannonia Superior will serve to illustrate the coarse-ware vessels: one is a cornice-rimmed folded beaker made of thin grey clay, with six lateral indentations (fig. 82); the second, a steeply-raked bowl or tazza in red ware, with everted rim and foot-ring (fig. 83). Both are wheel-made.[128]

LAMPS AND LIGHTING-EFFECTS

Mithras was the god of Sun, Fire and Light, and as such oil-lamps were lighted in mithraea in his honour. Charcoal too glowed in braziers; and all kinds of lighting-effects were used to illuminate the dark cavern-temples, as well as to increase the intensity of the initiates' mood. Lighting-effects were crucial to the presentation of the sacred drama. The evidence for this is the images of the torch-bearers, and the lion-headed statues, which both

82. *Carnuntum/Bad Deutsch-Altenburg, Austria: folded beaker from Mithraeum III. A quantity of very similar coarse-ware, of excellent quality, was found in the Mithraeum at Riegel in Upper Germany (unpublished).*

83. *The same: red-ware bowl. Considerable numbers of glass vessels, as well as coarse-ware, were found at Pons Aeni, Raetia (cf. fig. 77).*

symbolise fire and on occasion actually emitted it (p. 163). Further evidence are the marks of pitch on some altars, which had dripped from torches, and all the braziers, incense-holders and clay lamps that have been found. All of these objects may have been dedicated by initiates as votives. Stone braziers could easily be inscribed by the donor; one example, from Koenigshoffen/ Strasbourg, was dedicated *D(eo) I(nvicto) M(ithrae)* and had traces of pitch inside (V 1370, fig. 84).

84. *Koenigshoffen/Strasbourg (Argentorate): brazier dedicated* D(eo) I(nvicto) M(ithrae).

We may infer from the find-spots of some of the many small clay lamps that they were used to light up individual cult-images and votive inscriptions. A cult-image from Fellbach in Upper Germany shows a lamp of this kind, with a sword hanging from it, beside Mithras' head (V 1306, fig. 85). Apart from ordinary undecorated oil-lamps with a handle, such as the one illustrated in fig. 86 from Mithraeum III at Nida (Heddernheim/Frankfurt), lamps which offered the worshippers familiar symbols were especially popular. One example, from Romula in Dacia, represents the sun-god, Sol/Mithras (fig. 87). A single striking figure like this was much in demand for oil-lamps, and they were therefore easy for Mithraists to purchase. The other lamp illustrated, with Mithras killing the bull (fig. 88), is a mass-produced article, with the name of the manufacturer, Probus, stamped on the bottom.

85. *Fellbach, nr Stuttgart: cult-relief with lamp hanging from the ceiling of the cave, denoting the relation between mythic cave and mithraeum. The sword beneath it perhaps recalls the sword and radiate crown 'trophy' on German representations of the feast (figs 71, 72). Note the altar with volutes in front of the bull's throat, which may connote the sacrificial nature of Mithras' act.*

86. Nida/Heddernheim, Mithraeum III: clay lamp with enclosed spout and two lateral lugs imitating the suspension loops on metal lamps (late first/early second cent.). Numerous other lamps were found in this temple; over 50 at Pons Aeni, Raetia. Four bronze half-lamps were found at Martigny (cf. fig. 81), perhaps intended as appliqués to the unusual bronze cult-relief, of which only fragments survive.

87. Romula/Reşca, Romania: lamp decorated with a bust of Sol.

88. Provenance unknown (Italy): ornate lamp with Mithras killing the bull (V 766). Perhaps a forgery (Dressel), but accepted by Cumont as genuine.

Candle-holders are rather less common: the example illustrated also comes from Mithraeum III at Nida (fig. 89).[129] A Mithraist at Lentia in Noricum constructed and dedicated his own little votive plaque with holes round the rim for candles. On the obverse, shown in fig. 90, one can see the initial letters of a votive text, beginning *Iuppi[ter] / O[ptimus] / Ma[ximus* – Jupiter, like several other Roman gods, had been taken up into the cult of Mithras (pp. 158–62).

89. Nida: candle-holder. Others are known from Carrawburgh on Hadrian's Wall and the Walbrook Mithraeum, London; also a metal one from Pons Aeni, Raetia.

90. Lentia/Linz: terracotta plaque, with holes round the rim, perhaps for candles (V 1419).

We must try to imagine the flickering of the oil-lamps and the pine-torches casting all manner of shadows and reflections inside the gloomy mithraea. It was only in this irresolute light that the images' different properties could achieve their full effect. The rough finish of some reliefs, and especially the great wide-open eyes of some figures, must then have had a magical, even a spell-binding, effect. It may well be that the finish of many images took the dim light of the mithraea into account. By such flickering light, moreover, monuments which had been perforated by apertures at specific points 'came to life'. If a light-source were placed behind the relief from Biljanovac in Moesia Superior (Macedonia), Mithras, the bull, and especially the writhing serpent would stand out vividly (fig. 59). An image of Cautes at Carnuntum aimed at a similar effect. The body, with tunic and trousers, was worked in *alto-rilievo*, ending at the neck; the head, and the now lost raised torch, were free-standing, and could be illuminated all round (V 1688).[130]

Mithras is represented in the typical position on a limestone altar from Bingium in Germania Superior (Bingen) set up in honour of the imperial house to *Soli invicto Mitrae* (!): the god wears a radiate crown, and a cloak, and is holding a whip (fig. 91; see also pp. 127, 146). The face is now damaged, but the rays of the crown are in fact divided by perforated slits so that they could be illuminated from the rear: there is a hole in the back of

91. Bingium/Bingen: perforated altar with the bust of Sol (V 1241). The solar aspect of Mithras is emphasised by the layout of the inscription, with SOLI on the architrave above the relief. A complementary pair of elegant perforated altars with busts, one of Sol, the other of Luna, was placed on either side of the relief of the mithraeum at Mundelsheim on the Neckar (nr Stuttgart) (cf. fig. 3).

the altar large enough for an oil-lamp.[131] One occasionally finds traces of soot in such openings; at Stockstadt on the Main-*limes*, the lamp was actually still inside the altar (V 1198). In the rituals, perforated altars played a rôle analogous to that suggested by a passage in the 'Mithras-liturgy': 'You will see a youthful god, beautiful in appearance, with fiery hair, and in a white tunic and a scarlet cloak, and wearing a fiery crown.'[132]

Such lighting-effects must have been particularly impressive at Brocolitia (Carrawburgh) on Hadrian's Wall, which was equipped with a raised hearth where glowing pine-cones could slowly release their pungent odour.[133] In this mithraeum there was also a perforated altar, with a relief of Mithras in a radiate crown which could be illuminated like the one at Bingium (V 847); pine-cone ashes were found directly in front of it. Such cones did not merely burn slowly and emit a fragrance, but also possessed symbolic value – as we have seen (p. 70), on some reliefs the rock of Mithras' rock-birth is so worked that it resembles an ovoid pine-cone (V 344, fig. 92). The fruit of the pine could thus certainly be understood as a figure for Mithras' birth. Moreover, in medical usage, the fumes of kindled pine-cones were supposed to encourage giving birth (Dioscorides *Mat. med.* 1.69.1). It may well be that, as the pine-cones gradually began to glow, so the sun-god's radiate crown began to light up and Mithras seemed actually to be being born inside the cave. And, long after the cones had grown cold, the scent of pine still hung in the air as Mithras shone outside once more in all his glory.

92. Mithraeum of S. Clemente, Rome: statuette of the Rock-birth, with the rocks fashioned to resemble a pine-cone (cf. V 1088, Nida/Heddernheim). Carved marble pine-cones were found in the mithraea of S. Prisca and the Castra Peregrinorum in Rome, and at Lambaesis in Numidia.

Many different kinds of censers were in use to burn incense, which we know was used in the cult from a dipinto in the mithraeum beneath S. Prisca in Rome (p. 136). An open clay bowl-censer with flanged rim and two cordons, all finger-notched, from Mithraeum III at Carnuntum actually has traces of soot inside (fig. 93).[134] Charcoal or grains of incense could have been left smouldering in open vessels of this kind. A two-handled pot-like clay vessel with a perforated double rim and large central aperture must have served a similar purpose (fig. 94). Once the incense in the belly had been lighted, the fumes rose through the central aperture, and the small holes around the rim ensured a supply of oxygen to the remaining fuel. Fragments of a tower- or gate-thurible were found in Mithraeum III at Nida, roughly of the type illustrated in fig. 95. Arcuated clay towers of this kind measure up to 50 cm (20 ins) in height; open at the bottom, they were simply placed over the glowing incense.

93. *Carnuntum/Bad Deutsch-Altenburg, Austria: bowl-censer from Mithraeum III. Several examples were found in the Riegel Mithraeum (cf. fig. 82), and a sherd in the mithraeum of Gelduba (Krefeld-Gellep) on the Rhine in Lower Germany.*

Monuments that could be internally illuminated were, as I have said, widespread in the cult of Mithras. Altars of this kind were often erected in a central position on the axis of the mithraeum. Their designs are of many different kinds. Apart from the god's radiate crown (fig. 91; p. 125), we occasionally come across the crescent Moon, constructed in a very similar manner by perforation. At Ostia, there is an aperture in the form of a crescent above a votive inscription to *Deo Invicto Mithrae* (V 225). In a similar example from the 'Mithraeum of the Seven Gates' in the same town, the remains of window-glass were found inside a small altar in front of the

94. Dieburg: red-painted bowl-censer
(V 1269).

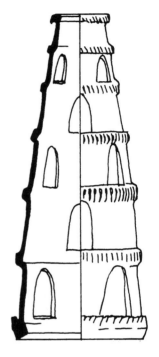

95. Verulamium/St Albans: arcuated clay tower-thurible
or 'lamp chimney' from the Triangular Temple (Henig,
RRB, 161 fig. 80). A fragment of a square or oblong
tower was found in Mithraeum III at Nida.

cult-niche; the crescent must therefore have been fitted with a piece of glass
(V 287). Rock-crystal was also sometimes used instead of glass to increase
the effect of the lighting arrangements (V 1198, Stockstadt I).

A kind of Sun→Moon transition could be enacted on a third example
from Ostia, this time from the 'Mithraeum of the Painted Walls' (V 267).
Once again, there is an aperture through the back of the altar. The front
carries a relief depicting the full bust of the sun-god in his *chlamys* and
radiate crown. At the height of his shoulders, there is preserved to left and
right the 'keel' of the crescent Moon, which could be illuminated from the
aperture at the back.[135] In the darkness of the mithraeum, therefore, the
relief could first be lit up from the front, so that the sun-god's radiate crown
would show up. When this lamp was extinguished, and at the same time the
lamp inside the altar lit, the Sun's rays 'disappeared', just as the Moon's
crescent began to shine.

An altar which stood in front of the grand relief in the mithraeum at

Koenigshoffen/Strasbourg differs from the examples just cited in being completely hollowed out at the back (V 1366/1367). Measuring 83 × 45 × 45 cm (c.33 × 18 × 18 in), this embrasure is substantially larger than the small apertures we have looked at so far. A person could fit into it. The altar-front is not perforated, but the top has a circular hole in it, about 4 cm (1 ½ in) in diameter. We may surmise that that an assistant crouched in the embrasure and produced pyrotechnic effects through this aperture.[136]

In the port-town of Rusicade in Numidia (Skikda = Philippeville, Algeria) there was found a conical Rock encircled by a snake, the bottom part of a rock-birth monument. The marble block has been hollowed out at the rear, and several perforations made through to the face of the 'rock' amid the serpent's coils (V 127, fig. 96). If a lamp or torch was placed inside the rear aperture, the light would shine through the little perforations, or even flames issue forth, just as on a relief from Civitas Montanensium in Moesia Superior (Golema Kutlovica, Bulgaria) (fig. 97). Mithras is the god born

96. Rusicade/Skikda, Algeria: rock entwined by serpent and perforated by small holes.

97. Civitas Montanensium/Golema Kutlovica, Bulgaria: detail of the Rock-birth from a cult-relief (V 2237). Flames issue from the ground below. At Dura-Europos, more naturalistically, fire comes shooting out of the rock as Mithras' body emerges (V 42. 5). Both of these are no doubt reproductions of the mythic narrative, otherwise represented 'symbolically' by the torch with which he is born. A papyrus glossary calls Mithras 'the Persian Prometheus' (P. Oxy 15: 1802 l.82).

from the rock, a god of Light: at Rusicade, his followers could experience the birth of this light out of the rock for themselves.

The importance of lighting-effects such as these should not be underestimated: we may recall the point quoted earlier from Servius/Donatus, that in religious contexts simulation is allowed to be veridical (p. 12).

CHAPTER 11

The priestly grades

St Jerome tells us that there were seven initiatory grades in the mysteries of Mithras, whose names were: Raven (in Latin: *corax*), Bridegroom (*nymphus*), Soldier (*miles*), Lion (*leo*), Persian (*perses*), Sun-runner (*heliodromus*), Father (*pater*). I should preface my discussion of these grades with one preliminary remark. Although it is not always clearly stated, most previous accounts assume that all Mithraists were members of one grade or another. Merkelbach, for instance, has tried to infer the initiatory grade of dedicators from the symbols on numerous altars and reliefs, even in those cases in which the grade is not mentioned in the corresponding inscription, or where there is no inscription at all. He also thinks it possible to discover representations of grade-membership in the series of by-scenes which frame the Bull-killing itself, whereas in my view they are to be understood, like Sol, Luna, the planetary gods, and so on, in relation to the legend of Mithras.[137]

We know the names of around 1,050 Mithraists, of whom about one hundred appear more than once in the epigraphic record. They had at their disposal when putting up an inscription a whole range of terms for titles, initiatory-grades and functions within the cult. Yet a mere 14 per cent make any mention of such matters, indeed considerably fewer, if we take the seven grades alone into account. Is it likely that the very people who scrupulously noted their real-world social status for the other members of the cult would have kept silent about their initiatory grade? Should we not rather conclude that in the cult there were, on the one hand, the great majority of Mithraists, who were simply initiated once, and, on the other, a small group of holders of the different grades, whom it would be appropriate to speak of as 'priests'? For this small group is in fact rather over-represented in the epigraphic record, as we can see from the fact that twice as many of them as of the simple initiates dedicated several inscriptions.[138]

A. Caecidius Priscianus was one of these priests, a *pater*, in the mithraeum of the *castra peregrina* in Rome (the barracks on the Caelian for soldiers of provincial armies seconded to the capital for special service); he was a Roman knight (*eques*) and at the same time one of the priests (*sacerdotes*) of the imperial palace during the years AD 180–4 (AE 1980: 48–50; CIL VI 2010b[22]). Among further Mithraists in this mithraeum who were involved in other cults is Aurelius Bassinus, who was the superintendent of the official cults of the *castra* when he dedicated a statue of the rock-birth; his son became *pater* of the mithraeum and later an *eques Romanus* (AE 1980: 48; CIL VI 273). Caecidius Priscianus, an *eques* and, as *pater*, holder of the highest initiatory grade, fitted well into this social milieu. He is one of only two members of his order whom we know to have been priests, who, in other words, took the trouble to proceed through all seven grades. This is not the case with the five known senators prior to the fourth century, nor with the other forty *equites*. These men made their dedications above all as military commanders in the provinces of Britain, Numidia and Pannonia Superior. Their initiation set an example to the soldiers under them; but they left the matter there.

The regional distribution of priests is quite striking. They cluster quite clearly in Italy, above all at Rome and Ostia. These two cities alone provide half of all cases, whereas only 17 per cent of all Mithraic inscriptions come from there. Two-thirds of all priests come from Italy, but only one quarter of all inscriptions. These figures give the impression that the cult in Rome and Italy, perhaps because it had existed for longer there, was more firmly rooted, and so more Mithraists were motivated to proceed through the grades one by one. In the provinces, the situation is reversed. One half of all inscriptions comes from the Danubian provinces, but only 15 per cent of these note a grade. In these provinces, the further we move away from the cult's place of origin, the fewer initiatory grades do we come across. From all Dacia, where more than one hundred Mithraic inscriptions have been found, we know of just one *sacerdos* (p. 138). Here again, we are faced with regional diversity.

In addition to the ordinary members of the cult, then, who were content simply to be initiated, there was a sort of hierarchy of offices or priesthoods. For these priests, theological, ritual, and surely also astronomical and astrological knowledge was required. We possess the funerary inscription of a *sacerdo[s] D(ei) S(olis) I(nvicti) M(ithrae), stu[d(iosus)] astrologia[e]*, which he erected for himself and his wife (V 708).[139] Initiates could take on rôles of this sort if they had sufficient interest, enough leisure for the instruction, and adequate financial resources, if only to be able to spare the time it all took.

As far as we are concerned, these initiatory grades are one of the cult's great mysteries. They stand in some relation to the planets: their number, seven, must have inspired the number of grades. In the important mithraeum beneath S. Prisca in Rome frescoes were discovered with figures depicting the different grades, each with a *dipinto* beside it commending the priests to the protection of the different planetary gods. They all begin with the word *nama*, a word, as we have seen (p. 8), of Persian origin, representing a particularly solemn form of greeting.[140] Further evidence is offered by the Mithraeum of Felicissimus at Ostia, where there is a mosaic floor to the central aisle, divided into seven panels each with devices akin to heraldic emblems (fig. 9). We may surmise that they are related to the grades, though it is possible that are just symbols of the planets.

RAVEN

Only a few smudges remain of the two Raven-dipinte at S. Prisca, but the grade must have been assigned to Mercury: that is the planet it is connected with at the Mithraeum of Felicissimus. Apart from the raven there, which is very naturalistic (fig. 98), one can see a small beaker and the caduceus, the usual attribute of Mercury. Ambrosiaster, whom I have already cited several times, mentions that some Mithraists 'flapped their wings like birds, imitating the croak of the raven' (p. 108). There thus appear to have been ritual occasions on which initiates wore raven-masks, as in the feast at Konjic in Dalmatia (Bosnia-Hercegovina) (fig. 69). Here we encounter the relics of ancient legends, originating from primitive rituals. The god was imagined in the form of an animal, and it was believed that one could identify oneself with him by taking on his name or his appearance. What survived the centuries was the custom of worshippers disguising themselves. These priests with their masks evidently acted as servants on special occasions – perhaps the beaker in the Mithraeum of Felicissmus is connected with this. One of the three priests of this grade whose name we happen to know donated the mithraeum and its furniture at Gimmeldingen in Upper Germany, by permission of the *pater* (p. 28).[141]

98. *Mithraeum of Felicissimus, Ostia: aisle mosaic (cf. fig. 9: mid-third cent.). Tokens relating to the lowest grade Corax, Raven. The carefully-selected bones of a raven were found on top of a rubbish-pit outside the mithraeum at Wiesloch nr Heidelberg (see fig. 76), covered by an amphora-sherd, and then a horse's skull. A wing-bone of a raven was also recovered from the Walbrook temple, London.*

BRIDEGROOM

Nama to the Bridegrooms, under the protection of Venus!

The manuscripts of Jerome's *Epistle 107, to Laeta* give two terms as the name of the second grade, *nymphus*, 'bridegroom' (or 'bee chrysalis'[142]), and *gryphus*, which seems to correspond to the word *cryfius*. This last occurs in one or two fourth-century inscriptions, apparently meaning 'One who is shrouded' (V 402, 403), whereas there is third-century epigraphic evidence for *nymphus*. Does this mean that the name changed in that time, a change which the copyists of Jerome's letters knew about? Or do they refer to two quite different things? For as a matter of fact we know of a good number of other terms, apart from the seven grades, which relate to particular functions and responsibilities in the cult (p. 138). The damaged mosaic panel in the Mithraeum of Felicissimus (fig. 99) shows an oil-lamp, a diadem and part of a now unrecognisable object. Firmicus Maternus records the ritual greeting: 'Hail Nymphus, hail New Light' (*Err. prof. rel.* 19.1). The lamp must therefore be connected with the grade, whereas the diadem symbolises the goddess and planet Venus.

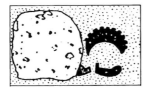

99. *The same: tokens relating to the second grade*, Nymphus, *Bridegroom*.

SOLDIER

Nama to the Soldiers, under the protection of Mars!

In the Mithraeum of Felicissimus, the Soldier's symbols are a soldier's sling-bag, a lance and a helmet, representing equally the priest's attributes and those of the planetary god Mars (fig. 100). Tertullian describes the following initiation rite relating to the grade *miles* (p. 36), in a passage challenging Christian soldiers who were unwilling to follow the example of one of their comrades and refuse to take part in the official army cult:

> Are you not ashamed, fellow soldiers of Christ, that you will be found wanting, not by him, but by some Soldier of Mithras? At his initiation in the cave, in the very camp of darkness, a crown is offered to the candidate at the point of a sword, as if in imitation of a martyrdom, and put on his head; then he is admonished to

put his hand up and dash it from his brow onto his shoulder, as it may be, saying: 'My crown is Mithras!'[143]

(*De cor.* 15.3, tr. E.A. Quain (adapt.))

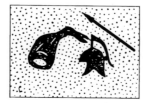

100. *The same: tokens relating to the third grade, Miles, Soldier.*

LION

Nama to the Lions, under the protection of Jupiter!

On the grade-frescoes at S. Prisca, the Lion wears a fiery red cloak. In the cult of Mithras, the Lion was, as Tertullian puts it, 'of a dry and fiery nature' (*Adv. Marcion.* 1.13.4). In the relevant panel in the Mithraeum of Felicissimus, the grade's symbol is the fire-shovel (fig. 101). The rattle, *sistrum*, and the thunderbolt refer to the planet Jupiter. Particular reference was made to this fire-symbolism during initiation into the grade. Porphyry tells us:

> So in the Lion mysteries, when honey is poured instead of water for purification on the hands of the initiates, they are exhorted to keep them pure from everything distressing, harmful and loathsome; and since he is an initiate of fire, which has a cathartic effect, they use on him a liquid related to fire, rejecting water as inimical to it. They use honey as well to purify the tongue from all guilt.
>
> (*De antr. nymph.* 15, tr. Arethusa)

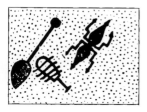

101. *The same: tokens relating to the fourth grade, Leo, Lion.*

Priests of this grade appear, like the Ravens (p. 110), wearing the appropriate masks, and are supposed to have 'roared like lions' (see n. 114). A procession of Lions bringing gifts to the Father was painted on the walls at S. Prisca on two occasions. On the earlier layer, metrical lines were painted above many of the figures. On the left wall, above the figure of Sol at the

Feast, we read the following two lines, which hark back to Roman sacral language:

> Receive the incense-burners, Father, receive the Lions, Holy One, through whom we offer incense, through whom we are ourselves consumed![144]

The other (souls) ascend in the offering of incense performed by the Lions.

In the epigraphic record, the grade *leo* occurs most frequently of all seven priest-grades apart from *pater* – just under forty times. It is possible that it was a sort of half-way house on the path up to the highest grade. Porphyry at any rate mentions a kind of dual grouping of the grades, albeit in a different context (*Abst.* 4.16.3). This would explain why there were so many Lions present that they could be shown in a procession. Moreover at S. Gemini in Umbria there was a *leonteum*, a special room or temple for the Lions (p. 45). Another Umbrian Mithraist, at Sentinum (Sentino), bore the title *pater leonum*, 'Father of the Lions', which also suggests a rather large number of them there (V 688).[145] The fact that we know more Lions from Umbria than from anywhere else apart from Rome may be pure chance, but it may also reflect a peculiar feature of the local cult of Mithras.

PERSIAN

Nama to the Persians, under the protection of the Moon!

Like those of the Lions, the hands of the Persians were purified with honey. But Porphyry tells us there was a difference: 'When . . . they offer honey to the Persian as preserver of fruits, it is its preservative powers that they treat symbolically' (*De antr. nymph.* 15, tr. Arethusa; see also p. 135). The sickle represented in the Persian panel in the Mithraeum of Felicissimus is to be understood in relation to the fertility mentioned here, and likewise the *akinakes*, the Persian dagger (fig. 102), which was doubly attached to the right thigh, the scabbard having ringed chapes both at the hilt and at the point. The crescent-moon and the star stand for Luna.

102. The same: tokens relating to the fifth grade, Perses, Persian.

RUNNER OF THE SUN

Nama to the Runners of the Sun, under the protection of the Sun!

The very name of the grade shows that its holder stood beneath the special protection of the Sun (which counted as a planet in antiquity). Its attribute is the torch (fig. 103); the seven-rayed crown and the whip belong to the sun-god.

103. The same: tokens relating to the sixth grade, Helio-dromus, Runner of the Sun.

FATHER

Nama to the Fathers, from East to West, under the protection of Saturn!

The highest grade was *pater*. Among his symbols in the Mithraeum of Felicissimus is Mithras' phrygian cap (fig. 104), and he can thus be seen as the god's earthly representative. Of the other symbols, the libation bowl recalls his functions in the performance of rituals. The staff and sickle stand for the grade's protective deity, Saturn.

104. The same: tokens relating to the highest grade, Pater, Father.

In the epigraphic record, the grade Father is mentioned most frequently of all seven grades: about half of all those whose grade is given are *patres*. It is a common phenomenon in Latin inscriptions, which in this case directly reflect social assumptions, that the occupants of the highest positions in any hierarchy are the best documented. The frequent mention of the Father, often twice or three times in the same mithraeum, is, however, also connected with the fact that, as head of the congregation, he supervised the setting up of the votive-offerings that furnished the mithraeum. The donor of an altar or a relief would thus sometimes mention the Father of the temple in his inscription, using formulae such as *permittente . . . patre*, or *permissu patris* (with the Father's permission).[146] The name of C. Accius Hedychrus occurs on four different votives at Emerita in Lusitânia (Mérida, Spain). Two he himself donated, but in the case of the two others he simply gave his approval, and in them he is referred to as *pater* (V 774, 793). In his own inscriptions, he calls himself once *pater* (V 781, fig. 115) and once *p(ater) patrum* (V 779). This last is probably not a higher grade, but is to be connected with the fact that there could be several Fathers in one congregation, so one of them became the 'Father of (the) Fathers'.

OTHER POSITIONS

It was in Italy, as I have already mentioned, that most use was made of the possibility of proceeding through all the priest-grades. Similarly, the different titles for Fathers may perhaps be traced to local traditions. There are two cases in which the Father bears the title of the ancient Roman fetial priesthood *pater patratus* (V 706, 803). The title *pater sacrorum*, conveying the idea that he is Father of the mysteries, is also rather uncommon (e.g. V 1243), as is *pater nomimus*, 'Father in conformity with custom' (V 76, 739).

After the Father, the grade found most commonly is the Lion (p. 135); the commonest post, on the other hand, is *sacerdos*. This is the usual term for a priest, which was also taken over by the Mithraists. The cases in which individuals are called *pater et sacerdos* (e.g. V 511) establish a relation to the grades. We should probably see here not two different rôles but an association of the specifically Mithraic term *pater* with the ordinary *sacerdos*, which may have corresponded to it. For it can hardly be a coincidence that, among forty occurrences in inscriptions, *sacerdos* is mentioned only in relation to *pater*. Because the Father was the head of the congregation, it was an obvious step to name Mithraic communities after their Father. An instance of this can be found in the mithraeum at Campona in Pannonia Inferior (Nagytétény/Budapest), where a Mithraist fulfils his vow by dedicating a votive *in templo Mucaporis sac(erdotis)*, 'in the temple of Mucapor the priest' (V 1808). Several other examples suggest that *pater* and *sacerdos* were interchangeable terms.[147]

Another word in ordinary use for the person in charge of a temple was the term *antistes*, and it too is found with both *sacerdos* and *pater* in Mithraic contexts. In the first mithraeum to be discovered at Ostia, the 'Mitreo Fagan', named after the English painter and excavator Robert Fagan who discovered it in the late eighteenth century, C. Valerius Heracles played a part in three votives. He donated the mithraeum as *pater* and *antistes*

(V 315). As *pater* he dedicated, together with two *sacerdotes*, a statue of the god of Time (V 313); and he terms himself *sacerdos* on a cult-image (V 311). The situation becomes even more fraught when we find M. Caerellius Hieronymus as one of two *sacerdo[tes et antisti]tes* at one Ostian mithraeum (V 223b), and as *pater et sacerdos* at another, where he is explicitly different from the *antistes* (V 282). It was not uncommon to move from one Mithraic congregation to another, and in this case the man could have been brought in as head of the community from another. A final example of the diversity of Mithraic congregations in the matter of naming officers or grade-holders is the last phase of the mithraeum at Dura-Europos on the Euphrates (V 34–70). There are one or two inscriptions on stone, but it is the graffiti scratched on the mithraeum walls which produced dozens of texts, and so provided us with a whole range of terms (cf. n. 141). Words such as *pater*, *pater patrum* and στρατιώτης (which might mean an ordinary soldier, or the grade Soldier) were usual elsewhere too, but quite what we should understand by *magus*, 'Persian magus' (V 61), στερεώτης, 'Fastener of the vault of heaven' (?),[148] ἀντίπατηρ (a preliminary stage to becoming Father?), or πετίτωρ (Latin *petitor*, candidate) remains unclear.

Just like other religious groups in the Roman empire, the Mithraists formed a group in the sense of a juridical person, a corporation with the right of holding property and the right to administer its funds according to certain rules. To look after their worldly interests, they elected or chose lay officers, whom we should perhaps not always identify with the initiates or the priests.

We only have information about the internal organisation of Mithraic congregations from Rome and a few other cities. The corporations were organised like the municipal councils: there was an official list of members, an *album sacratorum*, of which we possess an inscribed example from Sentinum (Sentino) in Umbria (V 688). The leaders of the *collegium* were the *decuriones*, who formed a sort of miniature Senate (V 519); in another mithraeum, the first ten members listed in the *album* bore the widely-used title *decem primi* (V 336). The chairmen were called *magistri*, and were perhaps newly elected every year (V 517–19). The *patroni*, relatively wealthy individuals, were expected to provide not merely effective protection for the other members through their political and social contacts, but above all material support for the community (V 688).

The main function of many *collegia* was to provide a decent burial for their deceased members, and the same seems to have been true of the cult of Mithras. The recent discovery at Virunum in Noricum (nr Klagenfurt, Austria) of a membership-list makes clear that the death of members might sometimes be recorded on such an *album* (AE 1994: 1334).[149] Moreover there are increasing indications that in some places graves were deliberately sited in the vicinity of mithraea.[150]

We may doubt whether the posts mentioned above, and the related allocation of functions, were to be found in all mithraea. In most of the smaller temples the *pater* or the *sacerdos* may have taken over the administrative side on the congregation's behalf.

Provided that the circumstances in which they were found make clear that they had actually been part of the temple-property, coins can tell us something about the often no doubt rather limited financial resources of Mithraic communities. This is the case with the mithraeum of Konjic in Dalmatia (Bosnia-Hercergovina), where ninety-one coins were found, many in remarkably good condition.[151] There are no signs of wear either to the portrait heads or to the legends, even on the often paper-thin silver coating of the coins of the third century, the Antoninianae, which proves that they were only in circulation for a short time and entered the temple's treasury soon after their emission. Given that even in this probably incomplete collection, all the emperors from Gallienus (253–68) to the end of the fourth century are represented, we may conclude that the temple enjoyed a regular income in the form of contributions from members, paid in small denominations.

CHAPTER 12

Mithras, swift to save

Initiation into a mystery cult such as that of Mithras enabled one to acquire knowledge of all the secret lore, prayers and rituals which guaranteed that the initiate's soul would one day find its way to the sphere of the fixed stars. The god was to provide the necessary help. This is not the place once again to rehearse the reasons that might prompt a person to have himself initiated into the mysteries of Mithras; they are anyway mostly opaque to us. The numerous votive-inscriptions, however, make one point sufficiently clear. The god's aid was expected not merely in the distant future but here and now, in the midst of life. Roman religious practice, especially under the Empire, regularly had an instrumental tinge. A person would vow to dedicate a particular offering to the god, provided that the latter first fulfilled a specific request. Sometimes the deity appeared to the person in a dream to request his or her gift (*somno monitus*: V 304).

THE EVIDENCE OF THE INSCRIPTIONS

Altars are just one of many kinds of votives, but the inscriptions on them often confirm the point just made. 'The dedicator has gladly fulfilled his vow in return for a benefit received': this is a rough translation of the most widespread of all votive formulae, which was so standardised that it is normally abbreviated in inscriptions to *v(otum) s(olvit) l(ibens) m(erito)* (e.g. fig. 46). This is also the case in the mysteries of Mithras, which was of course a Roman cult. The votive gifts are often mentioned explicitly: people donated entire mithraea or parts of them, or had them repaired when necessary; gave the land, altars, reliefs of marble or some cheaper material, cult-utensils of widely varying quality, sometimes silver plaques or bronze tablets. One text even mentions pine- and fig-trees which someone had planted round the mithraeum (V 1892).

We generally know only the donors of the more valuable votives, and of course it cost a further sum to have an inscription cut in commemoration. The names of those who contributed simple objects for cult-use, beakers or plates, candles, torches, the oil for the lamps or meals, are quite unknown.

Nor do we learn anything about the reason for making the vow in the first place. Mithraic votive-inscriptions, like most dedications generally, do not refer to the matter: it was enough that the two parties involved, the god and the dedicant, knew. Making an announcement to the god that one had fulfilled one's vow was in fact just an occasion for setting up a votive-inscription, and in Roman society perhaps not even the most important reason for doing so. Just as with public inscriptions, so in small religious associations the inscribed votive – even if few enough were ever in a position to see it – was primarily a means of calling attention to one's own financial resources. It also served to proclaim one's social position and, in the case of Mithras, the priests' initiatory grade. As a result, the specifically religious intention of a votive rather faded into the background: in fact only the name of the god, often severely abbreviated to *DIM*, and the closing formula *VSLM* allude to it (e.g. fig. 56). The crucial part came between these: the information about the person, his rank and what he had done for the congregation (and for the god).

Because Mithraic votive texts do not differ in this respect from those of other cults, we may take it that the same holds good for the donors' motives. Mithraists opened to their god all manner of wishes, as humankind has always done, but particularly wishes for advancement in their profession. Occasionally indeed the occasion for the votive is explicitly stated, and sometimes we can infer it from information given in the inscription. The following examples imply nothing uniquely true of the cult of Mithras, simply documenting the fact that, in terms of the help he could offer in everyday matters, Mithras was just like all other deities. So much is clear from the very first case I take.

Two persons of the same name, P. Aelius Clemens, dedicated an altar at Rogatica in Dalmatia (Bosnia) to Jupiter Optimus Maximus. Father and son thus expressed their gratitude that the son, who calls himself *veteranus*, had safely served his term in the army. On a later occasion, when he had become a *duovir*, one of the two annually-elected mayors of his town, the son put up another altar to Jupiter. Later still, as *quinquennalis*, he dedicated an altar to Mithras: he had become mayor for the second time, and this time the office was associated with special duties which only required to be performed every five years. Both offices are part of a career in local politics, and it is likely that Aelius Clemens jr. was in each case expressing his gratitude and fulfilling a vow (*VSLM*), first to Jupiter, and then to Mithras.[152]

Advancement and promotion are also aims of every soldier: that Mithras could help fulfil this aim was a natural conclusion from his epithet *omnipotens*, almighty (p. 62).[153] One of the few individuals to mention the reason for his votive is Claudius Marcellus, who dedicated his altar *D(eo) S(oli) I(nvicto) O(mnipotenti) M(ithrae)*: he had been promoted to *beneficiarius*.[154] And even if one had not managed to become a privileged soldier like this, at least one might hope to get through one's service honourably and without incident, like Aurelius Marcellus, who 'fulfilled as a veteran the vow he had made as a soldier': *quod miles vovit, ve(teranus) solvit* (AE 1926: 72). Invincible Mithras, to whom the altar is dedicated, has helped the soldier to become himself 'invincible', that is successfully to complete his period of service, so as to be able to enjoy his reward as a veteran and respectable citizen.

Promotion, and ultimately the status of a *libertus*, was also the focus of the wishes of the slaves whom we often meet in the cult of Mithras as officers of the customs organisations, and to attain which they invoked Mithras' aid. The imperial slave Apollonides was promoted from clerk (*contrascriptor*) in one station (*Vizi . . .*) to inspector (*scrutator*) at the *statio Lamud(ensis)* near Lopata in Moesia Superior (Yugoslavia). After his promotion, he fulfilled the vow which he had made as clerk, and had the venerable mithraeum at his new station repaired (V 2209). His is certainly no isolated case. Eutyches at Siscia in Pannonia Superior (Sisak, Croatia) was probably also a slave in the customs service: he dedicated an altar as Aurelius Eutyches to Mithras in honour of the Emperor M. Aurelius Antoninus, that is, Caracalla (V 1476); he may possibly have recommended the emperor, his patron, to the god on account of having been granted his freedom.

Mithras is thus a god who helps men in their daily lives, and as *D(eus) S(ol) I(nvictus) M(ithras)* he is explicitly called Helper (*adiutor*) on an altar at Angera on Lake Maggiore (V 717). He could assist in earthly matters like this because, as we have just seen, he could do everything. The idea that their god was almighty, *omnipotens*, suggested itself spontaneously to Mithraists, and they liked to stress it. Inscriptions make the point, though generally in a highly abbreviated form, as in Claudius Marcellus' case above, more than a dozen times. This must also surely indicate how familiar it was to them, at any rate in the Danubian provinces, where it is almost exclusively found. Mithras was in truth *omnipotens*, a quality he shared with other Roman deities, and which offered every one of his adherents security, well-being and aid. Their god was, after all, unconquered and unconquerable, *invictus* and *insuperabilis* (V 376, 741 with Supplement, s.v. 741). Hence, for some he became *conservator* (AE 1979: 426 = 1994: 1310), that is, the god who sustains a career, or safeguards health; with regard to the empire as a whole, protector, *fautor imperii* (V 1698, p. 28); with regard to the universe, finally, κοσμοκράτωρ, ruler of the kosmos.[155] For the slaying of the bull is the timeless, ever self-renewing re-creation of the world (p. 70).

The consequence of all this is that Mithras is Lord, *dominus* (V 333), or *dominus invictus* (V 767), lord of life, here and in the other world. Anyone may adopt this lord, subordinate himself to him, for to his followers he is, to be sure, mighty, but also and above all a good, just, forgiving god, beneficent, one who hearkens to requests.[156] People gave Mithras honorific epithets like this because he had taken up their needs, or because they wished to make him favourably inclined to them. They are in no sense attributes unique to Mithras, being found, in these or similar terms, in connection with many gods. Mithras was certainly for many of his followers the most important god of all; but as far as such expressions of reverence are concerned, as represented by the epigraphic record, he is barely to be distinguished from any other deity of the Roman world.

ETHICAL TEACHING

If Mithras was the good and just god who rewarded his followers, we may take it for granted that moral demands were made upon the members of his congregations. Porphyry mentions such moral values in relation to initiation into the Lion grade, that is, to priests: Lions must keep their hands pure from everything that brings pain and harm, and is impure; and the mystagogues purify their tongues from all sin with honey (p. 135). The Emperor Julian (361–3) mentions the existence of such injunctions in his so-called 'Caesares', a satire on earlier Roman emperors, in the form of a symposium hosted by Romulus-Quirinus. Towards the close, he makes Hermes address the following words to himself, Julian:

> As for you . . . , I have granted you to know Mithras the Father. Keep his commandments, thus securing for yourself an anchor-cable and safe mooring all through your life, and, when you must leave the world, having every confidence that the god who guides you will be kindly disposed.
>
> (*Caes.* 336C, tr. W.C. Wright)

We can get some hint of the content of such injunctions from a passage in which the apologist Justin Martyr discusses the fundamental similarities between Christian and Mithraic teaching. His remarks are important both for our understanding of the ritual meal (p. 108) and for the ethical teaching of Mithraism. In his *Dialogue with the Jew Tryphon*, Justin accuses the followers of Mithras of imitating the words of the Prophets, in fact an entire passage of Isaiah. In order to make his point clear to his fictive interlocutor, he cites a passage from Isaiah *in extenso*:

Hear you that are far off, what I have done; and you who are near, acknowledge my might . . . trembling has seized the godless. Who shall announce to you the everlasting place? The man who walks righteously and speaks uprightly, hates sin and unrighteousness, and keeps his hands clear from bribes, stops the ears from hearing the unjust judgement of blood, closes the eyes from seeing unright-eousness: he shall dwell in the lofty cave of the strong rock. His bread will be given him, his water will be sure.

(*Dial.* 70.2–3, citing Isaiah 33.13–16)

It is evident, Justin continues, that in this passage Isaiah is alluding to:

the bread which our Christ gave us to eat, in remembrance of His being made flesh for the sake of His believers, for whom also he suffered; and the cup which He gave us to drink, in remembrance of His own blood, with giving of thanks.

(*ibid.* 70.5, tr. A.C. Coxe)

In Justin's view, only Christians may legitimately interpret Isaiah: the Mithraists simply 'imitate' the Old Testament prophet.

Given that we otherwise know very little about these aspects of the cult of Mithras, the apologist's accusation is important, because it can give us some notion of the kind of rules and commandments which were impressed upon the initiates at their admission into the mysteries. It must, however, also be clear that we do not know how the priests interpreted these or similar texts: we can at best intuit their general cast.

By his act, Mithras created bread and water: by slaying the bull, he created the kosmos and life on earth. For his followers, therefore, as the text of Isaiah has it, bread and water will never fail, whether in the literal or in the metaphorical sense. Moreover, if the Mithraist will attain the 'everlasting place', he must walk in righteousness, hate sin and unrighteousness and follow many other precepts that reminded Justin of the language of the prophet. We must not, however, attempt to explain injunctions such as 'keeping the hands pure', which is Porphyry's analogous formulation, since we possess no further relevant information. But Justin's charge does at least make clear that Mithraic commandments did exist.

CHAPTER 13

Mithras and the other gods

Consideration of Mithras' relation to the rest of the divine world must necessarily begin with the deity with whom his relation is closest and yet at the same time, as far as we are concerned, the most difficult to understand – Mithras and Sol: one God in two different manifestations; two gods united as One.

MITHRAS AND THE SUN-GOD

Roman Mithras is the invincible sun-god, Sol Invictus.[157] This is the burden, repeated a hundred times over, of the votive inscriptions from the second to the fourth centuries AD, whether in the form *Sol Invictus Mithras*, or *Deus Sol Invictus Mithras*, or *Deus Sol Mithras*, or *Sol Mithras*. There do not seem to be any significant regional or temporal variations among such formulae. In the very earliest epigraphic evidence for the Roman cult of Mithras, the god is already invoked as Sol Invictus Mithras. These facts are confirmed by the numerous votive offerings to *Sol*, *Deus Sol*, *Sol Invictus*, and *Deus Invictus Sol* which were put up in mithraea. This is also the reason why an inscription at Carnuntum dedicated to Deus Invictus Mithras qualifies the god as *gen(itor) lum(inis)*, creator of light (V 1676; p. 64).

The identification of Mithras and Sol is effected as it were before our very eyes in an inscription from Bremenium (High Rochester) on Hadrian's Wall. The stone-mason originally carved *Deo invicto et Soli socio sacrum*, 'Sacred to the Invincible God and Sol his ally'. But before the slab was set up, the *et* was erased. The dedication was now *Deo invicto Soli socio sacrum*, 'To the invincible sun-god, (our) ally' (V 876 = RIB 1272).

Some further details help to complete this picture. A cult-image from Rome, in fact one of the earliest, datable to the first quarter of the second century AD (fig. 105), is dedicated, as the inscription tells us, to Sol Mithras (p. 22). On the altar from Bingium discussed above (p. 125), dedicated to

- 146 -

Sol Invictus Mithras, Mithras is represented as the sun-god, with radiate crown and whip (fig. 91). A cashier in the *familia Caesaris* at Caesarea (Kayseri), the capital of Cappadocia in Asia Minor, dedicated a doubtless similar bust, or statue, of Sol in willing fulfilment of a vow: *Solem / Soli invicto / Mythrae . . . Callimorphus arka / rius . . . votum solvi libens animo* (V 17). On some cult-images, an elongated ray from Sol's radiate crown descends towards Mithras (e.g. figs 51, 106). It perhaps symbolises the notion of their identity.[158]

105. *Rome (provenance unknown), now in the British Museum, London: cult-statue dedicated by Alcimus. The statue, which is heavily restored (see List of Illustrations), shows several signs of being early: uniquely, it shows ears of grain, rather than blood, exuding from the wound, and the torch-bearers (only their feet are original) are placed together on the same side.*

On the other hand, however, Mithras and Sol are two separate deities, as can amply be demonstrated. In marked contrast to the inscription from Bremenium just cited, the dedicant of an altar from Sublavio in Gallia Cisalpina (Chiusa/Klausen, on the Isarco/Eisack in the South Tyrol) specifies that Sol is Mithras' ally or companion: *D(eo) I(nvicto) M(ithrae) et Soli socio* (V 730). The commonplace title of Mithras is here heavily abbreviated, whereas the much less usual epithet for Sol is written out in full. When the two brothers M. Aurelius Frontinianus and M. Aurelius Fronto had a mithraeum built at Aquincum (Budapest) in Pannonia Inferior early in the third century, they also gave two bases, no doubt bearing now-lost statues of the two deities mentioned in the inscriptions. The texts of these are well-nigh identical, but their recipients were Deus Invictus Mithras and Sol *socius* respectively (V 1792, 1793). The siblings on earth dedicated the statues to the siblings in heaven.

106. Fiano Romano, nr Rome: obv. of double-sided relief, with an extended ray between Sol and Mithras (V 641, cf. fig. 51).

Mithras is Sol, and at the same time Sol is Mithras' companion. Paradoxical relationships of this kind are to be found between many deities in antiquity. People in the ancient world did not feel bound by fixed credos and confessions which had to be consistent to the last detail: in the area of religion, a truly blessed anarchy held sway. For that reason, we should not attempt to marshal the relationship between Mithras and Sol and their various exchanges into what we, with our knowledge and epistemological assumptions, would consider a strictly logical system. Perhaps we should not even assume that such a thing ever existed in antiquity.[159]

There is another reason too why it is difficult to account for the relation between Mithras and Sol in the cult-legend. The actions they perform together are, to be sure, frequently represented on the reliefs, and we can make out regular thematic clusters, but we cannot interpret all the events with any certainty. It is mainly the numerous Danubian complex reliefs that present a clear sequence of actions, in the virtually standardised panels of the lowest register. I take as an example the relief from Alcšut in Pannonia Inferior that we have already looked at (fig. 17, p. 57). The dimensions are only 21×15 cm (8×6 in). The division into three registers and the rounded upper rim are characteristic. In the wide central panel Mithras kneels on the bull; raven, dog, snake and scorpion are represented, in some cases very sketchily. Cautopates (l.) and Cautes (r.) are in their most common positions; Sol is above Cautopates and Luna above the bull's head. To allow for this close relation between the goddess and her animal, the Rock-birth, which is very common on these reliefs, has been pushed along to the top right-hand corner. Working from left to right, we can make out on the upper register: the bull in the temple; the 'water-miracle' with Mithras shooting on the left, and a torch bearer scooping up water on the right; the bull in the boat-Moon; on the right a scene that is quite difficult to make out: a figure with a staff (?) and a ram.[160] The bottom register finally, which is our concern here, contains three scenes: Sol's obeisance; the feast; and the ascension in the chariot. But despite the gross similarity between representations of these subjects (compare figs 57, 59, 111 for example), variation in detail predominates. The individual scenes of the bottom register are frequently depicted in niches, that is, probably 'caves'; but in the present case that is true only of the first two. We are no longer in a position to account for the arrangement of the cave-arches on these reliefs: some-times all three scenes take place in the cave, sometimes two, sometimes one, and the scene(s) picked out for this treatment also varies/vary. The diversity is still greater in the cases in which the register contains four panels.

SOL'S OBEISANCE

There can be no doubt that the relevant registers are to be read from left to right. They thus begin with the most enigmatic scene, which is sometimes interpreted as Sol's submission to Mithras. For it is characteristic of these scenes that Sol kneels on one or both knees in front of Mithras. The sun-god is often shown making gestures which emphasise the humility of his demeanour. On a fragment of a relief from Dacia, the sculptor has made the god hunch down and cover his face with both hands, while Mithras places the phrygian cap on his head (V 2190, fig. 107). Other versions express the idea of submission by making Sol stretch his hand out to Mithras, or clasp his knees in supplication.

107. Provenance unknown, now in Bucharest: fragment of a Danubian-style relief: scene of Sol's obeisance.

The meaning of the scene is problematic because of the minute size of the object that Mithras is holding in his hand on these Danubian reliefs. We may therefore look first at the corresponding panel of the relief from Osterburken, on the Antonine Main-Rems-*limes* in Upper Germany, where it is clearly visible (fig. 108). Sol is kneeling naked in front of Mithras, who is holding a phrygian cap in his right hand. Sol's radiate crown is lying on the ground between them. Unfortunately relief-scenes like this simply provide us with, as it were, stills from a film, so that we cannot see the frames before and after. Thus we cannot tell from them whether Mithras is taking Sol's phrygian cap off in order to put the radiate crown on, or the reverse.[161] In my view, however, Mithras is clearly holding the more decisive object, the phrygian cap, aloft in his hand. There are extremely few representations of this scene with the radiate crown lying on the ground (only at Osterburken and Dura-Europos). Slightly more common are scenes in which Sol, in his radiate-crown, is kneeling in front of Mithras, and the latter is holding the cap up high with his right hand, putting his left hand out towards the crown. An example is the relief-fragment from Virunum in Noricum illustrated in fig. 109 (see also pp. 153, 159). In this case, once

108. Osterburken: panel from r. jamb of the cult-relief (V 1292. 5d). Cumont was the first to argue that the object in Mithras' hand is a phrygian cap.

109. Virunum, Noricum/Zollfeld, Klagenfurt: detail of fragmentary r. jamb from the lost complex relief, showing four scenes (from top to bottom): Sol ascending in his quadriga with Mithras; the handshake (dexiosis) between Mithras and Sol; the obeisance of Sol; the 'Water-miracle'. Note how in the obeisance scene Mithras grasps Sol's forelock, which has been interpreted as a gesture of absolute superiority (S. Eitrem).

again, the more important object is in the hand held up high in a dramatic gesture. The large numbers of reliefs that show only a single object, namely the cap, being held up by Mithras, or being put onto Sol's head while he kneels, are surely decisive. The meaning, then, will be that Mithras is honouring Sol with the attribute which is properly his own.

THE PACT OF FRIENDSHIP

The 'pact of friendship', the scene in which Mithras and Sol, who is now an equal partner, stand erect to conclude a compact with one another, may have directly followed the narrative of the obeisance in the cult-legend. The scene is depicted in detail on the front of the large altar from Mithraeum III at Poetovio, where the sculptor had the entire surface at his disposal (V 1584, fig. 19). Mithras and Sol are shaking hands in front of a blazing altar, a sacred object intended to emphasise the solemnity of the event. They are clasping their right hands, and at the same time holding a dagger upright. Pieces of meat, kebabs, seem to be skewered on the blade. A raven is flying down to the dagger – or is it actually bringing the meat?: we cannot tell. In less detailed versions, the same event is represented by the two gods shaking hands (fig. 109).

Among the Greeks and Romans handshaking was not an everyday gesture as it is now, but normally a sign of notably close friendship. Guest-friends, and friends who had returned from a long journey, were received with a handshake. The same gesture was also used to settle undertakings and agreements, and consequently the *iunctio dextrarum*, the 'joining of right hands', was a means of solemnising marriages. With their handshake, therefore, Mithras and Sol are settling an agreement. The solemn character of the gesture is emphasised by the fact that it is performed in front of an altar. The pact between the deities was the model for a ceremony that concluded the acceptance of new members into the Mithraic community: the initiates were termed *syndexioi*, 'those who have been united by a handshake' (with the Father) (p. 105). The scene showing the solemn compact between Mithras and Sol perhaps anticipates the meal which they are about to share.

THE SACRED REPAST

On our relief from Alcšut (fig. 17) the scene that follows the Obeisance is the ritual repast between Mithras and Sol, the feast which was reproduced by the Mithraic congregations at their banquet (pp. 108–13).

ASCENSION TO HEAVEN

Next comes the two gods' ascension in Sol's quadriga. Since this is the scene which concludes the Danubian lower registers with three panels, we can assume that it is to be placed at the end of the sequence representing the joint actions of Mithras and Sol. Many reliefs depict Mithras driving with Sol, or mounting the chariot to join him. Sol is often extending his hand to assist Mithras. As with the other scenes, while the Ascension itself was canonical, the details were left for local taste or the sculptor's individual imagination to decide. The chariot may have up to four horses; Sol, as the driver, may wear the radiate crown, and carry a whip or torch. Sometimes just one of the gods is shown, or Sol is accompanied by Luna. The sculptor often indicates the act of ascension to heaven by representing the vehicle at an angle.

The chariot's journey over the Ocean, over the Great Water, is often also symbolised by a figure placed to the right of the horses, naked, with his arm raised as though greeting the chariot on its flight. A serpent twines itself around him, with jaws agape, its head following the direction in which his hand is pointing. This serpent, as a symbol of water, surely confirms the identification of the figure as Oceanus (fig. 110). The deity sometimes supports himself on a hydria with water pouring from it; or reclines amid the waves; or holds onto a boat (fig. 39).

110. Apulum/Alba Iulia, Dacia: bottom r.h. corner of a Danubian-style cult-relief (V 1958). The identity of the snake-encircled figure is uncertain: it does not resemble the conventional iconography of Oceanus (e.g. V 778), which never includes a serpent. Vermaseren identified him as Saturnus. On two other reliefs from Apulum, however, the figure beneath the Ascension is a full-bearded male sitting on a rock and holding a velum (V 1974, 2000). An identical figure at Tavalicavo, Moesia Superior, clearly has waves beneath him (V 2244, cf. 2272). The snake-encircled deity may be a variant on this Oceanus type. Oceanus is also represented in the context of the bull-killing itself, as at S. Prisca (V 478).

On a fragmentary relief from Radomir in Thracia (nr Sofia, Bulgaria), we find a hydria with water flowing from it in the place usually occupied by this divinity, namely under the horses' hooves (V 2316). On another, from Sarmizegetusa in Dacia, waves have been indicated beneath the quadriga because there was no space for a figure (fig. 111). On the panelled relief-jamb from Virunum just cited (p. 150, fig. 109), Mercury is guiding the two gods, recognisable by his winged helmet and caduceus. In Graeco-Roman mythology, Mercury is the guide of souls: just as Mithras, after completing his exploits on earth, ascends to heaven, so the initiate hoped that his soul would one day, by the aid of the god, return to the Sun's light.

111. Sarmizegetusa, Romania: Danubian-style cult-relief (V 2052, fig. 543). Water is clearly represented beneath the horses of Sol's chariot. There are seven stars in all. Note the lion's head between Mithras and Cautopates (l.) (cf. fig. 14).

MITHRAS AND PHAËTHON

It may have been this account of Mithras' journey up to the Sun that prompted the dedicator, donor and artist in one, to depict an incident from the myth of Phaëthon on a relief in the mithraeum at Dieburg (V 1247 rev., fig. 112).[162] The central scene is framed within a tondo, probably as a symbol of heaven, bearing an inscription with the name of the deity to whom the relief is dedicated, together with those of the donors of this face: *D(eo) S(oli) I(nvicto) M(ithrae), Silvestrius Sil<v>inu[s] et Silvestrius Perpetu<u>s et Silvinus Aurelius (donum dederunt)*. The monument is thus a donation by a family.[163]

112. Dieburg: rev. of complex relief, Phaëthon being granted his request to be allowed to drive the chariot of the Sun, modelled on a type created for Nero's Golden House. The interpretation is disputed. Cumont argued that it represents the Zoroastrian end of the world, the Frašegird, *with Mithras-Phaëthon about to cause a cosmic conflagration. In the Roman empire, however, Phaëthon was often associated with the immortality of the soul, and with the issue of cosmic order.*

Outside the tondo there are just the busts of the four wind-gods in the spandrels. The background of the main scene is formed by a pedimented temple-front supported by four Corinthian columns, with decorative swags extended between them. The figure represented on the pediment-cartouche is no longer identifiable. In the centre, we see Sol, defaced by the destroyers of the mithraeum, naked but for a robe, and shown in the act of descending from his throne. In his left hand, he holds a staff. In front of him, clothed only in a *chlamys*, is Phaëthon, his left hand resting on the throne, the right extended in a supplicating gesture towards Sol.

The other persons depicted are here only of marginal interest. Four female figures represent the four Seasons. There are also four youths, squires, attired like Phaëthon, and each holding a horse by the bridle. Below the main scene are represented Caelus, beneath a *velum*, Tellus and Oceanus, symbolising air, earth and water respectively. The fourth element, fire, is present in Sol himself.

The central scene can be explained with reference to representations on several Roman sarcophagi and a mural from Nero's Domus Aurea. The god sitting on the throne is Helios/Sol; the youth in front of him is Phaëthon, asking his divine father for the chariot of the Sun. The request has already been granted, because the god is shown just descending from the throne to conduct his son to the chariot; that is also why the squires are leading the Sun's steeds out to harness them to the vehicle.

In the last resort, we cannot explain what ideas the donor associated with the scenario represented by this unique piece.[164] But it is important to note that Mithras could be read into a context of this kind, that Mithras-Sol was so strongly felt to be a *single* god that he could be identified with other deities of light.

MITHRAS AND OTHER DEITIES

MITHRAS AND APOLLO

Many deities were honoured in Mithraic communities with votive inscriptions or images. There were several reasons for this. One had to do with the character of Mithras himself: since he was a sun-god, it was an obvious step to identify him with other sun-gods, or to range them by Mithras' side. This is how Phaëthon and Phanes (p. 70) found entry into mithraea. Apollo was another such solar divinity; he is, for example, invoked as *Sol Apollo Anicetus* in the mithraeum at Vindovala (Rudchester) on Hadrian's Wall (V 843 = *RIB* 1397). The epithet *Anicetus* is the Greek equivalent of *Invictus*: Apollo has here taken it over from Mithras, with whom he is equated. Apollo is also represented on an altar from Whitley Castle (nr

Alston, Northumberland), all four of whose faces are decorated with relief sculptures. Three of these depict familiar forms of Apollo. But on the back there is a deity standing on a sort of plinth, between two figures who are undoubtedly the torch-bearers (fig. 113). The god in the middle must be Apollo/Mithras.

113. *Whitley Castle, Northumberland: rear face of composite altar (RIB 1198 with pl. XVI), Apollo as Mithras with the torch-bearers. The other faces represent Apollo playing the lyre (front), Apollo as Helios in radiate crown (r.), and a man making an offering to ?Apollo Maponus. Statius' reference to Mithras (Theb. 1.719f.) is also in the context of a series of assimilations to Apollo.*

MITHRAS AND ATTIS

In addition to such identification with solar deities, local influences might also affect the way in which Mithras was represented. A clear example of this is the amalgamation of ideas from the cult of Attis with Mithras. Phrygian Attis was the dying and reviving god of vegetation, and so the guarantor of life; in this aspect he was akin to Mithras. His cult had been established in the area of the northern Black Sea long before the Roman empire. It is here, at Panticapaeum on the Thracian Chersonese (Kerch' on the Crimean Peninsula), that we occasionally come across small terracotta figurines, which show a god in a phrygian cap kneeling on a bull (fig. 114). He is grasping one of the bull's horns with his left hand, and wrenching back its head; the right arm is raised to deliver the death-blow. So far, this god must be Mithras. But in sharp contrast with the usual representations, he is dressed in a jacket-like garment, fastened at the chest with a brooch, which leaves his genitals exposed – the iconography typical of Attis. Both deities were the focus of mystery-cults, both shared certain exterior attributes, such as the phrygian cap; and so it was an obvious step to assimilate them one with another.[165] The cult of Mithras, or whatever remained of it, evidently spread in the Thracian Chersonese only in this syncretistic form, but was so popular that it was worthwhile for local artisans to make moulds to manufacture these little figurines of the god. This version of the cult did

114. *Panticapaeum/Kerch', Crimean Peninsula: terracotta figurine of Mithras, assimi-lated to Attis, killing the bull (V 11). Five such figurines are known; of the two from excavations, one was found, along with various statuettes of Aphrodite, in a woman's grave; the other in a coroplast's workshop. The model is the generalised classical and Hellenistic 'heroic animal slayer'. Date: ? second half of first cent.* BC.

also have some effect on the area of the lower Danube: on a relief from there now in Paris, Mithras is represented with a very similar gesture after dealing the death-blow (fig. 60).

MITHRAS AND NATIVE DIVINITIES

Native deities were generally admitted into mithraea in ways analogous to these assimilations. In Britain, Cocidius, a divinity related to Mars, was worshipped by Mithraists (V 866, 867). At Dura-Europos on the Euphrates, right at the other extreme of the cult's range, the god could be identified with the probably Commagenian mountain-deity Turmasgad (V 70). The absorption of indi-genous divinities in the German provinces is well documented. A votive altar (V 1351) was dedicated at Koenigshoffen/Strasbourg to the Celtic god Cisso-nius. This god was often equated with Mercury, a deity who himself, as we shall see, had a close relation to Mithras (p. 158). The mother-goddesses, extremely popular in Germany, gained entry to the mithraeum at Taunum (Friedberg) behind the Wetterau-*limes* (V 1066). At both Nida and Stockstadt we also find another female deity, Epona, the patroness of horses (V 1094; 1188).

Some Palmyrene soldiers who dedicated an altar at Doştat in Dacia also introduced their own native religious ideas. For them, the almighty sun-god Mithras was also *deus genitor*, the creator god (V 2008). Palmyrenes were accustomed to associating themselves with foreign cults if they were linked with the idea of fertility, so fundamental to their own religion, and were centred on a male divinity.[166] Hence the emphasis upon *genitor*, which is an aspect of Mithras not otherwise much in evidence; and that is why the word, unlike the god's other titles and epithets, is not abbreviated (p. 62).

MITHRAS AND THE GRAECO-ROMAN GODS

There are many examples illustrating the readiness of Mithraists to worship other divinities. Typical of them is the centurion of the *legio VIII Augusta* (stationed at Argentorate, Strasbourg), who in the mid-second century set up separate altars to Mithras, Apollo Pythius and Fortuna Respiciens at Böckingen/Heilbronn on the Neckar-*limes*.[167] The range of Graeco-Roman divinities to whom votives were offered in mithraea is quite considerable.[168] The most comprehensive list is provided by a governor of the province of Numidia (Algeria) on a late-third-century altar at Diana (Aïn-Zana): he dedicated it to *Iovi Optimo Maximo, Iunoni Reginae, Minervae sanctae, Soli Mithrae, Herculi, Marti, Mercurio, Genio loci, dis deabusque omnibus* (V 140). Individual deities honoured with altars or statuettes include Atlas (p. 87), Diana, the Dioscuri (perhaps identified with the torch-bearers), Fortuna (p. 21), various Genii, Hecate, Hercules, Isis, Juno, Jupiter (fig. 90), the Lares, Luna of course, Mars, Mercury (p. 93), Minerva, Sarapis, Silvanus, Tutela, Venus (fig. 117), Victoria, Virtus and Vulcanus. One could also include Jupiter Dolichenus here: not only have votives to him been discovered in mithraea (V 1208), but Mithraic inscriptions and cult-reliefs have been found in *dolichena* (V 70, p. 157; V 468–70; 1729).

Of all these deities, I would just like to stress the significance of Mercury for many Mithraic congregations. The point is underscored by the number of votive-inscriptions to Mercury, and still more statues, which have been found in mithraea.[169] The two Germanies and three Gauls, where native Mercuries were anyway deeply rooted, are central here. The evidence from Stockstadt is particularly telling: in one mithraeum were found three statuettes of Mercury (V 1176, 1178–79), and in the other, an inscription dedicated *D(eo) I(nvicto) M(ithrae) Mercuri[o]* (V 1211). Both Mercury – already indeed in his Greek form, Hermes – and Mithras were considered psychopomps, gods who guided the souls of the initiated to heaven: the parallel may have suggested the identification to this dedicant. A *pater* at Emerita in Lusitania (Mérida) donated a statue of Mercury in marble (fig. 115) in his mithraeum. The god is naked; his robe hangs over the rock on which he is sitting. The usual wings grow from the ankles; the lyre leans against a rock. On the lyre, in fact on the instrument's characteristic tortoise-shell body, is the votive-inscription to Mithras: *Invicto Deo Mithrae*. The notion of psychopomp is illustrated unmistakably on the panelled jamb from Virunum, where Mercury attends the ascension of Mithras and Sol (p. 153). But at the same time, of course, Mercury could be thought of as the protective deity of a planet, of a weekday, or of a sign of the Zodiac. For, quite apart from the individual traits of the Olympian gods, it was their function as guardians (*tutela*: p. 133) of the planets, the days of the week, and the zodiacal signs that prompted Mithraists to do them honour with inscriptions on altars and iconographically on reliefs (figs 13, 14, 59). It is as such that they appear in greater or smaller numbers on votives and images.

115. *Colonia Augusta Emerita/Mérida, Spain: statue of Mercury, naked, with lyre (V 780). Part of a cycle of expensive mid-second-cent. sculptures in Italian marble, one signed by a Greek craftsman, Demetrios (V 773). Two statues of Mithras-Mercury have recently been found in German mithraea, one at Mundelsheim (cf. fig. 91), the other at Groß Gerau, nr Mainz. The latter, found by the entrance, is dedicated to the hitherto unknown deity Mercurius Quillenius.*

They appear as the gods of the weekdays on the bronze plaque from Brigetio in Pannonia Superior that we discussed above (p. 85, fig. 51). The planetary week had been spreading in the Roman world since the early Principate, and in the third century became quite general. The days were accordingly named after the seven then-known planets which could be observed with the naked eye: Saturn, Sol, Luna, Mars, Mercury, Jupiter and Venus. Within this seven-day week, the Romans considered one day as exceptional, the day of Saturn (Saturday). Saturn was thought to be an unlucky planet, and so no important business was transacted on his day. It therefore became a day of rest, when people went to the baths and, if they could afford it, splashed out on better food.[170] That is why Saturn heads the sequence of the gods of the days of the week. The sequence on the lower register of the plaque then reads (l. to r.): Saturn with his sickle; Sol with a whip; Luna with a torch and ox-horns; Mars with helmet, cuirass and spear; Mercury with his caduceus and winged helmet; Jupiter with the thunderbolt; and Venus with her mirror.

The grand relief from Osterburken on the Main-Rems-*limes* offers all twelve of the divinities that presided over the Zodiac. Two rows of them are visible on the enlarged detail in fig. 116. In the upper row (l. to r.): Diana, taking an arrow out of her quiver (tutelary deity of Sagittarius); Pluto, with a beard, holding a sceptre in his raised right hand (Cancer); Proserpina, in a long robe and a veil (Virgo); winged Victoria, holding a palm-branch in her left hand and, with her right, placing a crown upon the head of Jupiter sitting on a throne beneath her (Capricorn); Neptune with a trident

116. Osterburken: centre panel of architrave of the complex relief (V 1292. 1), the twelve Olympian gods. It has been argued that they are to be identified as the tutelary gods of the zodiacal signs. Among the panels of the cult-fresco of the recently-discovered Mithraeum V at Aquincum (Pannonia Inferior) is one that seems to show the planetary gods feasting, perhaps as representatives of the grades they protected.

(Pisces). In the lower row are: naked Venus, checking her hair in a mirror (Taurus); Minerva, in tunic and helmet, with her left hand on her shield, and holding a spear in her right (Aries); Juno, dressed in a long robe and veil and holding a small box in her left hand (Aquarius); Jupiter sitting on his throne holding the thunderbolt, his robe falling about him (Leo); Apollo, dressed in just a *chlamys*, resting his lyre on an altar and holding the plectrum in his right hand, ready to play (Gemini); Mars in helmet and cuirass, his left hand resting on his shield, a spear in his right (Scorpion); Hercules, the Nemean lion-skin over his shoulder, holding a club and a Hesperidean apple (Libra).[171]

One has the impression that the interest of some Mithraic communities in these well-tried gods was a good deal more marked than – or at least as marked as – their interest in the special world of Mithraic imagery. The proportion of images from the two realms among the wealth of statuary at Mithraeum I at Stockstadt is roughly equal. At Emerita in Lusitania (Mérida), there are many more statues to Olympian deities, such as the Venus illustrated in fig. 117, so that the specifically Mithraic iconography is pushed into the background.

117. Emerita/Mérida, Spain: statue of Venus (V 784) from the Mithraeum. Other non-Mithraic deities here include a Sarapis-head, a possible Neptune, a deity enthroned, another Venus, and two unidentifiable female figures. Sarapis was regularly counted as a solar deity in the Principate, and as such found a place both at S. Prisca in Rome (V 479) and in the Walbrook Mithraeum, London (818).

Many themes taken from the mythology of this Graeco-Roman divine world, with its numerous tutelary functions, also found their way into mithraea. One common example is the Gigantomachy, which is sometimes represented on the monuments. The Giants were the fearsome, outrageously vast, gruesomely ugly behemoths of Greek saga, with scaly serpents in place of legs. Their battle against the gods is often depicted on the friezes of temples and on Greek vases: they hurl great boulders against heaven, but are finally slain by Jupiter, who despatches them with his thunderbolt, the divine weapon that humankind could experience at first hand, the lightning that strikes and annihilates. This battle is represented on a second panelled jamb-fragment from Virunum in Noricum (fig. 118). With the thunderbolt given him beforehand by Saturn aloft in his hand, Jupiter is about to stretch the Giants dead as they bluster defiantly before him.

118. Virunum/Zollfeld, Klagenfurt: detail from l. jamb of the lost complex relief (V 1430 B1, cf. fig. 109), Battle of the Giants. The indirect model for this scheme of Jupiter slaying a snake-legged Giant was the Great Frieze of the Pergamon Altar. The Gigantomachy, as a conventional statement of order triumphant over disorder, had many possible connotations, but fits well into the general Mithraic concern with the rhythms of the kosmos.

THE GOD OF TIME

In this section we have often had occasion to mention syncretism, the identification of several deities of different origins, which is everywhere observable during the Principate. The clearest example in the mysteries of Mithras is a divine figure whose actual name we do not even know.

In many mithraea one comes across the rigid image of a god whose outer form remains for us without a name, whose identity no inscription certainly reveals. The multiplicity of his attributes is fully consistent with the indeterminacy of his name and character: these images are hyper-freighted with emblems and mystic symbolism whose meaning remains in part opaque to us. He usually has a lion's head with mouth agape, or his trunk and legs are studded with lion-masks (V 326). The mouth is occasionally so formed that fire would spew from it (fig. 119) if a torch were held to the corresponding aperture at the back of the head (fig. 120). These statues really did emit flame:

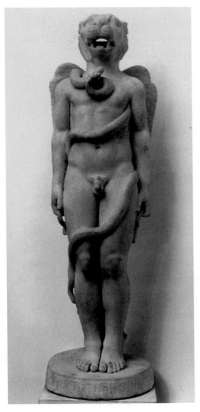

119. Sidon, Lebanon: front of a late-antique statue of the lion-headed deity (V 78) from the Mithraeum. This is one of only two examples in which the god's sex is unambiguously indicated (see also V 545): otherwise either the deity wears a loin-cloth, or the snake is draped in such a way as to obscure the issue. There is an interesting contrast between the two versions of the figure at Emerita (Lusitania): the lion-headed one (V 776) has a loin-cloth; the human-headed (777) exposes his sex.

120. The same: rear view. There are two further examples of a perforated mouth (V 543, 544). Note the double wings: on reliefs, where the detail was easy to indicate, the god generally has four.

and no doubt a fire could be kindled by the same means on an altar standing in front of the statue, as is suggested by a relief at Rome (fig. 121). Occasionally, as in this case, the god is represented holding torches. To make the Lion-head a still more effective symbol of fire, he might be red-leaded (Arnob. *Adv. nat.* 6.10). The deity is represented with a human trunk, hieratically obtected, with stiff legs, undraped: a male god. A snake entwines his body, sometimes as much as seven times, and may thereby enclose signs of the Zodiac. On the god's torso at Arelate in Gallia Narbonensis (Arles), one can see between the two uppermost coils Aries, Taurus and Gemini, and then, beneath them, Cancer and Leo; lower still, Scorpius (fig. 122).[172]

121. Nr S. Vitale (Via Nazionale), Rome: relief of the 'god of Time' (V 383). The four snakes may allude to the four seasons (cf. fig. 122). A flaming altar similar to that shown here is depicted on a relief from Oxyrhynchus in Egypt, balanced on the other side by a krater (V 103).

122. Arelate/Arles: fragmentary Lion-head with signs of the zodiac denoting Spring, Summer, Autumn and Winter (V 879). A statue at Rome carries four zodiacal signs (Aries, Libra, Cancer and Capricorn) (545). On one relief, the god's staff has twelve spirals (V 543). In some cases, such as the Marino and Barberini mithraea, the Lion-head, standing on a globe, is placed in the centre of the zodiacal signs spanning the arch of the cave.

This god was addressed as Aion, whom we know under this Greek name in Egypt, the god of Time.[173] He was born on the night of 6 January, a date which was at first also considered the date of the birth of Christ, before the birthday of Mithras/Sol, 25 December, became established for that feast. Aion's birthday survived in the end too, as the feast of Epiphany. But this deity is also Saturn, imagined in antiquity 'sometimes in the form of a serpent, because he is so algid, sometimes with a lion's gaping jaws, because he is so torrid' (*Mythogr. Vatic.* 3.1.8).

Mithras too is a god of Time, or rather was considered a god of the unfolding year. One Greek form of his name, Μείθρας, in which the ει was pronounced as long i, was regarded as an encoded play upon this reference. The Greek system of numerals was composed of the letters of the Greek alphabet, so that it was a common arithmological practice to convert the letters of a name into the corresponding numbers, whose sum thus provided the figure desired. A number of ancient authors mention that the following calculation could be performed on the basis of the name Μείθρας: [174]

$$
\begin{array}{rcl}
\mu & = & 40 \\
\varepsilon & = & 5 \\
\iota & = & 10 \\
\theta & = & 9 \\
\rho & = & 100 \\
\alpha & = & 1 \\
\varsigma & = & 200 \\
\hline
\text{Μείθρας} & = & 365
\end{array}
$$

By means such as this, Mithras could be shown to be god of the year, and was perhaps as such identified with the lion-headed god of Time.

But this deity also has lineaments of Sarapis, Apollo, Jupiter, Pluto, Aesculapius, Pan and other divine beings, a splendid example of the commingling of different religious conceptions which did not always need to be made fully coherent with one another. The point can be illustrated from a relief probably originally from Rome but now at Modena, whose imagery likewise draws upon a variety of elements of quite different provenance (V 695, fig. 123). What follows is merely a description of the individual elements, most of which cannot be fully explained, since we are unable to determine whether astrological, Orphic, Chaldaean, Persian or Graeco-Roman ideas predominate.

In the centre there stands a naked young man, holding a staff in his left hand and a thunderbolt in his right. He has wings, as lord of the Winds, and

123. *Probably from Rome, now in Modena: the 'god of Time'.*

stands with his feet, which are cloven-footed like Pan's, on the lower half of an ovoid form with flames pouring out of it. The other half of this object is above his head, which is itself surrounded by rays, symbolising the Sun. At the same time, the horns of a crescent Moon project above his shoulders. A snake winds around his body, its head directly above the youth's. On the breast is a lion-mask, on either side a ram's (r.) and a goat's head (l.), possibly symbolising past and future. The figure is encircled by an elliptical band, which again symbolises an egg – the World-egg, out of which the zodiac was formed: the signs of the Zodiac are arranged around it. Here, once again (p. 84), the heads of the four wind-gods are depicted in the spandrels. Finally, the relief is inscribed with the names of its donors, Euphrosynus and Felix, the latter of whom is a Father.[175]

Any account of this and similar images must remain hypothetical. One can now only note the variety of divine attributes and speculations that meet in them. For their own interpretations, the priests and members of the different Mithraic communities had plenty to start with.

Several factors contributed to the Mithraists' readiness to accept such a variety of deities. The cult developed as a Roman mystery cult in the early Principate and spread rapidly around the turn of the second century. It was not at all as well-established and consolidated as older cults, and was therefore more open to all manner of influences. Moreover, from the outset numerous figures and narrative elements from Graeco-Roman mythology were incorporated into the legend of Mithras. The cult's symbolic language was in many respects by no means exclusively its own: Sun, Moon, bull, dog, serpent, scorpion, krater and flames, just to name a few, were well-known in other cults. Again, the small size of the congregations meant that they were able to react flexibly to the wishes and enthusiasms of their members. The range of deities worshipped in the cult was anyway very large, if we include the tutelary gods of the planets and the divine representatives of the zodiacal signs, and this wealth was exploited by the believers. A Mithraist at Crikvine near Salona in Dalmatia (Croatia) pushed this development to its logical conclusion when he chose an extended formula for the votive-altar he was dedicating: to Mithras and the other immortal gods and goddesses, ceteris[que dis dea] / busqu[e immor] / talibu[s (V 1872).

Chapter 14

Mithras and Christ[176]

Ever since the middle of the second century AD Christian writers had commented, often enough in harsh terms, on the remarkable similarities between their own religion and the cult of Mithras. From their point of view, all these resemblances were clever ruses on the part of the Devil.

Mithras and Christ actually compose a fascinating chapter in the rich history of the religious movements of the Principate. From the late nineteenth century, that is, with the work of Franz Cumont, there has been an occasionally lively debate over the nature of the relationship between the cult of Mithras and Christianity. This long controversy was sparked off by a stimulating remark of Ernest Renan, in his book on the cultural history of the later Principate: 'If Christianity had been arrested in its growth by some fatal malady, the world would have become Mithraist.'[177] This rather pointed way of putting the claim naturally raised numerous voices for and against.

Yet the entire discussion is largely unhistorical. To raise the issue of a competition between the two religions is to assume that Christians and Mithraists had the same aims. Such a view exaggerates the missionary zeal – itself a Christian idea – of the other mystery cults. None of them aimed to become the sole legitimate religion of the Roman empire, because they all offered an entirely individual and personal salvation. The alternative 'Mithras or Christ?' is wrongly framed, because it postulates a competitive situation which, in the eyes of Mithraists, simply did not exist. The only people who could imagine a conflict between two religions were those who believed that their religion, their God, would eventually be victorious, and worked towards that end in whatever way they could. We should not simply transpose Christian views and terms in this area onto other mystery cults.

Most of the parallels between Mithraism and Christianity are part of the common currency of all mystery cults or can be traced back to common origins in the Graeco-oriental culture of the Hellenistic world. The similarities do not at all suggest mutual influence. The Church Fathers themselves must have had an inkling of this when they blamed the imitation not on the Mithraists but on the Devil. For example, water plays a significant part in the the two religions because of their common background: just as Moses caused water to gush out of the rock with his staff, so did Mithras with an arrow. Mithras was the god born from a rock (p. 62); in the Eastern Church, Mary, the *theotokos*, the mother of god, was linked with the rock from which Christ was born. But there are more substantial parallels at the ritual level, particularly the ritual meal (pp. 108–13).

To their followers, finally, Christ and Mithras were divinities of light and the Sun. Just as Mithras was for his followers the invincible sun-god, so Christ was for his the light of the world. Because of such parallelisms, the Christians distanced themselves from pagan ideas and accordingly Christ became much more *Sol iustitiae*, the Sun of righteousness. Where such evasion seemed impossible, they effected a take-over, as in the case of the observance of Sunday and the festival of the god's birth on 25 December. Here we may also adduce the depiction of the so-called Three Kings (the 'wise men [μάγοι] from the East': Matth. 2.1–11) as priests of Mithras, for example on a fourth-century lead medallion (fig. 124), an item which is itself a visual symbol of the triumph of Christianity over Mithraism.

124. Lead medallion from Italy: the Magi adoring the infant Christ. This is a version of the 'Hellenistic' type found in the catacombs and on Christian sarcophagi from the early fourth cent. The type was developed from the 'barbarians bringing tribute' image in Roman triumphal art. The best-known is that on the cypress-wood door of S. Sabina in Rome (c.430 AD). Here too the Magi are beardless and their gifts are carried on platters.

The Christian writers alone survived, and they made the Mithraists, like their other opponents, look ridiculous. 'Some of them flap their wings like birds, imitating the croak of the raven, while others actually roar like lions . . . how disgustingly abused are these people, who call themselves "wise"': these are the terms in which, as we have seen, Ambrosiaster, the anonymous fourth-century commentator, inveighs against the Mithraists, whose priests, as members of particular grades, dressed up on certain occasions as ravens or lions (p. 108).

In the reign of Constantine (306–37) conditions changed for the adherents of the cult. With the defeat of Licinius (308–24), whose troops fought the decisive battle against Constantine under the banner of the sun-god, Mithras – virtually indistinguishable now from the sun-god – also gave way before before Constantine's new favourite as sun-god, Christ. The agitation of Christian pamphleteers against the pagan cult of the Sun grew increasingly hectic under Constantius II (337–61), to the point at which, according to the slightly exaggerated testimony of the rhetor Claudius Mamertinus, people hardly dared to watch the sun rise or set, and farmers and sailors neglected to study the heavens for weather signs or guiding stars (*Pan. Lat.* 3 [11].23.5–6 ed. Mynors).

Under the successors of the Emperor Julian (361–3), there began a sharp and bloody persecution of all pagan cults, which also brought about the extermination of Mithraism. Around 400, Jerome, the translator of the so-called Vulgate version of the Bible, wrote a letter to a Christian woman named Laeta in which he praises the *praefectus Urbi* of the year 376/7:

> Did not your kinsman Gracchus, whose name recalls his patrician rank, destroy a cave of Mithras a few years ago when he was prefect of Rome? Did he not break up and burn all the monstrous images there? . . . Did he not send them before him as hostages, and gain for himself baptism in Christ?
>
> (*Ep.* 107.2, tr. F.A. Wright[178])

Quite unlike Vettius Agorius Praetextatus, his colleague in the same office in 367 (p. 30), Gracchus broke up one of the many mithraea in the former capital almost to prove himself worthy to be admitted a Christian. Jerome goes out of his way to praise him; he does not simply say that he destroyed the mithraeum – no, he relishes his words, nicely distinguishing between 'destroyed', 'broke up' and 'burned' (*subvertit, fregit, exussit*), and so catches exactly the Christians' fanatical intolerance.

We get a vivid impression of the results of such an onslaught from the finds in the mithraeum at Koenigshoffen/Strasbourg. On the floor of the cult-niche there originally stood, as in hundreds of other cases, a cult-relief measuring about 2.30×1.80 m (c. 9 ft 2 in $\times$ 5 ft 11 in), depicting the familiar scene of Mithras slaying the bull (V 1359). The excavation of 1911–12 brought more than 360 fragments of this grand relief to light. From the sheer number of the fragments, and the nature of the damage to them, there can be no doubt at all that the sculpture was deliberately destroyed. The destruction was carefully planned and extremely thorough. All the projecting features were knocked off, and then the remaining large panels were sledge-hammered into rubble. Not content with this, the intruders scattered the fragments all over the mithraeum: fragments of the sculpture were recovered all over the place, from the west wall, against which it had stood, to the eastern end of the temple.[179]

In destructions such as this, we catch a sudden glimpse of the mood of many groups in late-antique society. On the one hand, the innumerable accounts of the martyrs, with their simple, popular narrative style, kept green the memory of the persecutions that so many Christians in the past had had to endure. Among such accounts was one concerning four Christian sculptors who were supposed to sacrifice to the great god Sol, but had preferred death because for them Christ was the true Light.[180] The Christians could now at last repay the adherents of the sun-god, represented in the different localities by Mithras and his temples, for the misfortunes they had once suffered, and at the same time help to impose their own religion as the sole legitimate belief. We can even see traces of the same mentality in our own time, such as when we find Hans Lietzmann writing in his *History of the Early Church* that, 'Christ had placed his foot on the neck of the "Invincible One" ', just as 'Mithras had done to the bull'.[181]

It cannot yet be shown that any mithraeum continued to exist into the fifth century AD. The coin-series cease at the end of the fourth century at the latest. At Scarabantia in Pannonia Superior and Aquincum in Pannonia Inferior they come to an end with Gratian (383); at Nida (Heddernheim/ Frankfurt) with Maximus (388); at Skt. Urban (Noricum) with Valentinian II (392); at Pons Saravi (Sarrebourg) in Gallia Belgica, Lentia (Linz) in Noricum and S. Giovanni di Duino (NW of Tergeste, Trieste) with Theodosius I (395); at Pons Aeni in Raetia (Pfaffenhofen am Inn) with Honorius (408). The cult of Mithras disappeared earlier than that of Isis, for example, and, unlike her, almost without trace. Isis survived in legend, and was known still in the Middle Ages as a pagan deity, whereas Mithras was already forgotten in late antiquity.

Due to its lack of internal organisation, the cult of Mithras had barely any means of defending itself against attacks by Christians, and the abominations of the age. It was scattered in numerous small congregations which were not recognisably connected with one another. There was no hierarchy to bind several congregations together, which might have been able to organise some resistance; and there were no centres with super-ordinate temples.

It is impossible to compare the attractiveness of different cults in the fourth century. We should not depreciate the power of the Christian story, the rituals and the practical altruism of Christianity. But, equally, it is difficult to gauge the part played by such considerations in the success of that religion by comparison with the emperors' political ruthlessness, the many different kinds of oppression, or the violent incidents by means of which it came to be victorious in the late fourth century.

On the other hand, for many Mithraists, it may only have taken slight pressure to induce them to rally to Christianity: some of them had after all shared burial grounds with Christians in Rome during the fourth century.[182] The adherents of all pagan cults were in general prepared to involve themselves in more than one kind of worship. One consequence may have been that there was a certain latent curiosity about Christianity. The cult of Mithras had always had a large element of dutifulness, a strong connection with constituted political authority. This may have induced many to accommodate themselves to the demand for a new kind of loyalty in the fourth century.

Moreover, the similarities between the two religions adduced above must have encouraged Mithraists in particular to become Christians. They had no need in their new faith to give up the ritual meal, their Sun-imagery, or even their candles, incense and bells. Some elements of Mithraism may well have been carried over into Christianity, which partly explains why even in the sixth century the Church authorities had to struggle against those *stulti homines*, those simple clowns, who continued on the very church-steps to do obeisance to the Sun early in the morning, as they always had done, and pray to him.[183]

Notes

1. F. Cumont, *The Mysteries of Mithra* (New York: Dover, ³1956, ¹1903); *Les mystères de Mithra* (Brussels, Lamartin, ³1913, ²1902); *Die Mysterien des Mithra*, ed. K. Latte (Leipzig: Teubner, ³1923, ¹1903).
2. Particularly A. Dieterich's *Eine Mithrasliturgie*, ed. O. Weinreich (Leipzig: Teubner, ³1923, ¹1903).
3. Where appropriate, the material is cited hereafter by the number in this Corpus (V.).
4. M.J. Vermaseren, *Mithras, de geheimzinnige God* (Amsterdam: Elsevier, 1959), trans. as *Mithras, the Secret God* (London: Chatto and Windus, 1963).
5. R.L. Beck, 'Mithraism since Franz Cumont,' ANRW II, 17.4 (1984), 2002–115.
6. J.R. Hinnells (ed.), *Mithraic Studies: proceedings of the first international congress of Mithraic studies* (Manchester: Manchester University Press, 1975); J. Duchesne-Guillemin (ed.), *Études mithriaques: Actes du 2e Congrès international, Téhéran*, Acta Iranica 17, First Series (Actes de congrès), 4 (Leyden: E.J. Brill, 1978); U. Bianchi (ed.), *Mysteria Mithrae: Atti del seminario internazionale . . . Roma e Ostia*, EPRO 80 (Leyden: E.J. Brill, 1979).
7. R.L. Beck, 'In the Place of the Lion: Mithras in the Tauroctony,' in *Studies in Mithraism* (see next note), 29–50; M.P. Speidel, *Mithras-Orion: Greek hero and Roman army-god*, EPRO 81 (Leyden: E.J. Brill, 1980); D. Ulansey, *The Origins of the Mithraic Mysteries: cosmology and salvation in the ancient world* (New York and Oxford: Oxford University Press, 1989, ¹1991; enlarged German edition, Stuttgart: Theiss, 1998).
8. J.R. Hinnells (ed.), *Studies in Mithraism: papers associated with the Mithraic Panel organized on the occasion of the XVIth congress of the International Association for the History of Religions, Rome 1990*, Storia delle religioni 9 (Rome: L'Erma di Bretschneider, 1994).
9. His most important points are to be found in 'Franz Cumont and the Doctrines of Mithraism,' in *Mithraic Studies* (n. 6 above); see also J.R. Hinnells, 'The Iranian Background of Mithraic Iconography,' *Acta Iranica* First Series (Actes de congrès), 1 (Leyden: E.J. Brill,1974), 242–50; I. Roll, 'The Mysteries of Mithras in the Roman Orient: the problem of origin,' JMS 2 (1977), 53–68.
10. PhD diss., Cambridge 1972. The conclusions are summarised in 'Mithraism and Roman Society: social factors in the explanation of religious change in the Roman empire,' *Religion* 2 (1972), 92–121, repr. in id., *Image and Value in the Graeco-Roman World* (Aldershot: Variorum, 1996), no. III.
11. R. Turcan, *Mithras Platonicus: Recherches sur l'hellénisation philosophique de Mithra*, EPRO 47 (Leyden: E.J. Brill, 1975); *Mithra et le mithriacisme* (Paris: Les Belles-Lettres, ²1993; ¹1981)

12. R. Merkelbach, *Mithras* (Königstein/Taunus: Hain, 1984). I take the opportunity here of thanking Prof. Merkelbach for his help in procuring illustrations for this book.

13. A.D. Nock, *Early Gentile Christianity and its Hellenistic Background* (New York: Harper and Row, [2]1964, [1]1928), 58.

14. I was able to have new photographs of the reliefs taken thanks to a generous grant from the Fritz Thyssen Foundation.

15. On Iranian Mitra, see the general accounts by Turcan, *Mithra* (n. 11 above), 11–29; Merkelbach, *Mithras* (n. 12 above), 7–39. On the name: G. Bonfante, 'The Name of Mithra,' in *Études mithriaques* (n. 6 above), 47–57.

16. See G. Gnoli, 'Sol persice Mitra,' in *Mysteria Mithrae* (n. 6 above), 725–40.

17. See the relevant sections in Merkelbach, *Mithras* (n. 12 above), 43–72.

18. Cass. Dio 63 [62].5.2; cf. Suet. *Nero* 13.2; Plin. *HN* 30.16–17.

19. E. Schwertheim, 'Monumente des Mithraskultes in Kommagene,' *Antike Welt* 6 (1975), 63–8; F.K. Dörner, 'Mithras in Kommagene,' in *Études mithriaques* (n. 6 above), 123–33; J. Duchesne-Guillemin, 'Iran and Greece in Commagene,' ibid., 187–99.

20. Merkelbach, *Mithras* (n. 12 above), 23–30.

21. Hermes occurs in the texts as a fourth deity, no doubt as guide of souls: B. Lincoln, 'Mithra(s) as Sun and Savior,' in *La soteriologia dei culti orientali nell' Impero romano*, U. Bianchi and M.J. Vermaseren (eds), EPRO 92 (Leyden: E.J. Brill, 1982), 505–26, at 514–15.

22. References to the debate over the extent, indeed the existence, of traits common to both Persian Mitra and Roman Mithras may be found in Beck, 'Mithraism' (n. 5 above), 2063–71.

23. *De persica nobis adversaria gente progressa*: Cod. Gregor.14.4.4–7 = *Coll. Mos. et Rom. Legum* 15.3 .4–7 [FIRA 2: 580–1].

24. The point has been made most bluntly by S. Wikander, 'Études sur les mystères de Mithras', *Vetenskapssocieteten i Lund: Årsbok 1950* (Lund, 1951), 5–46.

25. As A. Schütze, *Mithras-Mysterien und Urchristentum* (Verlag Urachhaus: Stuttgart, [3]1972, [1]1960), tried to do.

26. M.P. Nilsson, *Geschichte der griechischen Religion* (Munich: C.H. Beck, 1974), 2: 675.

27. E.R. Dodds, *Pagan and Christian in an Age of Anxiety* (Cambridge: Cambridge University Press, 1965).

28. A.E. Imhof, 'Die verlängerte Lebenszeit – Auswirkung auf unser Zusammenleben,' *Saeculum* 36 (1985), 46–69.

29. *Sciendum in sacris simulata pro veris accipi*: Serv. ad Aen. 2. 116, cf. 4. 512.

30. See R. Bultmann, *Das Urchristentum im Rahmen der antiken Religionen* (Zurich: Artemis Verlag, 1949); W. Burkert, *Ancient Mystery Cults* (Cambridge, Mass., and London: Harvard University Press, 1987); M. Giebel, *Das Geheimnis der Mysterien. Antike Kulte in Griechenland, Rom und Ägypten* (Zurich and Munich: Artemis Verlag, 1990).

31. Symmachus *Relat.* 3.10: *uno itinere non potest perveniri ad tam grande secretum*.

32. M. Clauss, *Cultores Mithrae. Die Anhängerschaft des Mithras-Kultes* HABES 10 (Stuttgart: Franz Steiner Verlag, 1992).

33. The importance of the Platonic texts for the cult of Mithras has been stressed in different ways by Merkelbach and Turcan (nn. 11–12 above), but note the critical remarks of W. Fauth, 'Plato Mithriacus oder Mithras Platonicus? Art und Umfang platonischer Einflüsse auf die Mithras-Mysterien,' *Göttingische Gelehrte Anzeigen* 236 (1984), 36–50.

34. S. Laeuchli, 'Urban Mithraism,' *Biblical Archaeologist* 31 (1968), 73–99.

35. Origen C. *Cels.* 6.22; we can probably discern such influence in the 'Mithras liturgy' (p. 105).

36. I. Huld-Zetsche, *Mithras in Nida-Heddernheim* Archäologische Reihe 6 (Frankfurt: Museum für Vor- und Frühgeschichte, 1986), 21, 33–9. The case at Pons Aeni (Pfaffenhofen am Inn, Bavaria) is similar: J. Garbsch with H-J. Kellner, 'Das Mithräum von Pons Aeni,' *Bayerische Vorgeschichtsblätter* 50 (1985), 355–462.

37. P. Herz, *Untersuchungen zum Festkalender der römischen Kaiserzeit nach datierten Weih- und Ehreninschriften* (Diss. Mainz: in Komm. bei R. Habelt, Bonn, 1975), 1: 80–2.

38. V 1404, with G. Alföldy, 'Epigraphica Norica,' in his *Epigraphische Studien 8* (Düsseldorf: Rheinland Verlag, 1969), 27–8.

39. V 161, cf. M. Imhof, 'Invictus,' *Museum Helveticum* 14 (1957), 197–215; M. Guarducci, 'Sol Invictus Augustus,' *Rendiconti della Pontificia Accademia di Archeologia* 30/31 (1957–9), 161–9.

40. V 1013; cf. M. Clauss, 'Sol Invictus Mithras,' *Athenaeum* 78 (1990), 436.

41. Provincial high priest: V 2296 (Pontarch); *flamen*: V 2249 with CIL III 14211.2; *sacerdos*: AE 1980: 48, 49b, 50b.

42. Porphyry *Abst.* 2.56 (Pallas); 4.16 (Euboulus, Pallas); *De antr. nymph.* 6 (Euboulus).

43. R.M. Swoboda, 'Zu einer Inschrift aus dem Mithras-Heiligtum in Virunum: CIL III 4796,' *Carinthia* 160 (1970), 625–30.

44. V 522: *Antiqua generose domo, cui regia Vestae / pontifici felix sacrato militat igne, / idem augur, triplicis cultor venerandae Dianae, / Persidiciq(ue) Mithrae antistes Babilonie templi, / tauroboliq(ue) simul magni dux mistice sacri.*

45. V 406: *Olim Victor avus, caelo devotus et astris, / regali sumptu Phoebeia templa locavit. / Hunc superat pietate nepos, cui nomen avitum est: / antra facit, sumptusque tuos nec Roma requirit. / Damna piis meliora lucro: quis ditior illo est, / qui cum caelicolis parcus bona dividit heres?*

46. See H. Bloch, 'The Pagan Revival in the West at the End of the Fourth Century,' in *The Conflict between Paganism and Christianity in the Fourth Century*, A. Momigliano (ed.) (Oxford: Clarendon Press, 1963), 193–218.

47. V 76, 79, 85, with E. Will, 'La date du Mithréum de Sidon,' *Syria* 27 (1950), 261–9.

48. E. Sauer, *The End of Paganism in the North-Western Provinces of the Roman Empire: the example of the Mithras cult* BAR International Series 634 (Oxford: Tempus Reparatum, 1996).

49. F. von Fisenne, 'Das Mithreum zu Saarburg in Lothringen,' *Jahrbuch der Gesellschaft für lothringische Geschichte und Altertumskunde* 8 (1896), 119–75. Two hundred and fifty of the coins are of the fourth century AD. In this area at that period, small-denomination coins were commonly used as votives, in place of the stone monuments of a previous age: E. M. Wightman, *Gallia Belgica* (London: B.T. Batsford, 1985), 284.

50. See n. 30 above.

51. J. Beaujeu, 'La religion de la classe sénatoriale à l'époque des Antonins,' in *Hommages à Jean Bayet*, M. Renard (ed.), Collection Latomus 70 (Brussels: Latomus, 1964), 54–75.

52. V 1751–4, AE 1962: 26; note also the similar cases at Gimmeldingen/Neustadt (p. 29) and Tîrgusor (Bulgaria), V 2304–9.

53. G. Alföldy, 'P. Helvius Pertinax und M. Valerius Maximianus,' *Situla* 14/15 (1974), 199–215, repr. in idem, *Römische Heeresgeschichte* Mavors 3 (Amsterdam: Gieben, 1987), 326–48. The Mithraic dedications by this senator are V 137, 138B, 1950.

54. Third century: V 135; AE 1906: 8; V 134; fourth century: V 138F; 138D. On these, see M. Le Glay, 'Le mithréum de Lambèse,' *CRAI* (1954), 269–77.

55. Cumont (n. 1 above), 40–61; C.M. Daniels, 'The Rôle of the Roman Army in the Spread and Practice of Mithraism,' in *Mithraic Studies* (n. 6 above), 2: 249–74.

56. V 2350, with N. Reed, 'The Mithraeum on Andros,' ZPE 18 (1975), 207–11.

57. A.J. Ohrenberger, *Burgenländische Heimatblätter* 22 (1960), 7–8; V 1637–39; 1659, 1661.

58. P. Beskov, 'The Portorium and the Mysteries of Mithras,' JMS 3 (1980), 1–18.

59. M. Suić, 'Orientalische Kulte im antiken Zadar,' *Diadora* 3 (1965), 91–124, at 97; 124–5.

60. V 1484; CIL III 11674.

61. Respectively: AE 1971: 384; CIL III 1363; AE 1957: 273; V 2153, with I. Piso, 'Inscriptii din Apulum,'*Acta Musei Napocensis* 20 (1983), 103–111, at 109–10 no. 6 = IDR 3.1: 145.

62. Laeuchli, 'Urban Mithraism,' (n. 34 above), 86.

63. V 2296, with D.M. Pippidi, 'En marge d'un document mithriaque de Scythie mineure,' in *Hommages à M.J. Vermaseren*, M. de Boer and T.A. Edridge (eds) EPRO 68 (Leyden: E.J. Brill, 1978), 3: 967–73; the text is translated in Beard, North, Price 2: 310–11. On Mithraic membership in general, see R.L. Gordon, 'Mithraism and Roman Society' (n. 10 above).

64. V 423: *Hic locus est felix, sanctus piusque benignus, / quem monuit Mithras mentemque dedit / Proficentio patri sacrorum / utque sibi spelaeum faceret dedicaretque / et celeri instansque operi reddit munera grata / quem bono auspicio suscepit anxia mente / ut possint syndexi hilares celebrare vota per aevom; / hos versiculos generavit Proficentius / pater dignissimus Mithrae.*

65. H. Lavagne, 'Importance de la grotte dans le mithriacisme en occident,' in *Études mithraiques* (n. 6 above), 271–8.

66. U. Ciotti, 'Due iscrizioni mitriache inedite,' in *Hommages à M.J. Vermaseren* (n. 63 above), 1: 233–9. A translation of the text from S. Gemini in Beard, North, Price 2: 309.

67. G. Becatti, *Scavi di Ostia 2: I Mitrei* (Rome: Libreria dello Stato, 1953); Laeuchli, 'Urban Mithraism,' (n. 34 above); F. Coarelli, 'Topografia mitriaca di Roma,' in *Mysteria Mithrae* (n. 6 above), 69–79.

68. R.L. Beck, 'The Rock-Cut Mithraea of Arupium (Dalmatia),' *Phoenix* 38 (1984), 356–71.

69. CIL III 1096: *cryptam cum porticibus et apparitorio et exedra* (but see V 1978).

70. See n. 66 above.

71. Porph. *De antr. nymph.* 6; H. Lavagne, 'Les reliefs mithriaques à scènes multiples en Italie,' in P. Gros, J-P. Boucher, H. Lavagne, J-P. Morel and R. Turcan (eds), *Mélanges de philosophie, de littérature et d'histoire ancienne offerts à P. Boyancé* Collection de l'École française de Rome 22 (Rome and Paris: École française de Rome, 1974), 481–504.

72. G. Piccottini, *Mithrastempel in Virunum* Aus Forschung und Kunst 28 (Klagenfurt: Verlag des Geschichtsvereines für Kärnten, 1994), 18–19.

73. V 2265: τὸ στήλιον σὺν τῇ ζωγραφίᾳ.

74. *Deum vetusta religione in velo formatum,* '(the donor caused the image of) the God to be fashioned on a cloth according to the ancient requirements of the cult' (V. wrongly prints *vetustate*). See also p. 50.

75. R.L. Gordon, 'Panelled Complications,' JMS 3 (1980), 200–27.

76. W. Hermann, *Römische Götteraltare* (Kallmünz: Lassleben, 1961), 31–5.

77. Justin, *Dial.* 70: ἐκ πέτρας γεγενῆσθαι; Commodianus, *Instruct.* 1.13 (see n. 92 below); Lydus *Mens.* 3.26: τὸν πετρογενῆ Μίθραν; Firm. Mat. *Err. prof. rel.* 20.1: θεὸς ἐκ πέτρας; also M.J. Vermaseren, 'The Miraculous Birth of Mithras,' *Mnemosyne* n.s. 4 (1951), 285–301.

78. V 2007 (see p. 158); see also M. Clauss, 'Omnipotens Mithras,' *Epigraphica* 50 (1988), 151–61, at 157–8.
79. N. Gisdova, 'Ex-voto dédié à Mithra découvert récemment au village de Vetren, arr. Pazardjik,' *Archéologie (Sofia)* 3.1 (1961), 50–1.
80. Cited in CIL 1^2 338–9.
81. Compare Merkelbach, *Mithras* (n. 12 above), 376.
82. V 463.1, with G. Ristow, 'Zum Kosmokrator im Zodiacus, ein Bildvergleich,' in *Hommages à M.J. Vermaseren* (n. 63 above), 3: 985–7.
83. V 475 = IGUR 108, with Clauss, 'Sol Invictus Mithras' (n. 40 above), 430–1.
84. Nonnus *Dion.* 21. 248–9; 40. 400; Zenobius 5.78 ap. *Paroemiogr.* 1. 151; cf. H.J. Rose, 'Mithra-Phaëthon chez Nonnus' (with a reply by Cumont), *Revue de l'Histoire des Religions* 105 (1932), 98–103.
85. V 860, with C.M. Daniels, 'Mithras Saecularis, the Housteads Mithraeum and a Fragment from Carrawburgh,' *ArchAel* 4th series, 40 (1962), 105–15; also 277–9 with pl. 27.
86. *Fons concluse petris, geminos qui aluisti nectare fratres*: M. J. Vermaseren and C.C. van Essen, *The Excavations in the Mithraeum of the Church of Santa Prisca in Rome* (Leyden: E.J. Brill, 1965), 193.
87. M. Abramić, *Poetovio: Führer durch die Denkmäler der römischen Stadt* (Vienna: Verlag der Österreichischen Staatsdruckerei, 1925), 68.
88. G. Kazarow, 'Thrake,' in RE 6A.1 (1936), 478–88.
89. L. Zotović, *Les cultes orientaux sur le territoire de la Mésie Supérieure* EPRO 7 (Leyden: E.J. Brill, 1966), 63 no. 6.
90. According to Merkelbach, *Mithras* (n. 12 above), 343, 355, 358 and passim, this second carting-off represents the removal of the dead bull, but the fact that on several reliefs the tail is moving speaks against this. The detail was difficult to show on a tiny panel measuring 5×5 cm (2×2 in), or on a free-standing sculpture.
91. *Hunc quem aureis humeris portavit more iuvencum*: Vermaseren and van Essen, *Sta Prisca* (n. 86 above), 200–5. The shoulders are 'golden' because Mithras is an image of the sun here.
92. Commodianus, *Instruct.* 1.13:

> *Invictus de petra natus si deus habetur,*
> *Nunc ego reticeo; vos de istis date priorem!*
> *Vicit petra deum, quaerendus est petrae creator.*
> *Insuper et furem adhuc depingitis esse,*
> *Cum, si deus esset, utique non furto vivebat.*
> *Terrenus utique fuit et monstruosa natura,*
> *Vertebatque boves alienos semper in antris*
> *Sicut et Cacus Vulcani filius ille.*

93. P. Zanker, *The Power of Images in the Age of Augustus* (Ann Arbor: University of Michigan Press, 1988), 114–15; note also W.Wili, 'Die römische Sonnengottheiten und Mithras,' *Eranos-Jahrbücher* 10 (1943), 125–68, on the idea that Mithras, as sun-god, was well suited to the religious style of the Augustan age.
94. On the origin of the piece, note R.L. Beck, 'Four Dacian Tauroctonies,' *Apulum* 22 (1985), 45–61, at 55 n. 25.
95. Lactantius Placidus 1.719–20: *utrisque manibus bovis cornua comprimens. Quae interpretatio ad Lunam dicitur . . . his autem versibus sacrorum Solis mysteria patefecit. Sol enim, Lunam minorem potentia sua et humiliorem docens, taurum insidens cornibus torquet* (88–9 Sweeney: interpolated passage).

96. On the Brigetio plaque: A. Radnóti, 'Le bas-relief mithriaque de bronze de Brigetio,' *Archaeologiai Ertesitö* 7–9 (1946–8), 146–56. It should be noted that on the relief at Bologna, although the busts of Mars, Mercury, Jupiter and Venus have been added later, the order of the sequence is given by the position of Saturn.

97. Some examples are: A. Bausani, 'Note sulla preistoria astronomica del mito di Mitra,' in *Mysteria Mithrae* (n. 6 above), 503–11; D.R. Small, 'The Raven: an iconographic adaptation of the planet Mercury,' ibid. 531–49.

98. Merkelbach, *Mithras* (n. 12 above), 200–1.

99. V 1424 = AE 1953: 127, *D(eo) I(nvicto) M(ithrae) Verus pro salute / Comaci(a)e et Com(magenorum) v(otum) s(olvit) l(ibens) m(erito)*.

100. Vermaseren wrongly claims there is no dog: it is crammed in between the bull and Cautopates.

101. The exact provenance is unknown, but this ascription is supported by the similarity to the representations of Mithras-Atthis.

102. J.R. Hinnells, 'The Iconography of Cautes and Cautopates: 1,' JMS 1 (1976), 36–67, analyses all the reliefs with torch-bearers.

103. Merkelbach, *Mithras* (n. 12 above), 207–8.

104. Cumont, *Mysteries* (n. 1 above), 129–30.

105. The case is different where both torch-bearers hold their torches downwards (fig. 50: the Renaissance restoration is based on the surviving traces). This relief as a whole suggests that the sculptor was mainly interested in the symmetry.

106. E. Swoboda, 'Die Schlange im Mithraskult,' *Jahreshefte des Österreichischen Archäologischen Instituts* 30 (1937), 1–27.

107. *Quaestiones veteris et novi testamenti* 113, 11 = Migne, *PL* 34: 2214.

108. *Alii autem ligatis manibus intestinis pullinis proiiciuntur super foveas aqua plenas, accedente quodam cum gladio et inrumpente intestina supra dicta qui se liberatorem appellet.*

109. The best illustrations available are the colour photographs published by M.J. Vermaseren in the standard account of the Capua frescoes, *The Mithraeum at S. Maria Capua Vetere (Mithriaca 1)* EPRO 16.1 (Leyden: E.J. Brill, 1971). The podium panels mentioned here are in Vermaseren's list respectively: right podium: 1, 26–7 and pl. XXI; 2, 28–32 and pl. XXII; 5, 36–42, pl. XXV; left podium: 4, 45–47 and pl. XXVIII; 2, 43–4 and pl. XXVI.

110. V 498: *Natus prima luce / duobus Augg(ustis) co(n)s(ulibus) / Severo et Anton(ino) / (ante diem) XII k(alendas) decem(bres) dies Saturni / luna XVIII*, cf. Beard, North, Price 2: 316. M. Guarducci, 'Il graffito *Natus prima luce* nel mitreo di S. Prisca,' *Mysteria Mithrae* (n. 6 above), 153–64, takes the text to refer to the 'birth' of Mithras on this spot, that is, the dedication of the mithraeum; but a graffito of this kind would be an extraordinarily insignificant memorial of such an occasion.

111. M. Le Glay, 'La ΔΕΞΙΩΣΙΣ dans les Mystères de Mithra,' in *Etudes mithriaques* (n. 6 above), 279–303.

112. For the text, see PGM IV 475–829 (to which the line refs in the text refer); for full commentary, see Dieterich, *Eine Mithrasliturgie* (n. 2 above), and, in English, M.W. Meyer, *The 'Mithras Liturgy'* Society of Biblical Literature, Texts and Translations 10: Graeco-Roman religions series 2 (Missoula: Scholars Press, 1976). This translation is reprinted in H.D. Betz, *The Greek Magical Papyri in Translation* (Chicago: University of Chicago Press, 1993, 1986), 48–54. Note also R. Reitzenstein, *Die hellenistische Mysterienreligionen* (Leipzig: Teubner, ³1927), 169–78.

113. P.J. Sijpesteijn, 'Eine neue mithrische Gemme?', ZPE 64 (1986), 123–4. For the

relation between planets and vowels, see H.G. Gundel, *Weltbild und Astrologie in den griechischen Zauberpapyri* (Munich: C.H. Beck'sche Verlagsbuchhandlung, 1968), 42–3.

114. *Alii autem sicut aves alas percutiunt vocem coracis imitantes, alii vero leonum more fremunt . . . ecce quantis modis turpitur inluduntur qui se sapientes appellant,* 'some of them flap their wings like birds, imitating the croak of the raven, while others actually roar like lions . . . how disgustingly deluded these people are, who call themselves "wise" ': *Quaest. vet. et nov. test.* 113.11 = Migne, PL 34: 2214 (cf. n. 107 above).

115. M. Clauss, 'Mithras und Christus,' *Historische Zeitschrift* 243 (1986), 264–87, at 267–72.

116. Tertullian, *De praesc. haer.* 40.3–4; see E. Demougeot, 'Paganus, Mithra et Tertullien,' *Studia Patristica* 3 (Berlin: Akademie Verlag, 1961), 354–65.

117. R.K. Yerkes, *Sacrifice in Greek and Roman Religion and early Judaism* (New York: Scribner, 1952), 122–30; J.P. Kane, 'The Mithraic Cult-Meal in its Greek and Roman Environment,' *Mithraic Studies* (n. 6 above), 2: 313–51.

118. E. Schwertheim, *Die Denkmäler orientalischer Gottheiten im römischen Deutschland* EPRO 40 (Leyden: E.J. Brill, 1974), 188–9, no. 144.

119. K. Messelken, 'Vergemeinschaftung durch Essen: Religionssoziologische Überlegungen zum Abendmahl,' in M. Josuttis and G.M. Martin (eds), *Das heilige Essen* (Stuttgart and Berlin: Kreuz-Verlag, 1980), 41–57.

120. H.L. Werneck, 'Der Obstweihefund im Vorraum des Mithraeums zu Linz-Donau, Oberösterreich,' *Naturkundliches Jahrbuch der Stadt Linz* (1955), 9–39; cf. D. Schön, *Orientalische Kulte im römischen Österreich* (Cologne and Vienna: Böhlau), 129 no. 150.4.

121. See Huld-Zetsche, *Mithras in Nida* (n. 36 above), 16; 27 fig.13.

122. R. Forrer, *Das Mithra-Heiligtum von Königshofen bei Straßburg* (Stuttgart: Verlag W. Kohlhammer, 1915), 116.

123. Schwertheim, *Denkmäler* (n. 118 above), 116 no. 94.

124. A different, questionable, interpretation is given by H. Ogawa, 'Mithraic Ladder Symbols and the Friedberg Krater,' in *Hommages à M.J. Vermaseren* (n. 63 above), 3: 854–73.

125. Schwertheim, *Denkmäler* (n. 118 above), 233 no. 192.

126. V 1302–3: *Deo Invicto Mytrae vassa decem Tertius Rustici (filius) v(otum) s(olvit) l(ibens) l(aetus) m(erito),* cf. V 1304–5; for the probable provenance, see R. Turcan, *Religions orientales de l'Asie dans la Vallée du Rhône* EPRO 30 (Leyden: E.J. Brill, 1972), 37.

127. M. Hell, 'Das Mithräum von Moosham im Salzburgischen Lungau,' *Mitteilungen der Gesellschaft für Salzburger Landeskunde* 105 (1965), 91–111, at 100–5.

128. See W. Reichel and E. Bormann, 'Funde von Carnuntum, das dritte Mithraeum,' *Archaeologische-epigraphische Mittheilungen aus Österreich* 18 (1895), 169–201, at 193–4, pl. C.

129. Huld-Zetsche, *Mithras in Nida* (n. 36 above), 86 no. 52.

130. Illustrated in M.L. Krüger, *CSIR Österreich* 1.2, nos. 16, 17.

131. V 1242; the full text reads: *In h(onorem) d(omus) d(ivinae) Soli / invicto Mitrae / aram Privati Se /cundinus et Tertinus et Confinis / ex voto Privati / Tertini v(otum) s(olverunt) l(ibentes) l(aeti) m(erito).* For analogous perforated monuments, see D. Wortmann, 'Ein Mithrasstein aus Bonn,' *Bonner Jahrbücher* 169 (1969), 410–23.

132. PGM IV 635–7, tr. M.W. Meyer (n. 112 above).

133. A. Richmond and J.P. Gillam, 'The Temple of Mithras at Carrawburgh,' ArchAel 29 (1951 I), 1–44, at fig. 7.

134. See n. 128 above.

135. For an illustration, see M. F. Squarciapino, *I culti orientali ad Ostia* EPRO 3 (Leyden: E.J. Brill, 1962), pl. X, fig. 13.

136. Forrer, *Mithra-Heiligtum* (n. 122 above), 56–8; the dimensions given by V are considerably smaller.

137. The very basis for the scheme of the grades, as Merkelbach presents it (*Mithras* [n. 12 above], 77–133, esp. 85), would then disappear; see also Cumont, *Mysteries* (n. 1 above), 138–9.

138. M. Clauss, 'Die sieben Grade des Mithras-Kultes,' ZPE 82 (1990), 183–94.

139. From Lodi Vécchio in the Milanese hinterland; see A. Caretta, 'Culti e sacerdozi pagani a Laus Pompeia,' *Archivio Storico Lodigiano* 19 (1971), 18–20.

140. Vermaseren and van Essen, *Sta Prisca* (n. 86 above), 155–60 (upper layer), 167–70 (lower layer). These greetings provide the headings to the discussions of the grades below.

141. In the continuing absence of the relevant *Final Report*, the names of several, perhaps many, other Ravens at Dura-Europos remain unpublished.

142. Merkelbach, *Mithras* (n. 12 above), 88–93.

143. M. Clauss, 'Miles Mithrae,' *Klio* 74 (1992), 269–74.

144. Vermaseren and van Essen, *Sta Prisca* (n. 86), 224–32, lines 16–17: *accipe thuricremos, pater, accipe, sancte, liones, / per quos thura damus, per quos consumimur ipsi* (metrical hexameters); cf. Beard, North, Price 2: 319. The only colour photographs of these paintings are to be found in *Mysteria Mithrae* (n. 6 above), Appdx 1 (unpaginated), pl. I-XII; this dipinto is visible on pl. X-XII.

145. C. Aloe Spada, 'Il *leo* nella gerarchia dei gradi mitriaci,' in *Mysteria Mithrae* (n. 6 above), 639–48, at 645; also Laeuchli, 'Urban Mithraism' (n. 34 above), 86.

146. For example, AE 1979: 425; V 333.

147. For discussion of the issue, F. Mitthof, 'Der Vorstand der Kultgemeinden des Mithras. Eine Sammlung und Untersuchung der inschriftlichen Zeugnisse,' *Klio* 74 (1992), 275–90.

148. Suggested by Merkelbach, *Mithras* (n. 12 above), 121.

149. Piccottini, *Mithrastempel* (n. 72 above), 22–5.

150. A. Hensen, 'Mithräum und Grab,' *Saalburg-Jahrbuch* 50 (1999), 353–61.

151. K. Patsch, 'Das Mithräum von Konjica,' *Wissenschaftliche Mittheilungen aus Bosnien und der Hercegowina* 6 (1899), 186–209, at 205–7.

152. Respectively: CIL III 8387; 8366; AE 1976: 533.

153. Clauss, 'Omnipotens Mithras' (n. 78 above), 153.

154. *fac(tus) ex option(e) . . . beneficia[r(ius)]* (V 1881, with Clauss, ibid. 155).

155. V 463.1, with F. Cumont and L. Canet, 'Mithra ou Sarapis ΚΟΣΜΟΚΡΑΤΩΡ,' CRAI 1919, 313–28; Ristow, 'Kosmokrator im Zodiacus' (n. 82 above), 985–7.

156. μέγαλος (V 473); *bonus* (V 2276); δίκαιος (V 18); *propitius* (V 891); εὐεργέτης (V 463); ἐπήκοος (V 2264).

157. For the problem in general, Lincoln, 'Mithra(s) as Sun' (n. 21 above); I. Chirassi Colombo, 'Sol Invictus o Mithra,' in *Mysteria Mithrae* (n. 6 above), 649–72; J. Ries, 'Théologie solaire manichéenne et culte de Mithra,' ibid., 761–76.

158. The widespread notion that it denotes Sol's commission to Mithras (so e.g. Merkelbach, *Mithras* [n. 12 above], 81) is not convincing. These elongated rays have actually been interpreted as 'deadly rays', by means of which Sol is trying to destroy Mithras: Á. Buday, 'Neuere Daten zu den Problemen der Darstellungen des sogenannten Reitergottes,' *Dolgozatok (Proceedings of the Szeged Archaeological Institute)* 6 (1930), 26–48.

159. See W.K.C. Guthrie, *The Greeks and their Gods* (London: Methuen, 1977, [1]1950), 224–31.

160. Merkelbach, *Mithras* (n. 12 above), 378–9, who locates several of the scenes in a supposed 'Shepherd sequence' (111–12), sees here a shepherd putting up a fence.

161. Merkelbach, *Mithras* (n. 12 above), 123, has a different view. Since he interprets all these figures as human holders of grades, he takes the naked figure to be Heliodromus, whose cap is being removed by the Father, before the latter fits onto his head the radiate crown that is lying on the ground.

162. F. Cumont, 'Le nouveau bas-relief de Dieburg,' *Journal des Savants* (1927), 122–6; F. Behn, *Das Mithrasheiligtum zu Dieburg* Römisch-Germanische Forschungen, 1 (Berlin and Leipzig: Verlag W. de Gruyter, 1928); E. Wüst, 'Über einige Probleme der Mithras-Mysterien,' *Archiv für Religionswissenschaft* 32 (1935), 219–27.

163. We know Silvestrius Silvinus' profession, *artis quadratariae*, 'artistic stonemason', from one of the inscriptions on the obverse of this double-sided monument (cf. CIL XIII 6434).

164. On the various attempts to explain the relief, see Clauss, 'Sol Invictus Mithras' (n. 40 above), 428–30.

165. W. Blawatsky and G. Kochelenko, *Le culte de Mithra sur la côte septentrionale de la Mer Noire* EPRO 8 (Leyden: E.J. Brill, 1966), 14–22.

166. I. Tóth, 'The Cult of Iuppiter Sol Invictus Deus Genitor in Dacia,' *Acta Classica Universitatis Scientiarum Debreceniensis* 6 (1970), 71–4, at 74.

167. Respectively: V 1295; CIL XIII 6469, 6472.

168. This is the intention of an inscription from Rome, for Mithras and τοῖς συνναόοις θεοῖς (V 473 = IGUR 106).

169. Cf. A. Hensen, 'Mercurio Mithrae: Zeugnisse der Merkurverehrung im Mithraskult,' *Provinzialrömische Forschungen: Festschrift G. Ulbert*, W. Czysz, C-M. Hüssen, H-P. Kuhnen, C.S. Sommer and G. Weber (eds) (Espelkamp: Verlag Marie Leidorf, 1995), 211–16.

170. F.J. Dölger, 'Die Planetenwoche der griechisch-römischen Antike und der christliche Sonntag,' *Antike und Christentum* 6 (1940/50), 218–22.

171. For the identification of the deities, I follow Vermaseren, and Schwertheim, *Denkmäler* (n. 118 above), 192 no. 148a; Merkelbach, *Mithras* (n. 12 above), 352 differs, but alone sees that they are the tutelary gods of the Zodiac. On the twelve gods, see also C.R. Long, *The Twelve Gods of Greece and Rome* EPRO 107 (Leyden: E.J. Brill, 1987).

172. Virgo is also represented to the r. in the second row, Libra and Sagittarius in the third; Capricorn, Aquarius and Pisces are all lost with the lower part of the statue's legs.

173. R. Pettazzoni, 'The Monstrous Figure of Time in Mithraism,' in *Essays in the History of Religions*, H.J. Rose (ed.) (Leyden: E.J. Brill, 1954), 180–92; M.J. Vermaseren, 'A Magical Time God,' in *Mithraic Studies* (n. 6 above), 446–56; H. von Gall, 'The Lion-Headed and the Human-Headed God in the Mithraic Mysteries,' in *Études mithriaques* (n. 6 above), 511–25.

174. Jerome, *Comment. in Am.* 1.3.9–10 = CCL 76: 250; *Acta Archelaï* 98 Beeson: *iuxta computationem Graecarum litterarum Meithras anni numerum habet*; see also Merkelbach, *Mithras* (n. 12 above), 223.

175. In my view the reading is: *Euphrosyn[us] et Felix pp(osuerunt), Felix pater.*

176. Clauss, 'Mithras und Christus' (n. 115 above).

177. E. Renan, *Marc-Aurèle et la fin du monde antique* (Paris: Fontemoing, 1923), 579: 'Si le christianisme eût été arrêté dans sa croissance par quelque maladie mortelle, le monde eût été mithriaste.'

178. Reading *subvertit, fregit, exussit.*

179. Forrer, *Mithras-Heiligtum* (n. 122 above), 59–62.

180. *Passio sanctorum IV Coronatorum* 7, ed. W. Wattenbach, ap. M. Büdinger, *Untersuchungen zur römischen Kaisergeschichte* (Leipzig: B.G. Teubner, 1870; repr. Graz: Akademische Verlagsanstalt, 1973), 3: 324–38, at 335.

181. H. Lietzmann, *Geschichte der alten Kirche* (Berlin: W. de Gruyter, 1938), 3: 329. P. Karnitsch's remark: 'At the end of the fourth century the flames of the burning mithraeum on the Castle Hill at Linz could be seen far and wide, a last sign of Mithras the God of Light': 'Der heilige Bezirk von Lentia,' *Historisches Jahrbuch der Stadt Linz* (1956), 215, must strike one as simply macabre.

182. A. Ferrua, 'La catacomba de Vibia,' *Rivista di Archeologia Christiana* 47 (1971), 61–2.

183. Leo, *serm.* 27.7.4 = Migne, PL 54: 218, with Clauss, 'Mithras und Christus' (n. 115 above), 284.

Bibliography

The following is a brief list of a few important publications. Further references will be found in the notes, and in the supplementary list of titles mainly in English on the following pages. For a full-scale bibliographic survey up to around 1980, see R.L. Beck, 'Mithraism since Franz Cumont', ANRW II, 17.4 (1984), 2002–115.

U. Bianchi (ed.), *Mysteria Mithrae: Atti del Seminario internazionale . . . Roma e Ostia, 28–31 Marzo 1978* EPRO 80 (Leyden: E.J. Brill, 1979).

W. Blawatsky and G. Kochelenko, *Le culte de Mithra sur la côte septentrionale de la Mer Noire* EPRO 8 (Leyden: E.J. Brill, 1966).

L.A. Campbell, *Mithraic Iconography and Ideology* EPRO 11 (Leyden: E.J. Brill, 1968).

F. Cumont, *Textes et monuments figurés relatifs aux mystères de Mithra* (Brussels: Lamartin, 1896–9), 2 vols.

F. Cumont, *The Mysteries of Mithras*, tr. from 2nd French edn. by T.J. McCormack (New York: Dover, 1956).

A. Dieterich, *Eine Mithrasliturgie*[3] (O. Weinreich, ed.) (Leipzig: Teubner, 1923, repr. Stuttgart: Teubner, 1966).

J. Duchesne-Guillemin (ed.), *Études mithriaques: Actes du 2e congrès international . . . à Téhéran, 1–8 septembre, 1975* Acta Iranica 17, First Series (Actes de congrès), 4 (Leyden: E.J. Brill, 1978).

A. García y Bellido, *Les religions orientales dans l'Espagne romaine* EPRO 5 (Leyden: E.J. Brill, 1967), 21–41.

R.L. Gordon, 'Mithraism in the Roman Empire,' PhD Cambridge, 1972.

J.R. Hinnells (ed.), *Mithraic studies: proceedings of the first international congress of Mithraic studies* (Manchester: Manchester University Press, 1975), 2 vols.

J.R. Hinnells (ed.), *Studies in Mithraism: papers associated with the Mithraic Panel . . . of the XVIth IAHR congress, Rome 1990* Storia delle religioni 9 (Rome: L'Erma di Bretschneider, 1994).

S. Laeuchli (ed.), *Mithraism in Ostia: mystery religion and Christianity in the ancient port of Rome* (Evanston, Ill.: North-Western University Press, 1967).

R. Merkelbach, *Mithras* (Königstein/Taunus: Hain, 1984).

F. Saxl, *Mithras: Typengeschichtliche Untersuchungen* (Berlin: Keller, 1931).

A. Schütze, *Mithras-Mysterien und Urchristentum*[3] (Stuttgart: Urachhaus, 1972).

E. Schwertheim, *Die Denkmäler orientalischer Gottheiten im römischen Deutschland* EPRO 40 (Leyden: E.J. Brill, 1974).

E. Schwertheim, *Mithras: Seine Denkmäler und sein Kult*, in *Antike Welt* 10, Sondernummer (Zurich: Raggi-Verlag, 1979) (whole volume).

R. Turcan, *Mithra et le mithriacisme*[2] (Paris: Les Belles-Lettres, 1993).

M.J. Vermaseren, *Corpus Inscriptionum et Monumentorum Religionis Mithriacae* (The Hague: Martinus Nijhoff, 1956–60), 2 vols.

M.J. Vermaseren, *Mithras, the Secret God*, tr. T. and V. Megaw (London: Chatto and Windus, 1963).

V.J. Walters, *The Cult of Mithras in the Roman Provinces of Gaul* EPRO 41 (Leyden: E.J. Brill, 1974).

Further reading

Select bibliography of titles in English, compiled by the translator. Items referred to in the notes have mostly been omitted:

GENERAL

R.L. Beck, 'The Mithras Cult as Association,' *Studies in Religion/Sciences Religieuses* 21 (1992), 3–13.

U. Bianchi, 'The Religio-Historical Question of the Mysteries of Mithra,' in idem (ed.), *Mysteria Mithrae*, 3–47.

P. Bilde, 'The Meaning of Roman Mithraism,' in J. Podemann Sørensen (ed.), *Rethinking Religion: Studies in the Hellenistic Process*, Opuscula Graeco-latina 30 (Copenhagen: Museum Tusculanum Press, 1989), 31–47.

W. Burkert, *Ancient Mystery Cults* (Cambridge, Mass., and London: Harvard University Press, 1987), 47–53.

J.H.W.G. Liebeschuetz, 'The Expansion of Mithraism among the Religious Cults of the Second Century,' in J.R. Hinnells (ed.), *Studies in Mithraism*, 195–216.

R. MacMullen, *Paganism in the Roman Empire* (New Haven and London: Yale University Press, 1981), 122–7.

A.D. Nock, 'The Genius of Mithraism,' JRS 27 (1937), 108–14. Repr. in his *Essays on Religion and the Ancient World*, Z. Stewart (ed.) (Oxford: Clarendon Press, 1972), 452–8.

IRANIAN AND NE BACKGROUND

M. Boyce and F. Grenet, *A History of Zoroastrianism, 3: Zoroastrianism under Macedonian and Roman Rule* Handbuch der Orientalistik, I. 8. 1. 2. 2 (Leyden: E.J. Brill, 1991), 468–90.

C. Colpe, 'The Development of Religious Thought,' in E. Yarshater (ed.), *The Cambridge History of Iran, 3.2: The Seleucid, Parthian and Sasanian Periods* (Cambridge: Cambridge University Press, 1983), 819–65, esp. 853–6.

M.J. Edwards, 'Herodotus and Mithras: *Histories* 1.131,' *American Journal of Philology* 111 (1990), 1–4.

I. Gershevitch (ed., comm.), *The Avestan Hymn to Mithra* (Cambridge: Cambridge University Press, 1959), 61–72.

J.R. Hinnells, 'Reflections on the Bull-Slaying Scene,' in idem (ed.), *Mithraic Studies*, 2: 290–312.

P.G. Kreyenbroek, 'Mithra and Ahreman in Iranian Cosmogonies,' in J.R. Hinnells (ed.), Studies in Mithraism, 173–82.

J.R. Russell, 'On the Armeno-Iranian Roots of Mithraism,' in J.R. Hinnells (ed.), *Studies in Mithraism*, 183–93.

G. Widengren, 'The Mithraic Mysteries in the Greco-Roman World with Special Regard to their Iranian Background,' in *La Persia e il mondo greco-romano: Atti del convegno 11-14 apr. 1965* Accademia Nazionale dei Lincei, Quaderno 76 (Rome, 1966), 433–55.

The Possible Role of Commagene

R.L. Beck, 'The Mysteries of Mithras: a new account of their genesis,' JRS 88 (1998), 115–28.

Individual Monuments, Temples and Regions

J.T. Bakker, *Living and Working with the Gods: studies of evidence for private religion and its material environment in the city of Ostia (100–500 AD)* (Amsterdam: Gieben, 1994), 111–17, 204–7.

E.D. Francis, 'Mithraic Graffiti from Dura-Europos,' in J.R. Hinnells (ed.), *Mithraic Studies*, 2: 424–45.

J.P. Gillam and I. MacIvor, 'The Temple of Mithras at Rudchester,' ArchAel 4th series, 32 (1954), 176–219.

R.L. Gordon, 'Two Mithraic Albums from Virunum, Noricum,' JRA 9 (1996), 424–26.

W.F. Grimes, *The Excavation of Roman and Medieval London* (London: Routledge and Kegan Paul, 1968), 92–117.

K.G. Holum, R.L. Hohlfelder R.J. Bull and A. Raban, *King Herod's Dream: Caesarea on the Sea* (New York: W.W. Norton, 1988), 148–53.

L.M. Hopfe, 'Mithraism in Syria,' ANRW II, 18.4 (1990), 2214–35.

G. Lease, 'Mithra in Egypt,' in B.A. Pearson and J.E. Goehring (eds), *The Roots of Egyptian Christianity* (Philadelphia: Fortress Press, 1986), 114–29.

I.A. Richmond and J.P. Gillam, 'The Temple of Mithras at Carrawburgh,' ArchAel 4th series, 29 (1951), 6–92.

M.I. Rostovtzeff, F.E. Brown, and C.B. Welles (eds), *The Excavations at Dura-Europos: preliminary report of the seventh and eighth seasons, 1933–34 and 1934–35* (New Haven: Yale University Press, 1939), 62–134.

J.D. Shepherd et al., *The Temple of Mithras, London: excavations by W.F. Grimes and A. Williams* (London: English Heritage, 1998).

M.J. Vermaseren, *The Mithraeum at Santa Maria Capua Vetere* Mithriaca 1, EPRO 16.1 (Leyden: E.J. Brill, 1971).

M.J. Vermaseren, *The Mithraeum at Ponza* Mithriaca 2, EPRO 16.2 (Leyden: E.J. Brill, 1974).

M.J. Vermaseren, *Le Monument d'Ottavio Zeno et le culte de Mithra sur le Célius* Mithriaca 4, EPRO 16.4 (Leyden: E.J. Brill, 1978).

M.J. Vermaseren, *The Mithraeum at Marino* Mithriaca 3, EPRO 16.3 (Leyden: E.J. Brill, 1982).

M.J. Vermaseren and C.C. Van Essen, *The Excavations in the Mithraeum of the Church of Santa Prisca in Rome* (Leyden: E.J. Brill, 1965).

MITHRAIC ART

J. Elsner, *Art and the Roman Viewer: the transformation of art from the pagan world to Christianity* (Cambridge: Cambridge University Press, 1995), 210–21.

R.L. Gordon, 'Viewing Mithraic Art: the altar from Burginatium (Kalkar), Germania Inferior,' *ARYS: Antigüedad, Religiones y Sociedades* 1 (1998), 227–58.

R.Vollkommer, s.v. 'Mithras,' LIMC 6.1 (1992), 583–626; 6.2, 325–68.

S. Zwirn, 'The Intention of Biographical Narration on Mithraic Cult Images,' *Word and Image* 5 (1989), 2–18.

THE MITHRAIC CULT-ICON

L.H. Martin, 'Reflections on the Mithraic Tauroctony as Cult-Scene,' in J.R. Hinnells (ed.), *Studies in Mithraism*, 217–24.

ASTRONOMICAL INTERPRETATIONS OF THE CULT-ICON

R.L. Beck, 'In the Place of the Lion: Mithras in the tauroctony,' in J.R. Hinnells (ed.), *Studies in Mithraism*, 29–50.

R.L. Beck, 'Cautes and Cautopates: some astronomical considerations,' JMS 2 (1977), 1–17.

S. Insler, 'A New Interpretation of the Bull-Slaying Motif,' in M.B. de Boer and T.A. Edridge (eds), *Hommages à M.J. Vermaseren* EPRO 68 (Leyden: E.J. Brill, 1978), 2: 519–38.

J.D. North, 'Astronomical Symbolism in the Mithraic Religion,' *Centaurus* 33 (1990), 115–48.

M.P. Speidel, *Mithras-Orion: Greek hero and Roman army-god* EPRO 81 (Leyden: E.J. Brill, 1980).

N.M. Swerdlow, 'On the Cosmical Mysteries of Mithras,' *Classical Philology* 86 (1991), 48–63.

D. Ulansey, *The Origins of the Mithraic Mysteries: cosmology and salvation in the ancient world*[2] (New York: Oxford University Press, 1991).

THE TORCH-BEARERS

R. Hannah, 'The Image of Cautes and Cautopates in the Mithraic Tauroctony Icon,' in M.P.J. Dillon (ed.), *Religion in the Ancient World: New Themes and Approaches* (Amsterdam: Adolf Hakkert, 1996), 177–92.

J.R. Hinnells, 'The Iconography of Cautes and Cautopates, 1: the data,' JMS 1 (1976), 36–67.

M. Schwartz, 'Cautes and Cautopates, the Mithraic Torch-bearers,' in J.R. Hinnells (ed.), *Mithraic Studies*, 2: 406–23.

THE LION-HEADED GOD

J.R. Hinnells, 'Reflections on the Lion-Headed Figure in Mithraism,' *Monumentum H.S. Nyberg* Acta Iranica 2.1 (Leyden: E.J. Brill, 1975), 333–69.

H.M. Jackson, 'The Meaning and Function of the Leontocephaline in Roman Mithraism,' *Numen* 32 (1985), 17–45.

MISCELLANEOUS

R.L. Beck, *Planetary Gods and Planetary Orders in the Mysteries of Mithras* EPRO 109 (Leyden: E.J. Brill, 1988).

P. Beskow, 'The Routes of Early Mithraism,' in J. Duchesne-Guillemin (ed.), *Etudes mithriaques*, 7–18.

P. Beskow, 'Tertullian on Mithras,' in J.R. Hinnells (ed.), *Studies in Mithraism*, 51–60.

W. Brashear, *A Mithraic Catechism from Egypt* Tyche Supplementband 1 (Vienna, 1992).

I. Culianu, 'The Mithraic Ladder Revisited,' in J.R. Hinnells (ed.), *Studies in Mithraism*, 75–91.

R.L. Gordon, 'Who Worshipped Mithras?', JRA 7 (1994), 459–74.

J.P. Kane, 'The Mithraic Cult-Meal in its Greek and Roman Environment,' in J.R.Hinnells (ed.), *Mithraic Studies*, 2: 313–51.

M.J. Vermaseren, 'The Miraculous Birth of Mithras,' *Mnemosyne* (series 4) 4 (1951), 285–301.

L.M. White, *Building God's House in the Roman World: architectural adaptation among pagans, Jews and Christians* (Baltimore and London: Johns Hopkins University Press, 1989), 47–58.

MITHRAS AND CHRISTIANITY

H-D. Betz, 'The Mithras-Inscriptions of Santa Prisca and the New Testament,' *Novum Testamentum* 10 (1968), 62–80.

S.G.F. Brandon, 'Mithraism and its Challenge to Christianity,' *Hibbert Journal* 53 (1954–5), 107–14.

M. Gervers, 'The Iconography of the Cave in Christian and Mithraic Tradition,' in U. Bianchi (ed.), *Mysteria Mithrae*, 579–96.

S. Laeuchli, 'Christ and Mithra,' in idem (ed.), *Mithraism in Ostia*, 85–105.

G. Lease, 'Mithraism and Christianity: borrowings and transformation,' ANRW II, 23.2 (1980), 1306–32.

DECLINE OF THE CULT OF MITHRAS

R.L. Gordon, 'The End of Mithraism in the Northwestern Provinces,' JRA 12 (1999), 682–8.

O. Nicholson, 'The End of Mithraism,' *Antiquity* 69 (1995), 358–62.

E. Sauer, *The End of Paganism in the NW Provinces of the Roman Empire: the example of the Mithras cult* BAR International Series 634 (Oxford: Tempus Reparatum, 1996).

J. Wall, 'Christian Evidences in the Roman Period: the northern counties,' ArchAel 4th series, 44 (1966), 147–64, at 157–62.

The captions have been supplied by the translator. The following is a list of references to recently-discovered objects and mithraea referred to there:

Aquincum (Budapest), Mithraeum V:
O. Madarassy, 'Die bemalte Kultwand im Mithräum des Legionslagers von Aquincum,' *Kölner Jahrbuch für Vor- und Frühgeschichte* 24 (1991), 207–11.

Biesheim:
F. Petry and E. Kern, 'Un mithraeum à Biesheim (Haut-Rhin),' *Cahiers Alsaciens d'Archéologie et d'Histoire* 21 (1978), 4–32.

Doliche/Dülük:
E. Winter and A. Schütte-Maischatz, 'Neue Forschungen in Kommagene,' *Münsteraner Historisch-archäologischer Freundeskreis: Rundbrief* (1997), 31–7.

Forum Claudii Vallensium (Martigny):
F. Wiblé, 'Le mithraeum de Forum Claudii Vallensium/Martigny (Valais),' *Archéologie der Schweiz* 18.1 (1995), 2–15.

Gelduba (Gellep-Krefeld):
R. Pirling, *Römer und Franken am Niederrhein: Katalog-Handbuch des Landschaftsmuseums Burg Linn in Krefeld* (Mainz: von Zabern, 1986), 32–7.

S. Giovanni del Duino:
G. Pross Gabrielli, 'Il tempietto ipogeo del dio Mitra al Timavo,' *Archeografo triestino* 4th series, 35 (84) (1975), 5–34.

Groß-Gerau:
H. Göldner and G. Seitz, 'Ausgrabungen im römischen Groß-Gerau: Ein neues Mithras-Heiligtum,' *Denkmalpflege in Hessen* 2 (1990), 2–8.

Hawarti:
M. Gawlikowski, 'Hawarti,' *Polish Archaeology in the Mediterranean* 10 (1999), 197–204.

Künzing:

K. Schmotz, forthcoming in *Ausgrabungen und Funde in Niederbayern* 27 (2001).

Mogontiacum (Mainz):

H-G. Horn, 'Das Mainzer Mithrasgefäß,' *Mainzer Archäologische Zeitschrift* 1 (1994), 21–66.

Mundelsheim:

D. Planck, 'Römischer Gutshof mit Mithras-Heiligtum,' in *Führer zu archäologischen Denkmälern in Deutschland, 22: Heilbronn und das mittlere Neckarland zwischen Marbach und Gundelsheim* (Stuttgart: Theiss Verlag, 1991), 184–90.

Rome, *Castra Peregrinorum* (S. Stefano Rotondo):

E. Lissi Caronna, *Il Mitreo dei* Castra Peregrinorum *(S. Stefano Rotondo)* EPRO 104 (Leyden: E.J. Brill, 1986).

Wiesloch:

A. Hensen, 'Das Mithräum im Vicus von Wiesloch,' *Archäologische Nachrichten aus Baden* 51/2 (1994), 30–7.

General Index

Place-names are entered selectively; unlisted sites can be traced via the relevant province.

References to sites under the province exclude those listed by name. Place-names generally list the Roman name first, if known.

Index of ancient passages

Index of monuments and inscriptions

Numerals without a reference denote the number in Vermaseren, *Corpus*.

CIL
III 1096,   45 n.69
III 1363,   40
III 8366,   142
III 8387,   142
III 11674, 39

VI 273,   132
VI 510,   31
VI 736,   31
VI 1779,   31
VI 2010b,   132

XIII 6469,   158 n.167
XIII 6472,   158 n.167
XIII 11791a,b,   96

AE
1906: 8,   35 n.54
1926: 72,   28, 143
1953: 127,   91
1957: 273,   40
1962: 26,   34
1966: 314,   36
1971: 384,   40
1976: 533,   142

1979: 426,   143
1980: 48–50,   132
1994: 1310,   143
1994: 1334,   51, 139

IDR
2: 510,   36
3.1: 145,   40 n.61

IGUR
108,   70

RIB
3,   88
1198,   97, 156
1272,   146
1397,   155
1599,   71
1600,   71

I.Huld-Zetsche, Mithras in Nida-
    Heddernheim (1986), 81
    no.43,   114
    ibid., 85 no.51,   122
    ibid., 86 no.52,   124

E. Lissi Caronna, Il Mitreo dei
    Castra Peregrinorum (S.
    Stefano Rotondo) (1986),
    31–4, pl. VIII, X,   99

G. Ristow, Mithras im römischen
    Köln (1974), 26 no.24,
    64

E. Schwertheim, Denkmäler
    orientalischer Gottheiten im
    römischen Deutschland
    (1974), 116, no.94a,   116
    ibid., 188 no.144,   110–11,
    118
    ibid., 233 no.192,   120

M.J. Vermaseren, Mithriaca
    3: The Mithraeum at
    Marino (1982), pl. III,   81,
    164

L. Zotović, Cultes orientaux . . .
    de la Mésie Supérieure
    (1966), 63 no.6,   77